I0624269

C.L. MCMURRAY

# Air Guitar Rules – Chords of Life

*A Memoir*

First published by Soul Fire In C 2024

Copyright © 2024 by C.L. McMurray

All rights reserved. No part of this publication may be reproduced, stored or transmitted in any form or by any means, electronic, mechanical, photocopying, recording, scanning, or otherwise without written permission from the publisher. It is illegal to copy this book, post it to a website, or distribute it by any other means without permission.

C.L. McMurray asserts the moral right to be identified as the author of this work.

C.L. McMurray has no responsibility for the persistence or accuracy of URLs for external or third-party Internet Websites referred to in this publication and does not guarantee that any content on such Websites is, or will remain, accurate or appropriate.

Designations used by companies to distinguish their products are often claimed as trademarks. All brand names and product names used in this book and on its cover are trade names, service marks, trademarks and registered trademarks of their respective owners. The publishers and the book are not associated with any product or vendor mentioned in this book. None of the companies referenced within the book have endorsed the book.

First edition

ISBN (paperback): 979-8-9916826-1-9
ISBN (hardcover): 979-8-9916826-0-2

Editing by Patty Consolazio

This book was professionally typeset on Reedsy.
Find out more at reedsy.com

*For anyone on a journey of living authentically.*

# Contents

III   PART THREE

IV  PART FOUR

V  PART FIVE

# Preface

After being forced abruptly into the pool against my will, my body and mind couldn't keep pace with the unexpected and quickly unfolding peril. Experiencing the sensation a bullet might encounter being shot out of the barrel of a gun, the speed at which I was sinking was petrifying. The chlorine-fueled liquid invaded my lungs before instinct forced me to hold my breath as the frigid isolation of water surrounded me. As I crashed haphazardly to the floor in the deep end of nowhere, the moment became suspended in time. My only-child persona has never felt so scared and alone; ironic, since the concept of being alone doesn't typically faze me. I was filled with dread, staring head-on at what I believed would be the end to my brief six-year-long life.

It started innocently enough. The adults at the house party proposed that the kids go play in the pool. Dad wasn't aware I hadn't learned how to swim properly yet, given all the time I'd spent down the shore with Grandma and Pop. It didn't actually occur to me either—the pool had a shallow end, and I'd spent plenty of time in my cousin Christina's inground pool, splashing around where my feet could touch the bottom.

The house where we were attending this particular summer party featured a sprawling backyard, and the massive death trap in question was situated all the way at the back of the property. Our newly formed tribe of half-pints made our way excitedly through the lush green grass, running barefoot with soft blades tickling our soft pink toes as the scent of freshly manicured lawn filled our tiny nostrils. No parents followed—hey, it was the '70s.

Once we reached the pool, one of the kids suggested a game. In some warped form of tag, this game involved someone being declared the monster, assigned the unpopular duty of chasing down other kids to get released from this most undesirable role. None of us considered running around the pool hazardous, and certainly our parents assumed we'd play *inside* the pool, not scurry along the edges like a pack of maniacs. The current monster, a boy much bigger and stronger than me, startled me from behind as I was running for cover. Making up his own rules to the game, he pushed me forcefully into the deep end. My newly pronounced title after being tagged the monster led to the dangerous situation I now found myself in.

As my mounting fear grew, something deep down in my core snapped open wide—I suddenly comprehended my motivation to live was stronger than my fear of drowning. Peering up toward safety, I felt an invisible, comforting presence forcibly pushing me from my bottom. Flailing yet determined, I launched myself toward the cloud-filled sky as quickly as my unproven swimming skills would take me. Up, up, up, up, up, up, up, up . . . I greeted the sudden burst of air with indescribable appreciation.

As I climbed shakily out of the pool, I just wanted to get back to my father to visibly see him in order to convince myself I was safe. I'm not sure I even told him what happened—I was in shock and had no words to describe my experience.

While this event did not prove to define me or succeed in

ending my time prematurely, I learned three valuable lessons, which I've been reminded of throughout the course of my life thus far:

1) Wearing any type of mask, monster or otherwise, lands a person in deep water. It would take me 37 years to understand that living authentically is the key to happiness and fulfill-ment.

2) Acceptance of ourselves and others, including the monster, is critical to harmony on Earth. Being different is an invincible superpower, taking us higher than our wildest dreams can imagine. We need to tap into our uniqueness as well as the gifts of others to continue learning and evolving.

3) Whether innate or learned, with motivation, commitment, discipline, and unwavering faith, we can achieve absolutely anything, including the thing we initially believed to be impossible.

After I'd already long committed to writing this memoir and created the title, I discovered the instrumental "Chords of Life" by Joe Satriani. I've always considered Joe one of the best guitarists but wasn't familiar with this arrangement—it was fateful to stumble upon it one day during a random Google search. It's the perfect backdrop to my story, emphasizing stellar guitar playing, an erratically paced tempo, and the absence of words. My introvert persona would enjoy nothing more than to move you through this journey of nostalgia by feeling the power of the music and the ups and downs to which I hope you can all relate. You will come to discover I've always considered myself a poet, and I found an old one written years ago prognosticating the invitation I offer to you now. Are you ready to come with me? I'm pumped. Let's go . . .

## MEMORIES OF THE HEART

Save all good memories throughout life as you go

Treasure them dearly as you continue to grow

Cherish the moments without clinging to the past

Thankful good surpasses bad with the knowledge neither is meant to last

For each contains a shooting star created just for you

They console your aching heart when you're feeling blue

While bittersweet to recall those involving loved ones no more

They help you hold tighter to those who endure

Travel back with me as I glide through time and space

The heart is designed to trap that which the mind has erased

**USE THIS QR CODE TO REQUEST A COMPLIMENTARY AGR PLAYLIST!**

(Alternatively: request by going directly to https://www.clm cmurray.com/contact)

# Acknowledgments

There are many people I need to thank who have been critical to the success of this publication.

Michele, you have supported me unconditionally during the writing of this memoir while also suffering the brunt of me lighting the candle at both ends. Through it all you've been steadfast as I pursue my writing passion. For this and so many reasons I'm reminded of on a daily basis, I know there is no one else on this Earth I'd rather do life with.

Mom, there aren't any words that can properly express the gratitude I have for the never-ending sacrifice and love you have shown me over the last 54 years. I will spend the rest of my life thanking God for giving me the gift of you. I love you.

Dad, though we are far in distance, I am reminded often how much I am your daughter. Thank you for the gifts you have passed on to me, which have helped form the person I have become.

Grandparents, though you are no longer with us, I remember you as if I just saw you yesterday. I miss your strong faith, wisdom and courage.

Family and friends, thank you for supporting me throughout this process. Your enthusiasm motivated me on any given day I started to question myself.

Patty Consolazio, the editing you have done on this work is jaw-dropping. I am so thankful for our collaboration, and can't wait for our next project! I'm equally grateful to Katy Corrado for introducing us - without that first step not sure where I would be right now!

Chief Writers Critique Circle, your early feedback to me was profound and set me on a path of improvement of this work I wouldn't have otherwise achieved. As I've often commented during our sessions, I enjoy the time spent together greatly and look forward to our continued support of one another.

ARC readers, thank you for investing your time and energy into the preview prior to publication! Honest feedback is important to my future growth as a writer and it means a lot to me.

Social media community, it has been my pleasure to provide inside glimpses as I went through the process of writing this memoir. The support of all of you, including the fabulous writing community, has been hugely inspiring.

Above all, I want to thank God for providing me with this writing ability, and for being patient with me as I navigated life to get to the place I am today.

# I

# PART ONE

***AIR GUITAR RULE #1*** – *The most reliable way to master the craft is remaining true to one core conviction: believing there are no rules.*

# Chapter 1 - "Beginnings"

The four-year-old girl inhabiting my first memory stirs up conflicting emotions I've never quite been able to resolve.

Sitting cross-legged on the avocado-green sculptured carpet, she's surrounded by 33⅓ rpm vinyl record albums randomly pulled from the cabinet. As she curiously observes the artwork on each cover, these inaugural musical choices lodge permanent burn marks in her brain. Chicago Transit Authority's (now known as Chicago) minimalist cover displays the band's signature cursive bubble lettering. In contrast, this album's song "Beginnings" reveals instrumental diversity and complexity; the uplifting horn section sending a message that hope is eternal.

My younger self is experiencing something for the first time that will unconditionally carry her through life, and I watch over her with a feeling of contentment. Music will establish definition when life doesn't make sense, help her express emotions she isn't sure how to say out loud, and allow her to cry when the tears will not flow.

Inspecting Carole King's *Tapestry* album while "I Feel the Earth Move" plays in the background, she looks curiously at the cat on the front cover, unaware she'll have many cats one day. She'll eventually come to admire Carole as one of the greatest songwriters of our time. But on this day, the upbeat piano melody inspires spontaneous head-bobbing and finger-snapping while the girl jigs around on the floor.

The appearance of my mini me is foreign to me. Long, platinum blonde hair with flowing waves seemingly spun of gold, piercing blue eyes, and a girly red and white gingham dress that traveled all the way down to the floor (no socks—hey, it was the '70s). Those lengthy tresses were tossed away in grade school, and a dress has not occupied my closet in over 20 years. As there is such little resemblance to the woman I am today, I might have trouble selecting her in a lineup were it not for those intense crystal-azure eyes.

The Al Green cover now catches her attention. His *Greatest Hits* cover features Al donning tight white leather tie-up pants with a chic floral design and no shirt, posing with an undeniably magnetic appeal. I wouldn't have been able to define it as sexiness at this young age, but I remember being completely intrigued, unable to take my eyes off the cover. As "Let's Stay Together" blasts soothingly from the turntable, my concern for the young girl starts to mount as the irony of the song strikes me. She has no clue the world as she knows it is about to spin off its axis. All I want to do is protect her, but it's too late now—all I can do is tell her it's going to be fine.

I'm being rude—it might be helpful to share a bit more about myself. I was born on September 16, 1970 at Barnert Hospital in Paterson, New Jersey. My parents Sandy and Rich named me Cheryll Lynn, and the spelling choice is spot-on for my personality: precise and buttoned-up like a true Virgo can appreciate. It's also caused some grief for the last 54 years, as hardly anyone spells my name correctly. In addition to the conundrum whether to start with C or S, I've seen my first name spelled this way—with two Ls—a total of ONE other time. I asked my mom how this spelling decision came about, and she explained that my dad wanted my name to be uniform. My full name is Cheryll Lynn Turoff. This makes perfect sense to me. It is also undeniable proof I am my father's daughter. It's wonderful when spelled correctly, though each time I see my name butchered, bells and whistles in my brain fire off in silent protest. Knowing my parents were going to name me Scott if I had been born male, I think I'd have encountered less controversy. Fittingly, it may have made some other things a whole lot easier as well.

Mom, Dad, and I lived in a charming little brick Cape Cod house on a quiet tree-lined dead-end street in Elmwood Park, New Jersey, located in Bergen County. Eighteen miles from Manhattan, this suburb was a perfect landing spot for early settlers migrating to the area. Even today, this picturesque little borough lies close to the action, hidden from view. Unfortunately, a million others had the same idea—Bergen County is overpopulated, making us all a tad edgy and pushy to anyone not from the area.

Growing up, life was simpler; a time when you actually knew all of your neighbors. Collectively, we were a community that prided ourselves on looking out and helping one another, and we always felt safe. I made my first friend, Tracy, here at around two years old. Tracy's grandfather would walk her down the block from her family's Cape Cod, and we'd hang out, play, and eat lunch together. This launched a lifelong friendship for us, as well as my mom and Tracy's mom Barbara.

Tracy's auburn hair, brown eyes, and quiet, reserved, and sensitive nature made us—and still make us—notably differ-

5

ent. Though I appreciate my quiet time as an introvert, my social tendencies profess extroversion, and I'm prone to cause a stir. Also, while my sensitive side has reared its head more often in adulthood, most things roll off my back lightning fast.

Unique attributes aside, we've remained forever friends, bonded by humor and music. As kids, we engaged in a constant chuckle fest with our silly antics, which still comes out today in our text exchanges. Tracy was also drawn to music at an early age, and we'd hang out in her bedroom and listen to Frankie Valli & The Four Seasons, the essential doo-wop band hailing from nearby Newark, New Jersey. Their song "Sherry" brings me back to the spacious attic serving as our sound studio, where two friends attempted to replicate the wide-ranging harmonies.

I loved my own perfect house on this memorable street. Our attic was a storage room and also my playroom. The perfect sanctuary, it exuded the strong scent of cedar and possessed a comfortable stuffiness I claimed as all mine. I wasn't into dolls, though I did own the same Holly Hobbie every other girl my age was toting around. My parents probably spent a small fortune on Romper Room Weebles and Fisher-Price play lands. But I really didn't require a lot of stuff. As an only child, I could easily transport to whatever world I decided to temporarily take residence in.

Our side yard was filled with fruit trees I loved exploring; this dank and shaded mystery place was yet another world where I could escape and dream of faraway lands. Our level backyard wasn't huge, but surely delightful to a four-year-old girl, frolicking around in her frilly summer dress on a beautiful, sunny day with her toy fox terrier Dino. I can hear the welcoming vibe of "Summer Breeze" by Seals & Crofts playing softly in the background, as I drift off to sleep in the evenin' when the day is through.

Behind our property, a wooded area containing railroad tracks retired for freight provided a great deal of privacy and quiet refuge. One day, I returned from these woods with a turtle. Though my mom indulged me with a box to put it in, he quickly and mysteriously disappeared.

How funny that looking back now, I'm a bit envious of the idyllic existence my four-year-old self experienced, even though I was the one who got to experience it. For the average person, a young child could not want or need more; only the beginning of something I'd want to feel forever. Deep down, I wish I could freeze this moment in time without any recollection of what follows. But that's not life, and though Chicago failed to mention this, all beginnings must eventually come to an end.

# Chapter 2 - "Ain't No Mountain High Enough"

My mom, Sandra Jean Battinelli, was born on April 2, 1947 in Warwick, New York, about 10 miles from where I now reside. Considered a part of the Hudson Valley, Warwick is considered the country, or informally, "the sticks," by anyone from New York City or the surrounding suburbs. Abundant green mountains, pastures, and wildlife possess a beauty inspiring feelings of wonderment.

Sandy's maternal family, the Garrisons, were settled in nearby Greenwood Lake. I recently learned my lineage had roots in this area beginning in the early 1800s. When I was a young girl, my mom, her sister (and my godmother) Aunt Linda, and I would take regular road trips to visit the Garrisons. Though it was less than 30 miles away, we'd arrive after a majestically scenic car ride on a winding one-lane road called Skyline Drive. The unpleasant part of this journey occurred when we'd have to pull over so I could toss my cookies; a habit I was happy to eventually outgrow. Both my mom and Aunt Linda loved music, and we'd begin our journey by popping in an 8-track tape from a case in the car that held a variety of tapes for entertainment.

These adventures fueled my adoration for many popular hit

makers in the '70s, including Barry Manilow. He may not be for everybody, but for the millions of us who have bought his music, he is a national treasure—his music makes us happy. After watching *A Very Barry Christmas* recently and seeing him perform about seven years ago, I was dazzled by his infectious energy, stunning outfits, and stirring vocals. "Could It Be Magic" always brings me chills as the deliberate, anticipatory piano opening leads to a masterful expression of longing.

Another popular road trip choice was the Carpenters. Karen Carpenter's hauntingly melodic voice now brings to mind the tragedy of her untimely death. But when she sang the light, feel-good song written by the master Burt Bacharach, "(They Long to Be) Close to You," it was easy to visualize the angels getting together.

Sometimes we'd listen to the radio and tune in to Casey Kasem's Top 40. I became a fan of Carly Simon after her popular song, "You're So Vain," which many people don't know features Mick Jagger on backup vocals. She perfectly tells the subject (whomever "he" is) a thing or two! Another number-one hit played repeatedly at the time was Tony Orlando & Dawn's campy, bouncy "Tie a Yellow Ribbon Round the Ole Oak Tree." It seemed like everyone on the planet during this time knew them, and in addition to permeating the airwaves, Tony and Dawn helped popularize the televised variety show format upon which many other talented acts were capitalizing.

Most relevant to me about these journeys is the memory of all three of us singing at the top of our lungs in unison, creating an unspoken bond. I'm also ready to acknowledge I am "that" person—you know, the person who sings aloud to literally every song. I suspect it all started with these early memories in the car.

We'd arrive at the Garrison family home, a huge, worn white colonial directly across the street from the lake, where in the winters, I'd slide around on the iced-over water with my snow boots. In the house lived Mom's mother—my grandmother Ruth—who lived with my great-grandfather, Leslie, and Ruth's partner, Louie. A sense of unease lurked under the surface in my grandmother's house, so much so that I always felt trapped and had the urge to escape.

Fortunately, my grandmother's sister, Elsie, lived in a house directly behind the Garrison house with her partner Aunt Winnie, and both were an absolute joy. Aunt Elsie always came up with unconventional activities to entertain me, which were all outdoors and usually resulted in me returning to my grandmother's a filthy, happy mess. As a tomboy, I always cherished these moments, such as when we would dig for worms in the yard. I can still recall jamming the spade dramatically into the ground, causing the smell of natural earth to waft into the air. Breezy Aunt Elsie had an infectious laugh; she was a kid at heart and always hyped up our worm-digging as if it were an Olympic event. Aunt Winnie and I still laugh about the time Aunt Elsie decided to bring me down to The Ball Shop for ice cream, transporting me in a wheelbarrow. As Aunt Winnie describes it, by the time we returned, I was sitting in a puddle of chocolate with a sticky mess dripping down my face and clothes. My mom had a fit, but it was worth it—what a blast!

Back at the Garrison house, I believe the level of discomfort was due to a number of interpersonal dynamics at play, and I intuitively picked up on these vibes. It would have been difficult to completely wrap my head around it as a young girl, as I didn't know the backstory. I suppose Mom told me my grandparents were divorced, but I didn't know my mom had been estranged from my grandmother for a long time and had only reconnected with Ruth when I was around two or three.

The reason for the estrangement is not a feel-good story, but it's part of our family's history and solidified a trajectory for the Battinelli family. My grandmother cheated on my Papa Frank Battinelli when my mom was around 12. At the time, they lived on Falmouth Avenue in Elmwood Park, in a house my Papa Frank built for them. To make matters worse, the man Ruth was having an affair with was Papa's first cousin. The one nugget of satisfaction I get from this awful story is one day shortly after the truth was discovered, Papa caught Louie on the porch digging through the mailbox, prompting Papa to punch him square in the nose. I'm not one for violence but in this instance, I felt it was certainly warranted.

Initially, my mom and her sister Linda were remanded to stay with their mother at Papa's house. As strange as it may seem given the affair, apparently the authorities did not think two young girls should be separated from their mother, but were apparently okay with effectively cutting the girls off from their father. Papa had to leave the house he built for his family to stay down the street with his sister Louise and brother-in-law Joe.

This living situation turned out to be temporary after a physical altercation occurred. Once Papa and the rest of the family found out, they sought permission to take Mom and Aunt Linda out of the unhealthy situation. Ruth was still in Papa's house, so Mom and Aunt Linda joined Papa at Aunt Louise and Uncle Joe's.

For the next year, Papa's siblings worked together to ensure a roof was kept over their heads. Eventually, the court ruled that Ruth had to leave the home, and Papa was able to retain custody and take his girls back home, under one condition: Papa's sister, Millie, needed to live in the upstairs apartment to be a mother figure to the girls.

This series of events was heartbreaking in many ways, but the Battinelli family has always been a strong force, and I'm honored to be a part of them. Also, while it would be easy to put all the blame on my grandmother in light of the circumstances, and I'm certainly not excusing her behaviors, it's relevant that she suffered from mental illness.

Unsurprisingly, these events would shape the woman my mom has become. In a lot of ways, she was forced to grow up quickly as the older sister, helping Aunt Millie tend to the home, which cemented her status as a lifelong cleaning fanatic. Most notably, though, my mom possesses an unwavering loyalty to her family, independence with an innate ability to always figure out the way forward, and perpetual resilience. She also made it her life's mission to be the mom she never got the benefit of having.

"Ain't No Mountain High Enough" by Marvin Gaye and Tammi Terrell captures my mom's essence. When faced with adversity, coupled with her loyalty and protective nature, she is steadfast, and nothing will stop her from carrying out her plan. My mom is my rock, and I've learned more about the right way to act as a human being from her than from anyone else.

Mom's outer qualities match her inner ones, and there's a theme to the adjectives that have popped up by others to describe my mom: "Beautiful." "Pretty." "Gorgeous." At 77 years old, she still fits these descriptors as much as the day she was born. Over the years, my mom and I have chuckled about the various co-workers, acquaintances, and contractors who have tripped over her. So, it's not surprising to me she caught the eye of my handsome, popular, and charming father.

# Chapter 3 - "Sunshine Superman"

You're likely familiar with the term "All-American." Richard John Turoff, born on October 26, 1945, fits that bill. His parents John and Claire created a nurturing environment for their children to shine, and in my somewhat-biased opinion, they were successful as it relates to my dad. He is gifted with qualities most would dream to possess: highly intelligent, classically good-looking with blue eyes and a head of wavy hair, athletic, and charismatic, and armed with a humorous sense of wit. My grandparents created the proper conditions for him to thrive, working diligently to create a good, balanced, and wholesome home life. They strove to help their children (and their only grandchild later on) receive excellent schooling and become well-rounded, always encouraging their involvement in a broad range of social activities.

My dad's dominant social skills likely helped fuel his popularity. My great-grandfather, Jacob Turoff, owned a tavern in Clifton, New Jersey, and it was the family's livelihood for a number of years.

Though he was a couple years older, Mom and Dad started dating when they attended Elmwood Park High School and would go on to marry in August 1967. My dad got his undergraduate degree from Seton Hall University and went on to get his MBA at the prestigious Wharton School of Business.

My dad was also musically gifted, and sang and played guitar in a band called The Secret Seven when he was younger. Though I never got to hear any of their recordings, I have always held an image in my mind. My ears transfix on a string of melodious harmonies similar to "Cherish" by The Association. I can picture the band breaking into "Sugar Sugar," that compelling bubblegum pop song made famous by The Archies. They could keep the crowd engaged with "Happy Together" by The Turtles—I can hear my Dad's pleasant resonance ringing in the background, breaking into the "bah-bah-bahs." Maybe they'd end their set list with "Time of the Season" by The Zombies, taking us on a psychedelic train ride with hip voice work to end the evening. You may be wondering why I haven't asked my dad for a more factual representation, and I'm not sure. I've always felt compelled to come up with my own version—it's exciting to create images in my mind painting his persona before I was born.

Dad served in the U.S. Navy from 1968 to 1970 and moved around a bit. My mom and dad were in Philadelphia with my dad beginning at Wharton. When he learned he was getting drafted, he preemptively joined the Navy. After boot camp in Chicago, he met up with Mom at his station in Bainbridge, Maryland. After Dad journeyed to multiple places overseas, he got stationed in Newport, Rhode Island. They eventually moved back to Philly where my dad was able to continue his schooling. Actually my mom was pregnant with me when my dad was stationed in Rhode Island—I suspect that explains my fondness for New England.

Dad was honorably discharged from the Navy due to his

sleepwalking. My mom has told me some of the antics she witnessed in the middle of the night, which once included him sleepwalking out onto a hotel balcony, and another time attempting to rip up the carpeting in their bedroom. I'm thankful my dad didn't fall overboard (or off the balcony), or neither of us would be here. I've followed my dad's patterns in a number of ways, and unfortunately I inherited my own form of sleeping disorder. My dad has told me he eventually grew out of his—I'm still waiting for mine to conclude.

My dad's profound devotion to all sports is an integral part of his existence. I remember watching him when I was younger, as he tediously wrote down all the college sports game matches, spreads, and winners of each game. Observing this, I can now understand some of my own OCD tendencies— a mutual love of statistics is evident. He continues to run two NFL pools for fun for a small group of us every season. The teams we unite on most wholeheartedly—the Dallas Cowboys and the Seton Hall Pirates men's basketball team—provide a source of shared elation and frustration during their ups and downs each season.

My dad is now retired after a successful career as an under-writer in the insurance industry. When I was little, he worked in Manhattan for a company called Royal Globe. He's the reason I have such a strong appreciation for New York City— he also helped form the basis of my love for Broadway. My dad took my grandparents and me to all the popular shows, including *Godspell*, *The Wiz*, and *The Magic Show*. These trips were always exciting and flashy, as I got to immerse myself in the bustling vibe of the city I consider to be the best place on Earth.

I'm convinced my adventurous side also comes from my

dad. He loves travel, another subject we often discuss. My dad is an organized planner for any outings, and over the years, I have also grown to love the planning and coordination of any trip as much as the trip itself. Investing hours in research to discover the ultimate places to stay, play, and dine is my idea of a fun-filled afternoon!

Against the backdrop of my description of my "All-American" Dad, the song "Sunshine Superman" by Donovan comes to mind, hearkening a bright ray of confidence where the hero always wins. I just wish my idealized vision could wipe out the reality our small family faced next.

# Chapter 4 - "Too Beautiful to Last"

They sat me down in the living room on our regal gold velvet couch, which was covered in clear plastic. In cooler weather, you could navigate fairly adequately, but in the summer months, the plastic would stick to your legs, causing obtrusive red strawberries to form. If there was a way to peel myself off the plastic and out of this memory, I would. While I believe all is as it's meant to be, it is not one of my happier moments: the day Mom and Dad told me my dad wouldn't be living with us anymore.

I don't blame them, faced with an unforeseeable path to soften this bit of news. My four-year-old self knew nothing outside of the family we were. I can't say I remember everything said, because I likely spaced out after the initial delivery. I'm sure they tried to reassure me things would be okay. They were right. Still, it would take me years into my adult life to realize the full impact this sit-down had; specifically the unintended consequences of abandonment. As an alternative to investing a small fortune in therapy, I've selected a few appropriate tunes that help me work through some of the lingering issues created by this early, unwanted shift in my family dynamic.

The chapter title, "Too Beautiful to Last," refers to a song from Engelbert Humperdinck's *In Time* album. Engelbert doesn't write his own music, but he sings with a level of emotion that forces you to relive the sadness and regret coming from his soul. Apparently, his performances are what made him famous, but I've never seen him perform, so I'm speaking to the weight his voice alone carries.

In the '60s, early in Carole King's career, she teamed up with her first husband Gerry Goffin to collaborate on an endless stream of number-one hits before embarking on a solo career and creating the masterpiece album, *Tapestry*. Her now-classic "It's Too Late" captures the mournful essence of a relationship about to end.

Another resonating song of loss is "If You Could Read My Mind" by Gordon Lightfoot. I love how Gordon reveals his sentiments through colorful descriptions of movie scenes and paperback novels, with a vulnerability I suspect it would be hard for most to acknowledge.

But in my mind, no song better expresses the reflection period following a breakup than "The Way We Were" by Barbra Streisand. My love of all things Barbra began early, through my mom. Barbra's vocal range is unmatched, and when she hits the note I know is coming, I find myself holding my breath. I got to cross an item off my bucket list in 2019 when I saw her perform at Madison Square Garden. Apparently, Bill and Hillary Clinton had the same great idea, as they were also in the audience that magical night. The movie *The Way We Were* is one of my favorite breakup flicks—the moment Katie gently tousles Hubbell's blonde locks gets me misty every time.

So back to my four-year-old reality. After my dad left the house, life continued and we all adjusted in our own way. My dad moved back in with my grandparents for a time while Mom and I stayed in the house. I don't recall a formal schedule of splitting time between parents, but I don't think things were as regimented as they are now. I'm sure court appearances, division of assets, and alimony and child support decisions took place, but in credit to both of my parents, they ensured I didn't get dragged into those elements. Many of us have witnessed divorces where, sadly, parents use their children as pawns. While the pain and resentment two people experience during a divorce is understandable, their duty as a protector to their children comes first. I'm grateful I got the benefit of two parents who never forgot this.

In fact, I didn't feel any pull and tug at all. My dad's parents remained close with my mom even into my adulthood, and she treated them like her own parents—with my paternal grandparents, this was easy to do. As a child, I felt the protection of many people around me. In addition to my parents and grandparents, all of the Battinelli aunts and uncles watched over me like a flock, much like they swooped into action when my mom was a girl.

My mom's sister Linda, my godmother, held a different space to which no one else compared. One year younger than my mom, she was youthful, hip, and fun to be around; the cool aunt everyone wishes they could have. We were extremely close when I was younger. When my mom had the tough job of holding the line and trying to keep me on the straight and narrow path later in my teenage years, Aunt Linda was an escape who acted as a neutralizer when I needed it.

While the initial blow of separation was devastating, the aftermath was not negative in how it relates to the love I felt in my day-to-day life. There was one comical incident

I'd describe as an "I'll show them" revenge move. My mom sat me at the kitchen table one day with my lunch and went off, presumably to tend to household tasks. When she returned, she caught me in the act of carving my full name into the kitchen table with my fork. After a moment of shock, she stopped me in my tracks, and for years I looked at an incomplete work. The Virgo in me was compelled to complete my mission, but alas, I never dared!

I've always wondered how my parents felt around one another as I was growing up. I've fabricated a story around the song "Hello It's Me" by Todd Rundgren. Todd's gritty and slightly-off-key pitch proclaims it's important that you know you are free. I guess it was, in fact, too beautiful to last.

# Chapter 5 - "Sailing"

Over the last 20 years, a new music genre has coined the term "yacht rock" to describe a combination of soft and pop rock, smooth jazz and soul, rhythm and blues, and disco from the mid '70s to the mid '80s. According to Wikipedia, it originated by the makers of an online video series connecting this style of music with the popular leisure activity of boating. I find myself frequenting this channel on SiriusXM over the summer months when lazing around the pool, but you can listen year-round on the app. In addition to bringing a level of calm to my soul, the music transports me back to a time and place from my past that was filled with warm and happy memories.

My dad's parents had roots down at the Jersey shore for many years predating my birth. In reading my Aunt Eleanor's memoir, I learned that Aunt Jean was the first one of Grandma's siblings who purchased property in the Brick area of the Jersey shore. Many other siblings would eventually settle down in the area, including my paternal grandparents after Pop retired. Pop and Grandma bought land around the corner from Aunt Irene and Uncle Ray on Kettle Creek Drive in a quiet, serene shore neighborhood.

One pastime we all enjoyed together was crabbing. This shore activity was popular when I was growing up, and the crabs were always plentiful. Prior to Pop's retirement, when they still resided in Elmwood Park, we'd take frequent summer weekend excursions down the Garden State Parkway. Off we'd go, toting crab traps, lines, bait, and wooden buckets in the trunk. My grandmother would pack fresh rye bread sandwiches filled with ham, cheese, mayonnaise, and lettuce. They always had Top 40 radio playing so we could tune in to songs by bands like Crosby, Stills & Nash. The song "Suite: Judy Blue Eyes," written by Stephen Stills to his then-girlfriend, singer-songwriter Judy Collins, reminds me of our trips in Pop's spacious Buick with the windows open and summer wind whipping lullingly around the cabin.

Once we arrived down the shore, we'd seek out one of our favorite spots, usually along the banks of Barnegat Bay. If you're curious, "down the shore" is a Jersey thing. If you grew up in the northern part of New Jersey, you understand this is how many of us reference most of the southern part of the state—whether the area is directly or indirectly by water is irrelevant.

My Pop taught me how to bait fishing hooks, catch a crab on a line, and throw out and retrieve a trap—all tasks that I suppose most little girls would deem gross. Getting all smelly was no big deal to me, though. My favorite of these tasks was catching a crab on the line. It required two people— one person slowly pulling up the line, while the other person skillfully dropped the net underneath. Then together, they would calculate the precise moment to secure the crab in the net. While the fresh, intoxicating ocean air soaked into our pores, we'd turn on a little transistor radio. America's mellow tune, "A Horse With No Name," illustrated a love and appreciation for all things in nature. I never felt so connected as on these excursions.

Once caught, the crabs would stay alive in the wooden crab buckets covered with burlap until the end of the day. Pop adeptly dismantled them, pulling the claws off first; the bottom shell next, then throwing the guts back in the water for other marine life to enjoy, and finally rinsing them clean. He was respectful to throw any pregnant females back in the water—you could tell by the protruding rounded dark abdomen on their bottom carriage, whereas a male's abdomen had a narrow triangular shape.

My grandmother usually made the crabs one of two ways: steamed in butter and garlic or in her famous crab sauce. Eating a crab properly requires patience and can be considered its own art form. Using nutcrackers and the sharp part of the crab's claw, which can be pulled off and used as a tool, you can scoop out every delectable morsel. We'd sit for what felt like hours, savoring the sweet fleshy meat and slurping up the sauce saturating the body, which took on the sea creature's tasteful undertones.

Pop purchased a boat prior to moving to Brick. Always responsible savers over the years, my grandparents made this their splurge, and I admired how they lived their life to the fullest. I wish I could remember more details about the boat itself, but the extent of typical interest as a kid stops at the satisfaction that having a boat is super cool. It was a wooden cabin cruiser and research leads me to believe it may have been a Lyman or Carver. To me it was perfect, and also an ego-boosting experience, as I can humble-brag that Pop named the boat after me; specifically "Three C's," representing wife Claire, daughter Carol, and granddaughter Cheryll. I thought it was clever; it also emphasized family was the most important thing in his life.

Our boat expeditions were magical. I don't remember going particularly far, but we'd spend the whole day out on Barnegat Bay, an arm of the Atlantic Ocean. Parking out in the middle of the bay to crab and fish, you tend to encounter different fish than you'd see off the pier or dock. A sense of complete freedom surrounds you when you're out on a vast ocean, sun graciously beating down, the smell of salt and sea permeating your nose—it conjures limitless possibilities. My ultimate mood music for this experience is yacht rock song, "Sailing," by Christopher Cross. However, the music of The Doobie Brothers comes to mind next, with "Black Water" and its funky Dixieland a cappella segment. My dad's sister, Aunt Carol, came with us on a number of these boat trips, and we'd lie out on the bow together, listening to music, soaking the sun's rays, not far from never-never land.

Even now, when I'm in my car trying to decompress, no type of music is more relaxing or chill to me than yacht rock, and it brings me back to a time when my grandparents were alive, healthy, and thriving; truly enjoying their best life. I still think about them daily, chat with them in my reflections, and remember the profound impact they had on my life. Even after all these years, a void still remains where their presence once was.

Toto is another group in this genre I've always enjoyed; especially their songs that feature backdrops of jazz and soul. Listening to "Georgy Porgy" evokes an image of sitting in a dimly lit jazz lounge with red velvet couches, drinking a whiskey neat (I don't drink whiskey neat, but I feel it would be a perfect accompaniment). The song also includes the backup vocals of Cheryl Lynn, who adds the perfect touch (notice the one L in Cheryl; *her* parents spared her tons of angst). It's so easy to disregard the importance of a good background singer. The theory is that the vocal is secondary or complementary to the primary; meant to blend in, it provides more complexity, depth, and layering. As I look back on my early years with appreciation, I see how greatly the influence of my grandparents playing the figurative role of background vocals would gently weave in some of the most important threads of my existence.

# Chapter 6 - "That's Amore"

Remember my grandfather, Papa Frank, who popped Louie in the nose? He was still living in his house on Falmouth Avenue with Aunt Linda when I was growing up. I always knew where to find Papa—sitting in the same overused easy chair in his living room. The TV tray in front of him was always armed with several essentials: Zig-Zag rolling papers, a can of Captain Black Gold, and an immensely worn deck of cards. Papa rolled his own cigarettes, and as I got a bit older, he taught me how to roll them, which I'm sure Mom wasn't too happy about. A frail man with silver-gray hair, he was always a bit disheveled with a hint of yesterday's scruff. He loved westerns and country music, and by today's definition, Papa would be considered a recluse. I'm not sure he ever got over Grandma Ruth breaking his heart, and additionally, he was deeply affected by the war. He and his brother Tony were drafted during World War II, and Papa was shot while stationed in Germany in 1943. He received a Purple Heart for his brave service and returned with more than just physical scars.

What got Papa outdoors was his garden, chickens, and rabbits. As an old-school Italian would appreciate, the garden took up the entirety of his backyard, and he had a hothouse—a greenhouse of sorts—attached to the garage. The little lawn to speak of could be found in the front yard, with another narrow patch along one side of the white aluminum-sided house. In the warmer months, with the doors and windows all open (the old-school Italians I knew didn't believe in air conditioning), Patsy Cline's "Crazy" echoed through the stale tobacco-filled air, solidifying Papa's heartache. On the occasions when he was in high spirits, Papa would pull out his accordion to play, sparking streams of life back into his melancholy eyes.

While I always had fun rolling Papa's cigarettes, the more interesting part of being there involved observing the dynamic between Papa and his sister, my Aunt Millie. You may recall she lived upstairs in the second-floor apartment of Papa's house, originally ordered by the court to take care of Mom and Aunt Linda. Organized, orderly, and no-nonsense, Aunt Millie ran the ship, making sure the bills were paid, groceries fully stocked, dinner cooked, and house tidy.

The combination of Papa's passive nature and Aunt Millie's "let's git 'er done" approach led to moments of spontaneous combustion. She'd come in and bark out a command. He'd reply, "I don't wanna know nothin'." She'd raise her voice several octaves higher, and he'd proceed to kick her out. I watched this go on for years; it was what they did. A lot of love was present under the surface of those exchanges, but the casual observer might not recognize it. Though the garden was Papa's, Aunt Millie always planted her own patch of strawberries—bright red, and succulent—perfect for picking in the dog days of summer.

Aunt Millie and Mom were close, and Mom seemed to view her as a mother figure. Mom and I have frequently discussed how talented Aunt Millie was—she literally could

28

do *anything*. I'm not sure if this was due to her independence as a single woman or from taking care of everyone. When I was younger, Aunt Millie would come over to our house for dinner on Thursday nights and then drive me in her garage-kept blue 1969 Chevy Malibu to her home, where I'd sleep over. Her home was immaculate with all details ironed out, including a rail to prevent me from falling out of the full-size bed (which I did a lot as a kid). I was always jazzed because Aunt Millie let me stay up late to watch her shows. Her set television schedule involved somewhat of an obsession with the *TV Guide*. On Thursday nights we'd watch *Streets of San Francisco* with a young Michael Douglas and not-so-young Karl Malden. Sometimes I'd stay over on a Saturday night, after enjoying dinner at a nice Italian restaurant with her and her cousin Annie. The Saturday night lineup included *Love Boat* and *Fantasy Island*, two of the corniest shows with higher entertainment value than most reality shows today. Another thing I anticipated about my visits was the next morning's breakfast—that woman whipped up the perfect fried egg. With the mouthwatering smell of butter and grated cheese frying in the pan, the sizzle would permeate the kitchen as she expertly flipped the fluffy yellow pillow with precision, creating exactly the right sear.

Traveling down Falmouth Avenue, four doors from Papa's, lived another set of Battinellis. Papa's brother Tony and Aunt Helen lived on the bottom floor of a two-family home. Uncle Tony was always standing outside, taking in the scene and whistling so loud I could hear him from Papa's, and he'd greet me with his loud, reverberating tenor. Aunt Helen was always kind to me, and we bonded over our mutual Russian heritage. Aunt Helen's sweet mom lived with them as well, and though she didn't speak English, her crinkled eyes lit up when I visited, and she would grasp my face with both of her hands. Upstairs were Papa's sister Louise and her husband, Uncle Joe. Their home was the most stylish of all the siblings (lots of plastic on couches!). Aunt Louise carried the most emotion in the group; a good, sensitive person who didn't have a mean bone in her body. Uncle Joe was kind, gentle, and quiet, in contrast to Aunt Louise's somewhat excitable nature.

I reminisce often about the holidays we all spent together as a family. Aunt Louise and Uncle Joe always hosted on New Year's Day. And yes, there was music. While everyone in my family loved Elvis Presley, my Aunt Louise *adored* him. The song "Jailhouse Rock" reminds me of all the Elvis movies we watched, and I came to admire Elvis's one-of-a-kind dance gyrations and boyishly handsome face. The day Elvis died, I walked in to find my four aunts sitting around the table crying. I get it—entertainers sometimes become our heroes.

To get to the remaining two siblings, you had to travel to the end of Falmouth Avenue to East 54th Street and hook a right. A couple blocks down, two houses stood seemingly isolated from the others; unusual, given the typical compactness of our town. On the left was a huge lot rented by owners of trucks, carnival rides, and other large equipment. On the right was a parking lot for an office building located directly behind the houses. All of this land was originally owned by my great-grandparents, Fiore and Pasqualina Battinelli. Both immigrants from Naples, Italy, they married and planted their roots in America in an area originally called Dundee Lake, which became East Paterson in 1916, and ultimately, Elmwood Park in 1973. Their house was originally located where the office building parking lot was, and it was surrounded by farmland. My Mom lived in that house as a baby until Papa finished building his home on Falmouth Avenue. I gather the first siblings to get married were given a piece of land as a gift, and so the two houses were built next to their parents.

The oldest sibling of the Battinelli crew was Papa's sister, Aunt Rose, married to Uncle Tony (not to be confused with her brother Tony—you know, every family has a favored name or two creating the need for clarification). As the matriarch of the family, Aunt Rose was cool, calm, collected, and wise beyond her years. She had a saying for most situations, and one of her most-used expressions was, "It's a great life if you don't weaken." She encouraged all of us to stand firm through the ups and downs of life.

I have a beautiful cream-colored marble table from Aunt Rose. It sits between my sitting chairs in the family room with my family Bible on top; it's my favorite spot in my house. Aunt Rose was a great cook—I remember sitting around the dinner table watching Uncle Tony polish off a loaf of bread in one sitting. Where he put it I'm not sure; he was tall and rail-thin, causing me to check under the kitchen table to see if he might be throwing it on the floor.

In my family, bread was a staple complementing each meal, and not having it could be considered a mortal sin, leading to a lifetime of sins on my hips. Aunt Rose always gave us ice cream for dessert, and she introduced me to a flavor called butter brickle. It had an ice cream base better than plain vanilla and contained toffee bits, and I'd cheer (using my inside voice) every time the bowls came out of the cabinet. I've never been able to replicate that flavor, and I've had my share of ice cream over the years. I suppose a good pralines and cream or salted caramel will have to suffice.

31

Last but never least is Papa's sister, my Aunt Josie, who was married to Uncle Moe. These two were the social butterflies of our family. Never having had children, they accumulated a brigade of friends, and as members of multiple clubs and travel groups, they were constantly on the go. One of those clubs was the Italian-American Club, and every Christmas season they hosted a holiday party where all the kids could meet Santa Claus. This sparks memories of Bing Crosby's "White Christmas" playing in a room with wood-paneled walls and tile floors, while a novice Santa put me on his lap and handed me a nondescript gift that likely wound up in the needy children pile once we returned home. Seems cheesy now, but when you're a kid, everything's magical.

Aunt Josie was one of the most unique people I've ever come across. With no apparent filter, she held strong opinions, most of them highly unconventional. When I was a child, she created her own unique ways to keep me on my toes. One thing we did was hold hands in her kitchen and perform her version of the "Mexican Hat Dance" (I say "her version" because I question the cultural accuracy). Aunt Josie loved Bingo, and I came to learn something important through her: how to lose. Unlike most sympathetic adults who would let a child win, Aunt Josie reveled in winning and shoving it squarely in my face. Undoubtedly I'd cry, prompting her to pretend-play piano while singing an unapologetic "and the tears come floating down . . . " She offered me a dose of reality some kids may not encounter until they graduate from college and find out what life is really like.

Aunt Josie also exhibited some obsessive-compulsive be-haviors. She loved all the gossip magazines and would leaf through the pages and cross out people's faces she didn't like.

Her other unusual hobby was to go through the phone book and cut out information on certain types of places, which she'd stockpile in folders in no apparent order. She was a restaurant maven—she could tell you about practically every restaurant in New Jersey and rattle off the history of any name changes. If you gave her a street address, she could tell you the restaurant. I'm a bit of a foodie, and into my adulthood, Aunt Josie would pull out her restaurant folders and grill me on what new places I'd gone. She referred to this exchange as "Show and Tell." What a character.

To balance out some of Aunt Josie's crazy, my Uncle Moe was mild-mannered, kind, and attentive. Uncle Moe's family owned an oil company, and he came home after a hard day's work full of dirt and sweaty grime. His first order of business was to wash up after entering through the basement entrance. As soon as he emerged upstairs freshly clean and shaven, he gave me hugs and smooches. The pleasant smell of masculine soap and shaving cream contained a whiff of petrol underneath as I rubbed against his smooth face. He called me his "little sweetheart." As tired as I'm sure he was, he always made time for me. Our ritual was for me to stand on his feet while he walked me around the house. Sometimes, he'd grab my hand in his chubby bear paw and take me around the corner to Durante's Deli, which had a penny candy area where I could pick out a sweet treat.

Uncle Moe had an old turntable on which he played his 78 rpm vinyl records, and one entertainer I remember him playing frequently was Dean Martin, because, as an Italian-American reminiscing about old Napoli, "That's Amore" is kind of a theme song.

Is your head spinning from all these characters? Can you

picture them in one room, all together, at the same time? This actually happened, once a week, when the four sisters took turns hosting. They would enjoy a light lunch and spend the whole afternoon talking. And after my parents separated, my mom started working full-time, so I spent a lot of time with my great aunts before I went to school and in the summer months. You might think a young child would get bored with all these grownups, but it was the opposite for me—I sat and listened, fascinated by every word. The aunts could at times get a tad gossip-fueled. When they didn't want my ears to be able to interpret the discussion, they would start speaking in Italian. I picked up some words over time, and it prompted me to take Italian in college.

In the late afternoon, the aunts would start preparing dinner. The men would come home, my Mom would return from work, and we'd all sit down for dinner around a smaller table than most families would find comfortable. Sometimes after dinner, I'd choose to sit with the men watching television after spending the whole day with "the cacophony."

I'd imagine you're a little exhausted, but I'm not letting you off the family tilt-o-whirl yet! Spending major holidays together was common practice, and as with everything else, the time we spent together revolved around the simple pleasure of just being together, and of course, the meal. My favorite holiday was Thanksgiving, hosted by Aunt Josie and Uncle Moe. The house was small, but they had a partially finished basement where we sat down at one seemingly endless table. Beyond all the siblings and their spouses, all the cousins came, too. One word to capture it: pandemonium. Aunt Josie and Uncle Moe had a bar in the basement, with vintage Western saloon doors evoking a foregone era. At some point,

I'd sneak behind the bar to hide in a cool, dark cabinet—this introvert sometimes needs respite. However, I best relate to the stereotypical Italian persona: somewhat loud, in your face, and direct, balanced with a naturally warm, hospitable nature. I was brought up in a culture of kisses and hugs to say hello and goodbye, no matter how long or short the visit.

All of these great memories remind me of one of my family's favorite crooners, the legendary Frank Sinatra. When I reminisce about the extraordinary characters comprising my family, I can't help but snap my fingers while humming "Fly Me to the Moon."

# Chapter 7 - "Down in the Boondocks"

We've all been graced with certain individuals who make a profound impact in our lives. Some are constant and some are fleeting. They may be parents, family members, friends, teachers, mentors, or even adversaries. What's the thread they have in common? Perhaps as a result of their presence, you've become a better and more completely developed person. Think about those who, had they not been part of your story, would leave a gap separating you from the person you were meant to become.

Aside from my parents, no one was more responsible for shaping my formative years than my Dad's parents, Claire and John Turoff. Their influence manifested through how they existed as a couple as well as individually, and their love shown to me was unconditional; a devotion I can attribute to only a small handful of people in my life. I would not be the person I am today or able to create the successful path I've been blessed with, had they not been a part of it.

My grandmother Claire was part of the Sutowski clan. Her parents, of Polish descent, immigrated through Ellis Island in the early 1900s. I recently read Aunt Eleanor's memoir, a fascinating story about Wladislawa (Lottie) and Alexander Sutowski. Together they raised a tribe of 10 siblings in Jersey

City, New Jersey (technically 13; sadly, Alicia, John, and Phillip did not survive). But Walter, Charlie, Jean, Victor, Joe, Helen, my grandmother Claire, Terri, Irene, and Eleanor filled their home with joy.

In reading more about their background from Aunt Eleanor's perspective, I learned a few important nuggets highlighting why my grandmother was strongly driven to certain values. The Sutowskis were poor, but made it through with three critical elements: unwavering faith in God, love for one another, and respect for family tradition. I believe my sense of nostalgia and desire to dive deeper into my roots stems from my grandmother. She loved all her siblings and similar to the Battinelli clan, the sisters were a force. Observing them together in my youth, I found them bubbly, jovial, and comical. My grandmother used to claim the song "We Are Family" by Sister Sledge was their theme song, and I can see her now, dancing around the dining room table where they're all gathered with ice cold beers, the room overflowing with laughter.

Grandma executed her role as a housewife flawlessly. Aside from Mom, she was the best chef I've ever known, and it came down to the care and attention she put into each meal. All the items she prepared were homemade and fresh, most with a strong Russian or Polish bent. Common meals included *golabki* (stuffed cabbage), pierogies, and kielbasa. Pop would feed butcher meat through a grinder and fill the kielbasa skins, as pungent aromatic spices filled the air. Claire often made borscht (beet soup) and jellied pigs' feet (admittedly, a bit out of my comfort zone). She'd whip up cheese blintzes for breakfast or homemade macaroni and cheese for lunch. It didn't matter what day of the week it was; all her meals were a culinary pageant. Everyone raved about her chicken soup—nothing like a hot bowl of "Claire soup" when you were sick or cold in the winter months!

Grandma was always the most comforting person when I felt ill. During the day, she'd let me stay in her bed to rest, where I'd watch cartoons and game shows and let her dote on me. She swore by a spoonful of cod liver oil to cure the ails—I remember how the fishy mercurial liquid slithered mercilessly down my throat. At night, I'd move to my own bedroom, which took on elements of a healing chamber, and she'd rub Vicks under my nose and on my chest, putting the humidifier on with the door closed while I slept off whatever cold or flu bug had struck.

Grandma spent the majority of each day on her feet in the kitchen, usually listening to talk radio, which is how she stayed up on current events. At some point in the afternoon, she'd pour herself a cold mug of beer to enjoy. I used to laugh when, after cleaning up from dinner, she'd loudly proclaim "the kitchen is closed." In between the cooking, she cleaned house, did all our laundry and ironed it, too. I'd sit in the basement watching her iron every literal thing, down to our bedsheets and underwear! In the warm months, she hung the clothes out to dry—if you've never experienced line-dried clothing, the feel and smell of clothes freshly dried on a line are delightful, enriched with earthly nutrients and warm sunlight.

Grandma's one guilty pleasure while ironing was watching soap operas. This was my introduction to *The Young and the Restless* (always our favorite), *General Hospital*, and *The Edge of Night*. She also enjoyed music, and sometimes she'd ask me to select an album, so I'd put on Sonny & Cher's *Look at Us*, which included the iconic song, "I Got You Babe." As the Sutowskis had previously figured out, it's a great reminder that love and togetherness are stronger than your circumstances. Once in a while, Grandma and I would hop on the bus to Passaic where we'd go clothes shopping—always an adventure. Sometimes for a treat in the summer months, we'd walk over to Jo-Jo's Italian Ices, which was only open in the summer. I've never come across Italian ice like it anywhere since.

Also in the summer months, we picnicked on the wooden picnic table in her side yard, complete with barbecued meats, homemade salads, and corn on the cob. One of my favorite pictures is a black-and-white framed photo of Grandma and me sitting outside on the stoop in the side yard as she watched over me coloring. I remember the feeling of the cold concrete, heavily guarded by the neighbor's shade trees. I was also fond of my grandparents' fig tree—symbolizing wisdom and success in abundance, it matched my grandparents' personas. While enjoying each other's company, we'd bob our heads in time as The Beach Boys played on the turntable. "God Only Knows" reminds me how precious these moments were.

While Grandma tended to the home, Pop worked long, full days managing a machine shop, until he retired in 1984. I was too young to remember when Pop lost one of his pinky fingers in a machine in an accident. He didn't allow this to impact his ability to do anything at all, which always amazed me. When Pop came home, he'd walk the dogs before retreating to the comfort of his recliner in the living room, where he'd read the newspaper, light up his pipe, and watch television. Similar to my dad, my grandfather loved all sports. He also watched *Jeopardy* every evening, and I've finally come to appreciate what all the fuss is about.

While Grandma ensured the inside of the home was in top

form, Pop kept the outside meticulous. My grandparents' Cape Cod (popular choice for our family) stood on Stone Avenue in Elmwood Park. They owned a corner lot with the heavily trafficked Boulevard as the cross street, a block away from Route 46. Most of their lawn was on the right side of the house, which fronted the Boulevard. You could theoretically have fit another house on the lot, and this was where Pop walked the dogs. Their dog Cleo gave birth to a litter of pups when I was five. My grandparents kept one of the litter, a girl named Cha-Cha. This was the first time I fell in love with a family pet—a gentle, patient, and lovable retriever mix. My favorite part of the yard was at the edge, where you could sit on the stone wall barrier under the big willow tree and watch the cars speeding by on the Boulevard.

My grandfather's parents and my great-grandparents, Katherine and Jacob Turoff, also immigrated through Ellis Island. They were a combination of Russian and Polish descent. Jacob had changed his name to flee an area ruled by Russia during a time of great strife, so we do not know what our name was originally. The story goes Jacob knew or met someone with the last name Turov, and made up the rest; or perhaps when he got to Ellis Island, they misspelled the name.

I recently did DNA testing through ancestry.com and was able to trace back everyone except Jacob. I'm hopeful I can solve it and get closure—Pop would be proud of me if I cracked the code, and Dad is curious about this as well. Pop was an only child, and he and his parents resided in Clifton, New Jersey, where as I mentioned, they owned a tavern. Similar to Papa Frank, Pop was also drafted in the Army during World War II. He went to Alabama University, and to my knowledge was the first in my lineage to receive a college education. Pop possessed a dogged work ethic, a strong moral compass, and a savvy business mentality.

Luckily, Pop also knew how to have fun. You'll remember that Pop loved fishing, and of course, he was the one who taught me how to crab. He was also a regular golfer and attempted to teach me how to properly hold a club in their front yard. But one of his favorite sanctuaries was the workshop in his basement. After habitually following him downstairs to the cold, dank cavern to watch him tinker, build, and fix, I unwittingly got my grandparents to buy me my own tool set. Unfortunately, the skill set did not pass on to me. My spouse and I laugh about this, as I will try to put the square peg in the round hole nine times out of ten. Darn near perfect, if you ask me!

I've mentioned my dad played guitar, and long before I knew how to play, I'd monkey around on his. Having no actual knowledge of what to do, I'd pick up his out-of-tune acoustic or electric guitar and start strumming away. I immediately fell under the spell of this magical instrument. While The Beatles' "While My Guitar Gently Weeps" played softly in the background, my grandparents were probably weeping from the sounds I was making, but at least it illustrated the critical need for lessons.

I didn't hear my dad play too often, but he'd pick it up to play with our cousin Bob when we were down the shore spending time with aunts, uncles, and cousins. I hung around a lot in my younger years with my cousin Stacey, who was around my age. I'd often sleep over at her house, and we'd hang out in the pool or go the beach. One song entrenched in my brain my dad and Bob played together is "Down in the Boondocks" by Billy Joe Royal. It's funny the memories you hold on to, as I would otherwise never know this song existed. Ironically, the guy in the song is from the impoverished side of town, and he's professing his love for a girl out of his league. Does love overrule the circumstances? If you ask the Sutowski clan, it absolutely does.

# Chapter 8 - "You Light Up My Life"

Coming from a Roman Catholic family, I was introduced to religion at an early age. Exposure to beliefs outside of Catholicism wasn't overly present in my younger years, and I didn't fully grasp the concept of religious diversity until college. Into adulthood, I encountered different beliefs and practices that helped me gain knowledge and update my perspective. Earlier limitations aside, the foundation I received is tightly woven into my fabric.

My religious indoctrination came through my grandparents and Aunt Millie. My grandparents were members of St. Stanislaus Kostka Church in Garfield, New Jersey. The heavy Polish population made it a natural choice for them, as this church offers Masses spoken in Polish. Though my grandparents preferred the Polish Mass, generally they would take me to the English version, likely after witnessing my perplexity trying to understand the foreign language.

As active members of the congregation, my grandparents sang the hymns with fervor, and my grandfather always walked around with the basket for the weekly collections. I learned about every rite and ritual of a Catholic Mass by attending and watching them Sunday after Sunday.

To someone who does not regularly go to Mass, the number

of rituals can seem overwhelming. If you happen to be Catholic and have ever brought friends who are not Catholic to services, you know the general response is one of bewilderment. It is likely the same look I have on my face when I attend a Mass or service of a different religion.

Incredible power exists in religious and spiritual rituals, especially once you garner an appreciation of the meaning behind them, and understanding the "why" is important. Over time I've gained a great amount of reverence toward these rituals—not sure I've reached the depth of my grand-parents' understanding, but I certainly have tried. When I set foot in any church, my internal aura becomes immediately still; transfixed and at peace. The traditions of Mass, such as blessing with holy water, genuflecting, and praying together helps connect us. I fully ingest the smell of incense filling the air when the priest swings around the gold thurible. I look around in amazement at the vividly colored stained glass. My favorite religious hymn always moves me to tears as I remember how my grandmother sang so beautifully in her mezzo-soprano voice. A breathtaking Latin version of the hymn "Ave Maria" was recorded by Barbra Streisand—I recommend taking a listen, whether you're religious or not.

A few added benefits made attending Mass with my grand-parents even more worthwhile. One block from St. Stan's was Genevieve's, the best homemade chocolate shop I've ever set foot in. When you walk through the doors, your nostrils fill with an aroma so heavenly you might believe you are encountering God Himself. However, the myriad choices are a bit of a dilemma, as well as a pocketbook drainer if you're not careful. I was spoiled as a child on Easter—all my baskets were assembled with these fine confections including my favorite, the Jordan crackers. Russell who?

As if this stop wasn't enough, a quick car ride farther down the road landed us at Kohout Bakery, a Polish/Slovak establishment. The fresh rye bread felt like tasty, doughy pillows in my mouth when Grandma passed a piece to me in the backseat. My grandparents also bought my birthday cake there every year: yellow cake with fresh whipped cream and peach filling. The top overflowed with giant peach slices and a graham cracker topping.

On the car ride home from all of this, we'd listen to some Top 40. "You've Got a Friend" by James Taylor always warms the heart, reminding me of the people who are always there for me. My belief is these people are sent by God, who is also always there for us .

Back at my grandparents' home, evidence of their strong faith appeared in abundance, including crosses, crucifixes, religious statues, and framed Jesus and Pope photos. My grandmother believed in lighting candles in front of her statue, Infant of Prague (the Child Jesus), for people who were traveling or ill. I learned that this statue symbolizes the humanity and divinity of Christ, rejoicing in God's caring and protective love for us. I keep this statue on my dresser today, and sometimes when I feel like talking to my grandparents, I'll sit on my bed in front of it to chat with them. I also have an old glass "God Bless Our Home" adornment that once hung in my grandparents' kitchen, as well as the last bottle of holy water my grandfather had in his house. I deeply cherish these items; they remind me to keep the faith no matter what's happening in my life.

My Aunt Millie was also a devout Catholic. The Battinelli church of choice was St. Leo's Church in our hometown.

I'd sometimes go to Sunday Mass with Aunt Millie after sleeping over on a Saturday night and waking up with a *Love Boat* and *Fantasy Island* hangover. Unlike my grandparents, who preferred to sit in the front of the church, Aunt Millie gravitated toward the back. She always held a set of rosary beads, and went to church on certain days during the week to participate in the rosary society.

Next to the church stood St. Leo's School, which educated children in kindergarten through eighth grade. My parents decided to send me there, believing this program would prepare me well for college. My experience with Catholic school was that classes were smaller, with a highly targeted focus around reading, writing, and mathematics.

To go to St. Leo's, we were required to become parishioners, and part of the requirement was to give a specified donation in both Mass collections. In addition to school tuition, this was a lot for Mom, and while she never complained, I could see the monetary struggle as I got older. Mom and I began attending Sunday Mass together during this time, and on the ride home, listening to "You Needed Me" by Anne Murray, I was lulled by a feeling of comfort and connection to God's love.

Prior to kindergarten, I attended a non-religious preschool called Tiny Tots. The socialization with other children was important for me, given the only other little person I knew was Tracy from down the block. But I still remember kinder-garten being an adjustment. This many kids at once was new territory—I was used to spending my day with adults. The overwhelming feelings returned when I hit first grade, which brought on the introduction of school uniforms. The girls wore yellow blouses, navy blue and forest green scotch plaid jumpers, and navy blue saddle shoes with matching socks.

The boys wore navy blue pants and light blue collared shirts. On the cold days, the girls could wear scotch plaid pants, and in the warmer months, we switched to short-sleeved blouses. School uniforms were purchased at a place called Lobel's, which was the main game in town unless you wanted to schlep to Paterson. While uniforms could be considered boring, it did eliminate certain superficial comparisons. With plenty of things to worry about when you're trying to navigate your way through school, I found that dressing similarly made it simpler somehow.

I also began to intuit some things about my environment. Most notably, I was one of two or three kids who came from a home with parents who were separated. If I recall correctly, one of those kids left not long after, and it was down to one or two. Further, most kids had siblings. Initially, I tried not to think about this. As we all progressed together from grade to grade, it became apparent I was different from other kids because of these circumstances. In the grand scheme of things, the differences became nothing but a tiny blip. As I'd eventually come to realize, I had larger differences to wrap my head around.

When I reflect back now on those differences, it's not surprising I chose some unique kids to be friends with in those early days. I got along with boys on the playground better than the girls. One boy I spent time with was obsessed with Wonder Woman; pretty sure he thought he was Wonder Woman. Another boy had a fascination with all things science-fiction; pretty sure he thought he was an alien.

But I had my moments, too. I suffered from nosebleeds, which would turn on like a faucet with no warning. One Halloween, I was running on the playground in my costume when the blood started flowing, and my whole costume got ruined. Naturally, I was devastated. Another embarrassing moment occurred in second grade. At the end of one day, we were getting ready to say closing prayers, and I desperately had the urge to pee. I raised my hand, and my teacher scolded me for raising my hand during prayers. Unfortunately, my seven-year-old bladder couldn't hold it in. The warm yellow stream started flowing, and there I was, standing in a puddle (yes, the puddle of chocolate in the wheelbarrow was decidedly more pleasant).

A popular hit around the time I was receiving First Communion was "You Light Up My Life" by Debby Boone. This calming piano ballad has strong religious undertones, and along with Debby's strong, uplifting vocals, it subtly assures me that the good gifts on Earth have come from heaven above.

Another song with an otherworldly quality came along a few years later—"Eye in the Sky" by The Alan Parsons Project— which always reminds me God is watching. An interesting fact about this song: "Sirius," the instrumental piece that sometimes precedes "Eye in the Sky," has become a staple of many college and professional sporting events when they're introducing a starting lineup, and it definitely pumps up the crowd. Such duality goes to illustrate that music, like religion, is all up to our interpretation.

# Chapter 9 - "MacArthur Park"

When I started first grade, Mom dropped another unsettling fact on me: We were moving. I was in denial. I loved our home—it was my safety net, a grounding anchor, and the place I could pretend nothing in my life was different than before.

Mom was making what she felt was the best choice for us, and more specifically, for me. Despite this, similar to my parents' separation news, this was a big blow to my six-year-old reality. Mom gently tried to explain the reasoning without putting extra baggage on top. The truth was that the bills and home maintenance were a huge struggle for a single mom trying to raise her child and send her to private school. I now recognize Mom was doing the best she could to make ends meet, and in a sense she was also choosing my education over some of the comforts we had in our home. As an adult, I see this was the right answer and I'm grateful.

We were moving from a house into an apartment. We were also leaving Elmwood Park entirely. Mom needed to find a rental that fit her budget, and we landed in a second-floor apartment on East 6th Street in nearby Clifton. The car ride from Elmwood Park to Clifton was 10 minutes, but if you had asked me then, I'd insist we were traveling to Mars.

Unlike the laid-back suburbia we came from, the urban Lakeview section of Clifton possessed a gritty, edgy vibe. Our apartment in a four-unit dwelling offered only street parking, which cluttered up the narrow street. Unfortunately, our dog Princess (Dino had run away, making Princess the replacement) was also in for a big adjustment. In fact, the apartment wouldn't allow dogs, so she became a country dog, moving up to Greenwood Lake with my grandmother Ruth. At least I got to see Princess when I visited, and she seemed to live out her years happily.

My mom had her hands full, trying to navigate us through this life-altering adjustment. It was a lot all at once, and this place was entirely foreign to us. This was probably my first direct insight into how resilient my Mom is. As opposed to curling up in a ball (like I was at the time), Mom forged ahead. She transformed our small, clean, and well-maintained apartment with her comforting and elegant decorating touches, giving our space a homey, inviting atmosphere. She also demonstrated her unconditional love for me and a protective motherly commitment. As Captain & Tennille described, "Love Will Keep Us Together." The indoor transformation of our space and the love of the person I shared it with helped me slowly adapt to our new living arrangements.

The outdoor world was a different story. Okay, I did have a fire escape attached to my bedroom, which was cool. A giant park a few houses down was also a promising prospect, though it did not live up to the lush, green play areas I was accustomed to in Elmwood Park. On the airwaves, the queen of disco Donna Summer was telling us all about "MacArthur Park", and I connected to her sorrow, but one day I gathered up enough nerve to walk down to the park.

A bunch of older rough and tumble boys, not the Wonder Woman or alien-type boys I was used to, were playing basketball when I arrived. I had no idea what to do with a basketball at this juncture and didn't dare ask them if I could join. I sat down on an unwelcoming, squeaky metal swing and passed the time watching them. I felt a little intimidated, but something about the game and style of play was stirring intrigue within.

We eventually settled into the apartment and Clifton life. The three other apartment units housed older couples, and on the lower floor, one of the women became to us the caricature of a nosy neighbor, always peering around at everyone with an aura of skepticism. The other elderly couple on our floor were lovely and warm with us. Somehow, we wound up with their parakeet, and so Tinkerbell, white with a sky blue belly, became my official replacement pet. Not exactly the same speed as a dog, but it was kind of fun when she flew around the apartment.

I started getting used to busy Lakeview Avenue, where there was a popular clothes warehouse called Nussbaum's that sold designer jeans. When I was old enough, I traded in my Garanimals for Jordache. No disrespect towards Garanimals— I loved them as a kid—my outfits matched perfectly. While I'm no fashionista, I take color matching in my outfits seriously.

In those early days living in Clifton, we spent a lot of time with my Aunt Linda. She took a vested interest in me, coming up with craft activities like paint by number on velvet canvas and hook rugs. I still have the *Peanuts* Christmas ornaments we painted together. Aunt Linda had a cool black Monte Carlo with T-tops, and in the warm months I'd hop in with her so we could go cruising. The disco rage was in full swing, and my love of this music stems from Aunt Linda, who was single and spending time in dance clubs. But nothing was exclusive. Country music also got air time in our world thanks to Papa Frank—I remember us driving with those T-tops off, soaking up the warm sun and gentle breezes while tap-tap-tapping and foot-stomping to "I Love a Rainy Night" by Eddie Rabbitt.

At school, first grade was in full swing. Shy and reserved, I was trying to figure out all these different dynamics, and it was a bit overwhelming; especially the feeling of not entirely fitting in. At St. Leo's, tuition was much higher if you weren't a resident of Elmwood Park. We used my grandparents' address to avoid the added expense, but in reality, I was not a resident. In my perspective at the time, this made me different from other kids.

Through experiences like this, I've learned uniqueness is power. Embrace yourself fully—this is what ultimately breeds confidence and contentment with self. If I could somehow go back and cement this one lesson in my brain as fluidly as the threads of music I picked up, I wonder . . .

While the car rides from Clifton to Elmwood Park were short, it sure felt like Mom and I spent a lot of time in the car. In the morning she'd drop me off at St. Leo's. After school I'd take the bus to my grandparents, eat a snack, and do my homework as quickly as possible to move on to kid stuff. I loved activity books with dinosaurs and amphibians, Colorforms, and Lite Brite, and I've always been able to keep myself entertained endlessly, content in my own little world.

After work, Mom would pick me up at my grandparents' on the way home. Once in the car, we'd catch up, but mostly— you guessed it—we were singing. I would beg Mom *not* to sing when we were stopped at traffic lights, but it didn't stop her. With the windows open, she bopped in time to "*Cherchez*

*La Femme/Se Si Bon*" by Dr. Buzzard's Original Savannah Band. This disco tune with an upbeat big band infusion brings you back in time. By the next traffic light, Mom would be gitchie-gitchying to "Lady Marmalade" by LaBelle (there's a remake from the movie *Moulin Rouge* with the power vocals of Christina Aguilera, M'ya, Pink, and Lil' Kim). Though she embarrassed me as a kid with her musical car performances, in those moments Mom was being authentically herself. Why wasn't I paying more attention? I might have actually learned something.

# Chapter 10 - "Don't Fall in Love With a Dreamer"

When Mom returned to the workforce, the first role she landed was as a secretary for Arrow Carrier Corporation, a trucking company in North Bergen. Mom started building a resume of skills, eventually leading to her role as an office manager at a different firm. But as fate would have it, Arrow is where she would meet the future love of her life.

Charles Thomas Davies was well-established as the controller at Arrow when Mom started working there. In those days, C-Suite titles were not as prominent in most industries. At a small private firm, a president of the company (typically the owner) would run the shop in a hierarchical environment, with a couple different management positions running the day to day. Even by today's standards, Charlie had a high-profile role at Arrow and was considered an executive, with benefits including a luxury company car.

This was not an overnight love affair. Charlie began asking my mom out soon after she started, but Mom rejected his propositions. She's typically sensitive, warm, and caring, but in certain instances she can put up a hard front. Unfortunately for Charlie, this was one of those times. I have to hand it to him, the man was persistent. He continued to ask Mom out for over a year before she finally relented.

I'm not entirely sure what caused my mom's hesitancy, though I have some opinions. For starters, she is proper, so her behaviors are always structured around the straight and narrow path. She likely didn't feel comfortable working in an environment where she was dating someone of authority. This ultimately became a non-issue, as she left for a different firm after an alarming incident involving her and one of the other higher-ups. More importantly, I believe the willpower driving her rejections was fueled by my presence. She was likely sheltering me, wanting to ensure no unintended negative consequences would occur as a result of her decisions.

Once Mom finally accepted his date offer, the first hurdle Charlie had to navigate was my acceptance of him. I'm guessing Mom was crystal clear about no "them" without "me." Charlie was 12 years older than Mom, but the age difference held zero weight. Unlike Mom, when I met Charlie, I instantly fell in love.

While not traditionally so, Charlie was a handsome man. I think it was the way he carried himself—with confidence, intelligence, and a dry, sharp wit. A sense of greatness came out of his pores. Like Mom, he paid attention to what he wore and his outward appearance. When he came to pick us up in his Lincoln Continental, I was instantly impressed, and it was the first time I recognized a higher level of wealth. When I climbed into the middle of the front leather seats, sandwiched between those two, I felt like a rock star getting valeted to a night on the town. As Rita Coolidge's "We're All Alone" (written by the talented Boz Scaggs) reverberated through the interior cabin, I discovered that a car of this caliber also features a superior stereo system.

All of my initial physical observations were complemented by Charlie's personality. He somehow pulled off being businesslike, well-spoken, proper, and suave with humor and childishness. His sense of humor was so corny, yet I found him hysterical. His repetitive jokes never got old to me. As we drove by a cemetery, he would ask, "How many people are dead in that cemetery?" I'd fall into the trap, replying, "I don't know," and he'd drop the punchline: "All of them."

When I was around Charlie, I had one speed: giggle. He paid attention to me, dropping down to my level of comprehension. This was what most endeared me to him. Charlie would say or do things meant to stir things up. Mom, often exasperated, implored him not to encourage me at times when she was afraid I'd pick up a bad habit. Unfortunately she was outnumbered in this regard, as I became magnetically attracted to every improper thing he ever taught me.

Charlie liked to go out to eat, so on Friday nights we'd hop in the car and drive to what became our favorite Italian restaurant, Villa Paisano. On the short trip, we might get transported to another place and time through the soulful voice of Linda Ronstadt singing "Blue Bayou." Don Henley performs excellent backup on Linda's version of the song originally written by Roy Orbison. At the restaurant, Mom and Charlie enjoyed a well-deserved Friday night cocktail, and I was treated to a Shirley Temple. Italian food has always been my favorite, and here I grew to love all their dishes, especially anything baked—stuffed shells, manicotti, ziti, ravioli. Nothing has changed.

The three of us quickly assimilated into sort of a familial unit. Charlie came over during the week for dinner and elevated the conversation with his jokes and diatribes. He also taught me to burp and fart like a champion, much to Mom's (and now my spouse's) displeasure. After dinner, Charlie transformed the kitchen table into a workspace, laying out his 12-ledger paper, adding machine, and mechanical pencils and working for a little while. As boring and nerdy as this sounds, I was enthralled. I loved the concept of all the numbers, neatly printed, ticked, and tied.

After a little work, we'd maybe watch some television together, and both of them would tuck me in. Charlie never slept over—he kissed my mom goodbye and vanished until the next evening, when he'd reappear. At some juncture, I found this to be unusual given the serious nature of their relationship. On some holiday occasions he'd leave or wasn't around, and it didn't make sense to me. I wouldn't learn the reasoning until years later, but we should have been heeding Kenny Rogers and Kim Carnes' warning in "Don't Fall in Love With a Dreamer."

Weekends with Charlie were always adventurous. The three of us would head off early on a Saturday morning for a full-day trip, frequenting places like Wild West City, a country-western theme park, or Bushkill Falls, a popular falls view destination in Pennsylvania. We went to Pennsylvania often, because Charlie had a cabin in Dingmans Ferry, part of the Poconos. A rustic wooden coffee table with a built-in chessboard in my library came from that cabin—it's one of my favorite pieces of furniture.

Heading back from the cabin after a long weekend, we often stopped to eat; one of our favorite places was the Walpack Inn in the rural setting of Walpack Township, New Jersey. And by rural, I mean rural—a population of six, according to the 2024 census. To get there, you drive off a main drag for miles when suddenly out of nowhere, a restaurant appears. The food is good and the bread even better, but to me, the main appeal is the expansive backyard landscape you gaze over while eating—in addition to the beautiful scenery, they feed the deer. This wonderful establishment still exists if you ever want to take a country drive on a nice day.

Our car rides were serenaded with the relaxing easy listening Charlie favored. Neil Diamond remains a powerhouse, and the nostalgic "September Morn" brings me back to our rides on country highways, passing cows grazing in the pasture. While Johnny Mathis became famous through his older hits from the '50s and '60s, I discovered him with his album *You Light Up My Life*, when he remade the title song originally sung by Debby Boone. Johnny's charisma exudes through his vocals, singing with Deniece Williams on "Too Much, Too Little, Too Late."

Charlie also took a strong interest in my development of hobbies and activities, and got me into stamp collecting. Having one of his own, he bought me my own book to start collecting and we'd work on them together. I thoroughly enjoyed learning about all those old stamps and their values. And while I wasn't into dolls, I did love the wooden dollhouse Charlie built for me by hand, with intricately detailed furniture. It's the one piece of childhood memorabilia I held onto.

I vividly remember him teaching me how to ride a bicycle, patiently guiding me down the bumpy sidewalk in front of our apartment until I was comfortable on my own. He was instrumental in showing me how to shoot a hoop, which started getting me over my stage fright of the children down at the park, though I still preferred to go there when the boys weren't around and I could practice quietly by myself.

Similar to Dad and Pop, Charlie also loved all sports and cultivated my love for the New York Yankees and New York Rangers. Most importantly, he got me over my fear of the water after my near-tragic episode by taking us to Lake George on vacation when I was around seven. By the end of the trip, I was diving in the deep end of the pool like a pro! Later, in my teen years, he taught me to drive a car, for which I am grateful; otherwise, I'd still be driving in the slow lane like Mom.

For all of Charlie's positive qualities and the influence he had in my formative years, it's no wonder I grew attached to him. He became a father figure to me and loved me like his own daughter. Without a ton of psychoanalysis, I believe it helped me level the playing field with the other school kids, and I began to feel slightly less different. But let's please remember, he's a dreamer . . .

# Chapter 11 - "You Should Be Dancing"

I've always had somewhat of an obsession with Studio 54.

The famed location at 254 West 54th Street in Manhattan enjoys an interesting history extending back to the 1920s. According to Wikipedia, it formerly operated as an opera house, theater, and studio for CBS, and continues to live on today as a popular Broadway theater and cabaret club. My particular fascination exists in the three years between 1977 and 1980. This period, garnering the most attention and notoriety, resulted in a documentary and movie (if you haven't seen it, the 1998 film 54 starring Ryan Phillippe, Salma Hayek, Neve Campbell, and Mike Myers has great entertainment value).

The nightclub Studio 54 instantly became the place everyone wanted to be. Opening as the disco era was exploding onto the scene, 54 gained attention due to the expansive celebrity guest list frequenting the establishment. This place popularized the admission policy—an exclusivity granted by Steve Rubell, one of the club's owners. It's been documented that well-known stars and celebrities were turned away. As the place to see and be seen, it generated headlines over the outlandish outfits and props witnessed there, such as a famed image of Bianca Jagger riding in on a white horse.

Several elements add to this fascination for me. I'm a bit enthralled with the idea of celebrity; I enjoy observing how an individual lands into the stratosphere, creates a newsworthy buzz, and makes their attempt to rise even further. When I discover someone I connect with, I want to know where they came from before they "arrived," which explains why I read a ton of memoirs. The backstory gives an appreciation of what they endured, and typically at least one life-changing obstacle pulls at the heartstrings. I draw inspiration from discovering the strength that enables them to rise above and turn the negative into a positive. Okay, another factor is the excessive grandeur of it all. I'm a keen observer of spectacles; my energy thrives on being able to sit back and soak it all in.

The underlying theme of acceptance present at Studio 54 during that period in time also appeals to me. Acceptance sounds counterintuitive given the club's infamous admission policy, but at the same time, the club was transparently an equal opportunity venue, open to people of all races, religions, and lifestyles.

Of course, the music of the time was a huge draw. While it's probably fortunate I wasn't old enough to actually go to Studio 54 (I've never used hard drugs, and given my addictive personality, being part of this madness may not have gone well), I would have loved to be part of the debauchery. If I could travel back in time and age myself by about 10 years, I'd have grabbed the opportunity. Indulge me if you please, while I share a vision of how it might have gone down . . .

The air is hanging like damp wash on a clothesline as I step out of the back of the stretch limo my friends and I rented for the evening. We've already informed the driver not to expect us back in this spot until dawn. It's 11 p.m., and anticipation is running high for our first time to the club—we intend to make the most of every moment. The Moet & Chandon we polished off has provided us with a buzz at the appropriate level—where tipsy meets confidence. As we stride toward the entrance, we see the unkempt crowd spilling out onto the street. The darkness brings no reprieve from the unmovable heat—the gritty smells of overheated asphalt, garbage, and an international food smorgasbord hit my nose with a vengeance.

We're hoping for a quick entrance into the club. As a collective group, I'm certain we have the "it factor" required. We're an attractive, shapely bunch, at the perfect age (barely legal), ready for anything—we look incredible. We all got our hair and nails done together after a late lunch, where we plotted out our evening. I'm loving my new bell bottoms— they're jet black and flowing wildly with astrological and planetary patterns across the bottom and coupled with a tight, white satin top showing a hint of all the necessary places. But the *pièce de résistance* is the sparkling silver platform boots. READY, SET, GO.

Once we arrive at the scene, we assess our quickest point of entry. Time to be bold—no waiting in the back of the line for these divas. We suss out Steve Rubell; his eyes are darting like balls in a jukebox. While I'm short even with the platform shoes, we have our smoking gun. My buddy Linda is tall, lean, blonde, and gorgeous, and at 5 foot, 10 inches barefoot, she's impossible to ignore in high heels. Game time. We cross in front of oncoming traffic to create a stir of honks and yells to get Steve's attention, and hit him with our group of five, side by side. He takes a step forward and motions us with one quick wave of the hand—we're in!

It's the most exhilarating feeling when we slip past those

red velvet ropes, squeezing through the crowd as their per-spiration floats in the balance behind us. Our next challenge is to manage not getting separated. It's a mob scene, and increasingly loud as "Shame" by Evelyn "Champagne" King rises an octave for every foot deeper we step in the room; the fast-paced beat drawing us in. First order of business, though, is to stoke our Moet buzz. We shimmy through the crush to the first bar we encounter. The bartenders are all tall, shirtless, ripped, and gorgeous in their tight black satin shorts.

Once replenished, we head upstairs with our drinks. Michael Jackson's "Don't Stop 'til You Get Enough" is pumping through the air. His *Off the Wall* album is the hottest in the world right now; it's hard to imagine him topping it. On the top floor, we take in the entire scene. The infamous moon and spoon hang ominously over a dance floor packed with bodies. It's a frenzy of characters, and everyone seems to be gravitating toward one old woman in the middle of it all. Directly behind us, velvet couches are occupied by couples intertwined (in some cases maybe more than a couple?), and off to the sides, small cocktail tables provide space for friends taking turns snorting white powder. Not what we came here for, but hey, it's all good.

Our friend Lauren has to hit the bathroom—we go as a unit. We discussed the rules of engagement on the limo ride over: We go everywhere in lockstep tonight. There's a huge line for the ladies' room, and Brooke Shields walks by with an entourage behind her. *Hmm.* I wonder if Michael Jackson is here tonight; rumors have been swirling around they're an item. We watch her all the way to her destination . . . and shucks, it's George Burns. After the endless wait for a stall, we return to freshen up our drinks and head downstairs. Time

63

to put our dancing shoes to the test.

Dot leads the way as the shortest of us; it's easier not to lose each other in height order. We're trying to figure out our ideal placement on the floor as "Get Down Tonight" by KC & The Sunshine Band comes on, urging us to do a little dance. In a millisecond, the dance floor is swarmed, and we're thrust into the crowd seemingly by osmosis. As people of all ages, races, colors gather, we become part of one amorphous mass of sparkles, sequins, and glitter. The colored strobe lights and disco balls spin wildly overhead, creating illusions on us; around us. We're drenched after one song, but won't rest anytime soon. "You Should Be Dancing" by The Bee Gees comes on—the *Saturday Night Fever* craze still has its grips on pop culture. My friend Sandy starts goofing with the signature John Travolta pose—she thinks she's Donna Pescow.

We dance for hours, the surrounding area swallowed by the combination of alcohol, perfume, and sweat. Morning is approaching, but before the witching hour, we make our way to the sound stage. France Joli is performing her new smash hit, "Come to Me." We all grab a cute partner and dance in a group; in their arms, we feel safe and warm. Outside of our circle, the crowd's starting to get a little sloppy—it's time to go. As we head outside the club, the rising sun is peeking at us. The damp sweat on our bodies starts to dissipate as we hit the crisp, early morning air—it'll be nice to cool off in the limo. We find our stretch and file in, exhausted but gleaming from the evening. One more stop to soak up the alcohol we just overindulged in—we ask the driver to head to the Parkway Diner . . . cuz hey, it's Jersey.

# Chapter 12 - "Smoke on the Water"

Holding a guitar has always made me feel like I'm suspended in the air above the clouds. The first time I held my dad's Gibson Les Paul, I knew something bordering on sacred was in my possession. Crafted by the master who perfected the electric guitar, it commanded reverence, though I blatantly disregarded the idea that such an instrument was intended for a trained musician. I reveled in the weighted heaviness on my thighs and the feeling of the wide leather strap pressing against my upper back. My left hand clutched the sleek, smooth guitar neck while my right hand delicately balanced a pick as light as air between my thumb and index finger. I knew exactly how to do this from observing my dad. Beyond this, my knowledge came to a screeching halt. I'd attempt to mimic different placements on the fretboard, hoping greatness would ensue by osmosis. I don't give up on anything I'm committed to easily, if at all. It's a blessing and a curse. After my persistence attempting to make music who knows how many times, without any formal study, my grandparents took action.

First came the birthday present of a more suitable guitar for a child. It's best to learn on an acoustic. Though I was in awe of Les Paul, my dad had an acoustic guitar as well, so the familiarity to it worked fine. Of course I was excited, and I came to find because the guitar was designed for a smaller person, I could more easily manage my fingers around the neck and navigate it better. With a more suitable guitar at the ready, the next obvious step was to obtain some guitar lessons. My grandparents found a local guy to come to our home. Mac was a soft-spoken hippie dude with a massive head of curly hair. Imagine the Bob Ross of guitar-playing.

I don't recall how often I had lessons or for how long, but I'm guessing I was around nine. I owe Mac a world of gratitude for teaching me all the basics. Over the course of some initial lessons, he instructed me on how to properly hold and tune a guitar. By using a tuning pipe, if you have a good ear it's not so difficult. Eventually I ditched the pipe and could do it without any aids.

I also learned some basic chords, properly staging my fingers around the fretboard for each. For the added layer of learning to read music off a song sheet, it's easier to do when the chord letter is on the sheet, and beginner pages help with this. In addition to the chord letters, I eventually learned to read notes and memorized what chord each note represented. This isn't all something that happens overnight, but with desire and curiosity, anything is possible. In addition to not giving up easily, once I commit to something, I will work exhaustively to attempt to master it. I may not always perfect whatever the thing is, but you can be damned sure I'm going to give it all I've got. These inherent qualities are the primary gifts getting me through life with a sense of pride and accomplishment. In fact, they've gotten me through the most challenging times in my life.

The first song I learned to play on guitar was corny, though

I can't place what it was—I likely blocked it out. Once we moved on to popular music, I became more invested. I'll claim the first official song I learned is "Oh, Pretty Woman" by the legendary Roy Orbison. The song, in addition to being a national treasure, is an excellent song to practice on guitar due to its repetitive, upbeat rhythm. In the '80s, the song made it back to the charts when Van Halen remade it—that music video was one of my favorites at the time. The song enjoyed an even bigger resurgence when the original was used in the 1990 blockbuster *Pretty Woman* with Julia Roberts and Richard Gere (the best rom-com ever, in my humble opinion). Once I had that song under my belt, I was ready to start exploring. Outside of Mac's lessons, I attempted to learn songs on my own, purchasing the Rolling Stones' greatest hits songbook. But Mac also taught me "Smoke on the Water" by Deep Purple, containing one of the best riffs ever created.

My musical tastes began expanding outside of my family members' preferences, and it was around this age when I started discovering artists based on their sound, look, and style. Naturally, what other kids my age were listening to was a factor, though I'd say I discovered much more on my own. The natural curiosity I held became the fodder for wanting to learn the songs I liked and wanted to play. I couldn't afford to buy sheet music and this was long before the internet. So, one day as I was listening to my record albums, I had the idea to pick up my guitar and recreate the song that was playing. While I may not have been able to instantaneously pinpoint each chord, through a pattern of listening and application, I could find my way through the main chords after a few takes. By either accident or instinct, I discovered I had the ability to play music by ear.

Once I untapped this potential, my interest exploded. I was enjoying this hobby tremendously, but my lessons with Mac were feeling a bit stale. For the next couple of years, I continued to practice on my own using my newfound technique. I'm certain it bordered on obsessiveness. At some juncture, Mom surprised me one Christmas with the ultimate gift— my own electric guitar. While I'm sure the candy-apple-red Hondo All-Star was a decision fitting into Mom's budget, to me it was made of pure gold! As the rocker in me was coming out of her shell, I obtained an awesome black leather silver-studded guitar strap. To make matters sweeter, the guitar was complemented by a Peavey amp—now we're talking. I still have these treasures.

At first, I spent a lot of time learning songs by some of my favorite idols. Female front women were a bit of an anomaly when I was growing up. The first female rocker I gravitated to was Pat Benatar. Though she didn't play guitar, she created a sound unique for the time with her husband Neil Geraldo and the band. And as a formally trained opera singer, she had power and range that was off the chain. I found myself easily settling in with some of her popular hits, and I'd put her albums on repeat to practice. One of the more complex songs expanding my chops a bit was "Promises in the Dark." I'd switch between playing rhythm and lead to try and get better.

A little further down the road, Joan Jett and The Blackhearts exploded onto the scene. While I'd later discover more about Joan's first band, The Runaways, which included a talented group of females including Lita Ford, my initial introduction to Joan was over the airwaves. I loved to play "Crimson & Clover," a cover tune originally written and recorded by Tommy James and the Shondells. The original used a technique called tremolo, creating a reverberating effect between the vocals and guitar—cool stuff. Joan is still rocking it today, and we recently saw her perform at Bethel Woods. If you looked up the word "cool," I'm pretty sure a picture of Joan's face would pop up.

As my play-by-ear talent got stronger, I also began to learn the Top 40 songs playing on the radio. By this point, cassette tapes were the rage. I'd record music from the radio on my boom box using blank cassettes and create mixes. Once I had them recorded, I could practice them again and again. I filled a notebook with the songs and chord progressions. Another of my favorite songs to play was The Cars' "Just What I Needed." Ric Ocasek's deep, powerful, and masculine voice coupled with an excellent guitar riff made it an exciting piece to practice.

Over at St. Leo's, Mr. Cassella was a new teacher when I entered seventh grade. A younger, hipper guy than we typically encountered, Mr. C. was more relatable and took an interest in us as individuals. He engaged in a well-rounded concept of learning the person behind the student and encouraged us to grow in our talents. I learned Mr. C. played in a rock band outside of school, and eventually his band would play at our school dances. I shared my love of guitar playing with him, and he came to my grandparents' home to help me expand my guitar skills. He taught me techniques on my electric guitar, but the thing I most appreciated was having someone else I could jam with! I consider Mr. C my first mentor; someone who had a positive developmental impact on my life. Through guitar playing, I was developing a confidence in my abilities that exceeded my talent.

As things in my young musical career progressed, I decided to start a band of my own with my pal Tracy. Many days we'd walk the couple blocks from St. Leo's to her house and hang out after school. Sometimes when Mom came to pick me up after work, we'd all eat dinner together. Tracy's mom, Barbara, is a great cook and I loved her baked macaroni. Tracy has two younger sisters, Amy and Lori, and I consider them my family and love them all dearly. Regarding the band, I'm sorry to say we never made it off the ground. The name I chose, Dead End, was probably a warning sign. Tracy was the more gifted singer of the two of us, so we practiced popular songs with me on guitar and Tracy on vocals.

I also began composing music and lyrics and running them by Tracy for adjustments, and Tracy wrote a song of her own as well. We'd practice first and record ourselves on a cassette tape to improve them. Before we knew it, we had a full album's worth of songs recorded. I wish we had taken it a step further by adding other musical members into our circle, but school and other activities got in the way. Tracy thought she had our tape somewhere, but alas, it hasn't turned up. And through a series of house moves, I also lost my book of songs. They weren't good, but for the age I was when I wrote them, I'd love to have them for sentimental value. Over time, as my schooling and other extracurricular activities demanded more of me, my guitar playing slowed down. By the time I hit college, it dwindled into oblivion. One of these days, I want to pick it up again—maybe when I'm not writing a memoir!

# Chapter 13 - "Don't Stop Believin'"

As my love affair with my guitar blossomed, so did my personality. My parents and grandparents were always encouraging me to get involved in multiple extracurricular activities. One of the first clubs I joined was the Girl Scouts affiliated with St. Leo's. I was a Brownie from first grade and it was natural for me to graduate into Girl Scouts. A majority of the girls starting from the beginning remained throughout—we grew up together. Our meetings took place in St. Leo's basement. Our troop leader, Chickie, was a real character—at less than five feet tall with flaming red hair, she had a personality that matched her physical attributes.

If you're not familiar with Girl Scouts, the organization focuses a lot on goals and achievements, and you can earn badges for different aspects of service and skills. While I wasn't a fan of the mint-green uniforms, I did come to appreciate the badges on my sash. When I earned a badge, my mom would proudly sew it on for me (albeit tiredly, as I'm sure I was asking her to do it at night after a full day of work, cooking dinner, and schlepping me around). I remember being excited about earning my first small, circular prize, but I started noticing certain girls around a little bit longer had many more, and I determined my one lonely badge needed a lot more partners. In a weird way, I think this may be where my overachiever mentality took hold—a focused mission to fill up my sash resembled some type of internally fueled contest.

In addition to badge hunting, we Scouts did a lot of fun things together. My fondest memories are of our camping trips. A few places I remember visiting regularly were Camp Te Ata, Rocking Horse Ranch and Lake Rickabear. They were such adventures—they seemed so far away, but in reality, two of the three are close to my current home, and one is less than a half-hour ride from Elmwood Park. Camping was exciting and fun, and the concept of "roughing it" didn't faze me. I enjoyed the cold, crisp air and waking up to the sound of rustling wind whipping through the forest. One of the funniest things I remember was my mom's one overnight camping experience as a chaperone (note the word "one"). Somehow I convinced her to go, though camping was not at all her speed. I was fascinated with amphibians, notably snakes—in fact, a collection of rubber copperheads, pythons, and boas took up space in my room, dresser drawers, and bedroom closet. The practical joker living inside me concocted the scheme to prank someone, and Mom fell victim. As she slipped into her sleeping bag, the aptly placed prop touched her feet, and she flew up in the air screaming wildly. It was decidedly her last time camping.

In addition to Girl Scouts, I joined softball through the Elmwood Park town league. This was my introduction to a world outside of the kids I knew at St. Leo's and my first official organized sport outside of gym, which doesn't count—dodgeball and kickball are fun, but I thought gym was otherwise kind of a joke.

I quickly began to learn something about myself: I'm not a

natural athlete (though I have always had that sporty look!). I'd watch some girls in amazement as they pitched, caught, and batted effortlessly. Some people might get frustrated making comparisons, but I suppose as a result of my stubborn, no-give attitude, this observation didn't deter me. Instead of hanging up my spikes, I turned my energy toward practicing and working with girls who were inherently more gifted than me. I took some cues from Jeanne (a friend also in my Girl Scout troop), who was a year older than me and one of the best on our team. She loved Journey and brought her boom box to the field. "Don't Stop Believin'" is one of my most inspirational anthems, taking me on an optimistic voyage to anywhere. My Mom bought me their *Escape* album as an Easter present, and it was probably my most-played album— it eventually needed replacement due to a skip in the track.

On the field, I always listened to the coaches' constructive criticism in an effort to improve. Over time, I became a decent outfielder who could make a base hit, but stopped short of ever becoming a power hitter. One thing I always had on my side was my speed (at least in those days—I think my legs remain my strongest body part). In the four or five years I played softball, I began to understand and appreciate the element of teamwork. I firmly believe involvement in organized sports teaches you most of what you need to know about life.

With my confidence improving through guitar, softball, and Girl Scouts, back at St. Leo's I was evolving quickly out of the shy, reserved girl from back in first grade. My popularity rose as I began to form friendships with the girls as well as the boys. A tight group of us girls started to form, though we were friendly with everyone. We hung around together after school, at each other's houses for parties, at sleepovers, and around town. We'd travel on foot or bicycle to popular places in town, such as Borough Field, The Trestle, and The Wall. We did both best friend and boy swapping—I guess at their core, girls can be cliquish and fickle.

Our musical tastes also continued to evolve. One shared influence was the group Kiss during the release of *Destroyer*. All the boys started coming in wearing face makeup and acting out "Calling Dr. Love" in our talent shows. It was impossible not to get swept up in the Kiss Army. I started exploring them on my own, and they have consistently been one of my favorite bands of all time. We recently went to see their last-ever performance at Madison Square Garden, which transcended a typical concert experience for me—I was completely absorbed into the crowd's nostalgic energy—20,000 fans celebrating 50 years of awesomeness. As a thank-you for my attendance, I caught my second bout of COVID. If you're wondering, of course it was worth it!

I was always a smart kid, though not the smartest in our class. I can now acknowledge I skated through grammar school. The three basics of reading, writing, and arithmetic have always come naturally to me. Challenges surfaced in other subjects, like science. Instead of working hard in the challenging areas, I accepted my limitations (a direct correlation between my interest level and commitment level). I was unconsciously deciding how to expend my energy. In grammar school, most of it stemmed around fun activities.

Don't get me wrong; I was kept on track. Every day after school, Grandma grilled me about my class assignments. She gave me an afternoon snack and made me complete all my homework before anything else. I even had to show her my work. When Mom came home, Grandma provided a full report, and all the tests Mom had to sign were placed on the kitchen table along with the pen. I'd always pile the tests from best to worst, hoping it would soften the blow. I'll never forget my mom's lifetime school mantras: "Cheryll Lynn, you need to apply yourself more," or more sternly, "Cheryll Lynn, you better buckle down!" I always knew when the sentence started with Cheryll Lynn, I wouldn't want to hear what was to follow.

At some point, the girls started having more parties with the boys. Listening to Debbie Harry's intoxicating vocals in "Heart of Glass" by the iconic new wave band Blondie, or the rhythmic stuttering in "My Sharona" by The Knack, we'd play games like Spin the Bottle or Two Minutes in the Closet. Though I was out of my shell and no longer focused on the differences of my home life, something was off. My friends were suddenly boy crazy, and I just didn't get it. Sure, I thought some of the boys were cute, and would develop crushes, but for the most part, I was following the lead of what other girls were doing as opposed to reacting to internal feelings or emotions. Under the surface, other signs of who I was were starting to swirl around deep down inside.

My first girl crush happened when I was in around fifth grade. The interest was toward a girl not in my class, and truthfully I'm not sure how it began—she wasn't in my clubs or circle of friends. My guess is it all began when I noticed her in the schoolyard, and all I knew was that feelings started stirring; feelings not present during my boy encounters playing Spin the Bottle. Nothing ever happened with this girl, because I didn't understand what any of it meant.

The second girl crush came when my girlfriends were starting to advance "bases" with boys. I was not doing those things with boys, yet was intrigued. In truth, I was becoming more curious about how it would feel if I did those things with a girl instead of a boy. As with the first girl crush, the second never amounted to anything other than continued confusion. No one in my world was exhibiting anything close to what was going on in my mind. All I know is when Mr. C's band was playing Eddie Money's "I Think I'm in Love" as I danced with my first boyfriend, inside I was contemplating if my girl crush could, in any possible scenario, be thinking of me the same way I was thinking about her.

Had anyone been paying attention, they'd have spotted a few early "warning" signs. Back in second grade, I insisted on wearing a Donny Osmond Halloween costume to school. While everyone loved Donny & Marie, no other girl I knew wanted to dress up like Donny, though everyone thought his purple socks were "far out!" My Mom seemed to accept my choice without any protest—was she perplexed about my choice? Her second tip should have been when I started my formal boycott of wearing dresses and began cutting my hair like Dorothy Hamill. The change is noticeable when looking back at my class pictures in order. The long, flowing blonde hair and frilly dresses disappeared by fourth grade, replaced by unisex shirts and pants with my hip new hairdo. Externally, I was decidedly comfortable with this transformation, but inside, the war of conflict was only beginning.

# Chapter 14 - "The Spirit of the Radio"

In my humble estimation, the diverse, groundbreaking music of the '70s and '80s can't be matched. Despite this, foundations upon which each genre was built are clear. Without Elvis Presley, Chuck Berry, and Little Richard, there would have been no Beatles or Rolling Stones. Absent the Motown and psychedelic soul eras, no disco would have ignited out on the dance floors. The crooners wooing the crowds, such as Frank Sinatra, Sammy Davis Jr., and Dean Martin, paved the way for a guy like Josh Groban.

The foundation of rock 'n' roll itself led to multiple offshoots like heavy metal, glam, and punk rock. Similarly, the tracks laid by rock artists in the '70s and '80s led to the grunge explosion of the '90s. The truth is, influences exist in each genre of music, deriving from somewhere and sometimes multiple sources; in turn, all the genres created evolve into a different style down the road. Behind all of this are two qualities conspiring in perfect unison: inspiration and creativity.

Where am I going with this diatribe? Oh yeah, '70s and '80s music can't be beat. It became apparent to me when I was going through a somewhat loony song-selection process writing this memoir. Because I'm guessing a part of you is curious, *did she really pluck all these songs out of her memory?* In many regards I did. I've been connecting songs to memories my whole life. I'm sure many of us do this, but the difference may be the extent to which I've pondered the reasoning behind it.

The initial thought to make music a focal point of my memoir came to me years ago. It popped into my brain like the pearly white gates were opening and took permanent residence. A game of multi-ball started playing out in my head—wouldn't it be cool if I used "Welcome to the Jungle" to name the chapter describing one summer as a young college student? Or the title "Enter Sandman" to talk about my sleeping disorder? Things continued to randomly rapid-fire anytime I was listening to music. For a long time, I did nothing, but the thoughts kept spitting out at me like an oncoming train.

When I began writing my memoir, the subjects and memory associations came first. I did this as chronologically as I could, arriving at almost 100 subjects with pages of associations to each subject; an outline of sorts. My initial intent was to start writing and layering in songs as I went—I certainly felt enough had rolled around in my brain for a number of years, so I could have easily gone in this direction. Still, I wanted to dig deeply to illustrate my connection to music and its importance to me.

I determined my sources; originally my personal CD and vinyl collections and older iTunes purchases. It occurred to me I might miss something since despite what you may think, I don't spend all my hard-earned wages buying music! I decided to do further research by reviewing the billboard charts from the '50s through today, as well as diving into internet lists on some of my favorite genres. I started making lists by decade. With over 500 CDs, more than 100 vinyls, and

200 iTunes purchases, not to mention the 70 years of billboard hits reviewed, I soon realized choosing would be a tedious and time-consuming endeavor.

However, the cumbersome nature did not strike me when I was making the lists—I was having fun. It became much harder when I had to start narrowing down the field. I love music deeply, and my selections were vast. I'd be in the car commuting to work and hear something and decide *I need to include this!* I'd take pictures of my navigation screen to add them the next morning. My first complete list included around 750 songs, but realizing this was out of control, I pared it down to 500. I rewrote the list, going through the difficult process of weeding out by comparing, listening, and deciding if the song deserved to be part of my life story.

Once I had my full list of around 500 songs sorted by decade, I finalized my chapter order and started placing songs into each chapter. I settled on five songs per chapter—enough to weave into the fabric but not overwhelmingly so. Given the number of chapters, I still had more songs than I could use. I'm continuing to weed out as I go, and your guess is as good as mine as to which songs will complete this work!

By far, the '70s and '80s were the most populated lists, leading to my logical deduction that they contain the best music. Naturally, this presumption is going to spark debate, but since this is my memoir, I'm here to provide my feelings on these matters. I hope I've inspired you to make your own memoir to music. I will cheer you on and promise not to subject you to my viewpoints, reading with no judgment if you come to a different conclusion than I would. While I love multiple genres of music, at my core I'm a rocker (maybe I fooled you with the early mentions of Barry Manilow and the

Carpenters?). Before moving farther out into the fringes, I want to give some appreciation for a few foundational rock bands leaving an unmistakable impact on the world.

It almost goes without saying, The Beatles are in a class by themselves. I'm certain the songwriting by Lennon and McCartney has inspired and generated more artists than anyone. It's impossible to guess a number, and it's still happening today. Their extensive music catalog could easily take up a whole book, but four other British rock bands have also achieved legendary status.

There's Led Zeppelin, combining Robert Plant's angelic voice, Jimmy Page's edgy guitar playing, and Jon Bonham's iconic drumming. Their songwriting by Plant and Page was deep and complex; their sound launched hard rock as its own category. I wish I could have seen them live. More on them later. Let's move on to The Rolling Stones.

Holy cow, where do I begin—the fact they are still actively touring is miraculous. They originated in 1962, eight years before I was born. True pioneers, Mick Jagger and Keith Richards as a songwriting team and anchors for the band are testaments to their longevity. "Gimme Shelter" reminds me of multiple movies by Martin Scorsese, one of my favorite directors. More than this, it brings back a snapshot in time from September 2002, when a few of us went to see the Stones with the Pretenders at the original Giants Stadium at the Meadowlands in East Rutherford. During the show, my buddy Linda and I went for a bathroom break and another beer. The opening riff of "Gimme Shelter" began as we were standing in the middle of the concourse—Linda and I looked at each other and bee-lined as fast as we could back to the stadium floor to join our crew and the massive crush of screaming fans. Mick was just a kiss away. I absolutely love love love the background vocals of this song—the woman who originally did them in 1969 is a gospel singer named Merry Clayton, who has a remarkable story of her own.

Another band continuing to impress as long as the Stones? The Who. Also originating in 1962, they were also born of the British rock explosion. With the anchoring team of Pete Townshend and Roger Daltrey, they went on to popularize rock operas such as *Tommy*. Watching Pete Townshend with his signature guitar move before smashing it to bits on the floor is a thrilling sight. And for a man of his years, Roger Daltrey is still sexy and can rock it on stage with the same charisma as ever. The synthesizer-on-steroids song "Baba O'Riley" became an anthem for an entire teen generation.

Quick funny story regarding the last time I went to see them. The show at MSG ended later than we anticipated and we were rushing to get back to the PATH to catch the train back to our home base. We packed into the elevator, and in a bit of bad timing and misfortune, our elevator got stuck. It wasn't a big elevator, and about 12 of us were packed in like sardines. I instantaneously freaked out, feeling trapped in despair and claustrophobia. Seamus (whom you'll meet later) was trying to calm me down, but I was at the point of no return. He should have knocked me out—I would have understood. We eventually got released after 45 minutes of paranoia.

The last British rock band getting props: Queen. Freddie Mercury left us way too soon. "Bohemian Rhapsody" is a masterpiece, coming back into the stratosphere with the movie *Wayne's World*, in the iconic headbanging-while-driving scene with Mike Myers' Wayne, Dana Carvey's Garth, and their goofy friends.

With all of these bands, you can easily see the recipe for success. A strong collaborative writing team, stellar mastery of instrumentals, and a charismatic front man. While Britain owns the limelight for legendary rock bands, fabulous rock music was also created elsewhere.

Hailing from Canada with a limelight of their own, a three-man band called Rush entered my world, literally blowing my 14-year-old mind. Their sound was completely unique, taking advantage of the generous use of synthesizers. The thing about Rush is if you didn't know any better, you'd easily think the band was comprised of many more members—that amount of sound coming from three guys? Crazy. And in my opinion, Neil Peart was the greatest drummer of all time.

Listening to a song like "The Spirit of the Radio" kicks my adrenaline into high gear. The drums, keyboards, guitars, finished off with the incredible vocals of Geddy Lee; it doesn't get more perfect, but their songs also have depth in meaning. The regard I have for them has been codified because they were the first concert I ever attended. I've been to many concerts in my lifetime, each of them bringing profound experience into my world, but you never forget the first time (wink).

Other bands performing up to this level of excellence, however, come to mind. I think about Fleetwood Mac, The Eagles, and Aerosmith and want to keep writing. Though when deciding my last song to end part one of this book, I considered influence. In the last chapter I mentioned a couple of my female idols, Pat Benatar and Joan Jett. One more female-fronted rock band from the early '70s helped to define a future generation of women powerhouses: That band is Heart.

Ann and Nancy Wilson started the band in 1973 in Seattle, Washington. With Nancy's masterful guitar playing and Ann's electrifying voice, they went on to create some of what I consider the best rock music on the planet. Listening to their songs, you feel like you've endured a round on an electric chair—currents pulse through their songs to your veins. I've had the benefit of seeing them several times, and their talent has not wavered. While I'm an equal fan of many of their hits from their highly successful 1985 self-titled album, I had to bring it back to one of their first hit singles, "Crazy on You." A song like this helps illustrate that women can create music equally to men.

Generally speaking, the path for a woman to succeed at this level is a tougher hill to climb. I think this can be said about almost any industry. I don't consider myself a feminist, yet I do subscribe to equal opportunity. When I see the path women such as Ann and Nancy traveled, I can't help but look up to them. I recently watched the American Music Awards, and it was saturated with female performers as the winning choices. Maybe we're finally, after all this time, getting somewhere . . .

# II

# PART TWO

***AIR GUITAR RULE #2*** - *The technique can be applied to any guitar-forward music, but in my view, the louder, the better.*

# Chapter 15 - "When Doves Cry"

The year 1984 was a milestone in my young life. Commencing with Confirmation in February after previously receiving the sacraments of Baptism, Penance, and Eucharist, I was now being accepted as a full-fledged member of the Roman Catholic church. Though my relationship with the Catholic church is a bit different today, these elements and what they represent has never wavered. I've received five of the seven sacraments (I added matrimony to the list in 1993.) Last Rites will complete the journey; hopefully not for a long, long time as I'm not ready yet, though when the time does come it is critically important to me to receive. If you're curious, a seventh sacrament referred to as Holy Orders is reserved for someone going into the priesthood. I'm relatively certain that will never be part of my story. Six out of seven is still a commendable percentage for a Catholic!

My eighth-grade school year was speeding by before I could realize the magnitude of what was happening. As the big dogs in the grammar school pecking order, we enjoyed our "power," and our collective confidence was never higher. We had become a tight unit as a class, savoring our last year together, celebrating our friendships and the experiences we'd gone through. As adults, many other milestones occur and we often forget how important grammar school is to setting our foundation. Our class had spent the last nine years together, including kindergarten. We knew this was our time to make the most of things, and boy did we ever—sleepovers with the girls, trips to Wallington Roller Rink, huge parties at various friends' houses, and school dances. At our last dance, reverberating vocals with a big band throwback emanated from the loudspeaker with David Bowie's "Let's Dance."

While eighth grade passed quickly, the important decision of where to go to high school loomed. Since public school was not on the table for me, on top of Confirmation and preparing for eighth-grade graduation, Mom and I were touring Catholic high schools. Some nearby schools I can recall were Paramus Catholic, St. Paul VI, and Mary Help of Christians. We ultimately decided on Immaculate Conception High School in Lodi, an all-girls school with a smaller enrollment, as we felt the strong curriculum coupled with small classes would best help me prepare for college. Also, my pal Tracy had already started as a freshman there, so having an inside track and perspective gave me comfort in what was a huge decision.

After graduating grammar school, my friends and I continued to party before the reality of a new chapter hit us. And there's no harm in a little innocent debauchery from time to time. On our last day of school, a large number of us decided to leave our mark. We targeted the boys' and girls' bathrooms, making a huge mess by toilet papering and throwing sopping-wet paper towels all over the walls and ceilings. After school, we all went over to our friend's last day of school pool party bash. But when the mess was discovered, we were called back to the school to promptly clean up our artwork. Imagine 39 kids running down the school halls in

dripping wet bathing suits! Say hello to my immaturity—
YES, I still find it hysterical—and NO, I'm not embarrassed by
our delinquent actions. Crisis averted, we left school for the
last time *again* and hustled our way back to freedom-filled
dives and cannonballs in the pool, while "Wanna Be Startin'
Something" by Michael Jackson blasted in the promising,
soon-to-be-summer air.

Summer was a blast—we soaked in majestic sunbeams and
Bartles & Jaymes wine coolers. Friends' basements turned
into free-for-alls, and on the airwaves, one of the best movie
soundtracks of all time was churning out hit after hit. We
already loved Prince from the *1999* album the year before, and
when *Purple Rain* arrived, we went batshit crazy. Talented,
sexy, and badass cool, Prince was the whole deal, and his
guitar playing, electrifying. "When Doves Cry" reminds me
of this particular summer—we felt as free as Prince speeding
through town on his purple motorcycle.

After Labor Day, the sun-washed heydays of summer came
to an abrupt, screeching halt as the reality of freshman year
of high school stood before us. My first glimpse came at
freshman orientation, when I suddenly realized the lax-vibe
"high" I was currently experiencing was going the way of the
dodo bird. Immaculate Conception was going to be my "good-
time Charlie" rehab center.

The simplicity of grammar school was no longer my reality,
and the new reality overwhelmed me. Though the school and
classes were small for a high school, I was accustomed to 39
students split into two classes. We had spent most of our day
with our primary teacher and when we swapped to the other
teacher for a class or two, an orderly chaperoned transport
was provided by our teacher down the hall. We didn't need to

think about anything other than homework and grades (spare the occasional duty cleaning erasers in the schoolyard; not too mentally cumbersome).

In high school, I was assigned a homeroom teacher, learning how to navigate new and unfamiliar halls and my locker, and carrying a stack of books that could be used as dumbbells. At least I was used to the whole uniform experience—our navy skirts (the only skirts I'd wear), light blue blouses, and saddle shoes were a welcome comfort. The one new element was blazers, which were always to be worn during Mass and assemblies, with no exceptions (included in the plethora of things for which you could earn yourself demerits).

Waiting in a stupidly long line crawling slower than an inchworm, I pondered my new prison sentence and my newly provided class schedule. Fate intervened when my perceptive mom, ever-supportive and hugely observant (unlike her daughter who exists in a solitary existence most of the time), excitedly announced that the girl in front of me would be in the same homeroom as me. *Mooomm . . . embarrassing to the max . . . why are you looking over her shoulder at her schedule . . . why are you yelling it out like a crazy person . . . gosh . . . I want to curl up in a ball and die.* Embarrassment aside, the bond around our shared homeroom became something we both had to look forward to on day one and took some of the edge off our freshmen jitters. Little did we know, 40 years later, Linda and I would still be laughing about this introduction like the 14-year-old girls we were then.

The other adjustment was my new wake-up time, which commenced on the first official day of school. My trek from Clifton to Lodi required me to get up at the butt crack of dawn to hop on the assigned school bus on Lakeview Avenue, which made stops through Paterson, Clifton, Passaic, and Wallington before getting to school. Mom had to drive me to the bus stop in pitch darkness to wait for the little yellow bus to arrive. However, it became another good opportunity to meet some of my classmates. I became fast friends with one of the girls, Liz, who was also a freshman—we're still friends to this day. Knowing other people helped me adjust to high school life. While both nuns and lay teachers were strict about following all the rules, I soon felt comfortable, safe, and at home.

As my inaugural school year and 1984 came to a close, the following year brought our family some major devastation followed by unexpected drama. Papa Frank got diagnosed with cancer of the liver and colon, and by the time it got uncovered, it was highly advanced. Papa needed care beyond what Aunt Millie and the siblings could provide, and the decision was made that Mom and I would move in so she could take care of him. Mind you, the house was small: just two bedrooms, a kitchen, living room, and one bathroom to share. My mom slept in the living room on a pull-out couch and I moved into the other bedroom. It was tight quarters, but at least we were together, with one upside—we were back in the comfort of Elmwood Park.

Mom is an excellent caregiver and did everything she could to keep Papa comfortable. Papa Frank passed away in July 1985. This wasn't my first encounter with death. When I was 10, Mom woke me up in the middle of the night to tell me Uncle Joe had died of a heart attack. Jarring news to a kid, but here's the thing I quickly assimilated about death. It is something to be respected and revered as equivalent to someone's birth. Our Catholic rituals around death—mourning, gathering, attending wakes, Masses, and burials—are symbolic to help us grieve and pay last respects to the person who left us behind. This is another place where I feel my religious foundation has helped me to accept and understand something incredibly heart-wrenching and difficult to wrap your head around.

In addition to Uncle Joe, we also lost Uncle Tony Battinelli, Papa's brother, a year earlier to lung cancer. This broke Papa's heart—maybe he decided he needed to follow his younger brother to paradise. In honor of Papa Frank, "Always on My Mind" by Willie Nelson echoes with sentiments of regret and sadness. I hope Papa left them all behind and is resting easy, playing his accordion for a group of goombahs from old Napoli.

After Papa passed, the business of settling his estate became the priority, as well as the added complication of what to do about us residing in his house. Mom thought the best course of action would be to buy out her sister Linda's half to avoid uprooting us again, and besides, Aunt Millie already lived upstairs. The rest is not my story to tell, so I'm going to leave it at things got complicated, and a massive rift between Mom and Aunt Linda was the outgrowth. From my singular point of view, I lost my godmother as well as my only two first cousins, Danielle and Peter, Jr. They were babies, and I had anticipated watching them grow and becoming the best older cousin, figuring I'd be the cool cousin like Aunt Linda was the cool aunt.

I'll admit I've never gotten over this rift—I don't have closure, because all these years later, we've never mended fences. This is one situation where my Mom and I have different viewpoints, and while I respect her perspective and reasoning, I've desperately pleaded for us to come back together as a family. In my view, it is never too late. Time is meant to heal all wounds. I'm going to leave this topic by putting out a direct request: Mom and Aunt Linda, hasn't it been long enough? Do you **really** want the story to end like this? The past can't be changed, and it no longer matters. What does matter is we have complete control over our present and future, with the power to bring our family back together again.

As 1985 drew to a close, we spent our first Christmas ever without Papa Frank, and apart from Aunt Linda and the latest generation to enter our family. As the legend Elvis Presley mournfully described, it was a "Blue Christmas" without them. Reflections of my childhood trailed behind in scattered particles of dust and crumbs left on an unswept floor.

# Chapter 16 - "Photograph"

In the early '80s, a new byproduct of heavy metal began to dominate airwaves, record stores, and a novel televised phenomenon called MTV. With its hard, edgy style, hair metal (or glam rock) added elements of flash, glitz, and over-the-top theatrics. While credit must be given to the true pioneers of metal—most notably Black Sabbath and Led Zeppelin—I was a personal witness to the glam explosion.

The domination didn't happen in typical fashion—these were not the bands making Casey Kasem's Top 40. The landscape was shifting, and bands viewed as "cool" were creating an anti-establishment order. These were bands causing havoc in the music industry, responsible for causing the need for explicit content and age-appropriate rating labels to start popping up on cassette tapes and vinyls. While some of these bands were able to pierce through the Billboard, the ones that did were viewed as sellouts or posers. I'm not sure what was happening in the rest of America, or the rest of New Jersey. What I do know is in Bergen County, my friends and I were getting swept up into a new sound and style of hard, fast, and loose reckless abandon.

A couple of bands kicked off the avalanche. One of the first was Van Halen. The band originated in 1973 and had been making kick-ass music for a number of years. The first album I started paying attention to was *Diver Down*. The popularity of MTV had carved out a pocket for certain bands absent from the Top 40, enabling their introduction to the world. In my view, this was how the Top 40 started to become irrelevant. Through music videos, we started paying attention beyond the music, homing in on the fashion style, charisma, and overall cool factor of the artists.

Earlier, I referred to the video "(Oh) Pretty Woman" by Van Halen. This was the first of a series of videos by the band that created a story around the songs and launched their image. By the time the album *1984* was released, they were the hottest thing going. In high school, my friends and I mimicked the dance to "Hot for Teacher." My song choice off the *1984* album is "Panama" for its stellar guitar playing and masterful slide rules—I consider Eddie Van Halen the greatest lead guitarist of all time.

While Van Halen was laying tracks in the United States, across the pond another band was making its presence. Britain-based Def Leppard was enjoying success with their album *High 'n' Dry* and they pierced into the States with their album *Pyromania*. I can remember sitting in my friend Tabby's bedroom listening to this album for the first time, going crazy over "Photograph." When their drummer Rick Allen lost his arm in a tragic car accident, everyone thought he'd be replaced. This courageous man learned to play the drums with one arm—his story's incredibly inspiring. Linda and I have seen Def Leppard twice in the last couple of years, and Joe Elliott still sounds like he did 40 years ago—a-mazing.

Another band I loved during this time was Quiet Riot, and while not as flashy or charismatic as some of the other bands in this category, they played great loud music and employed awesome marketing with the infamous mask on their album cover. The song "Metal Health (Bang Your Head)" became fodder for a whole generation of headbanging. Another band to come on the scene around this time was Ratt—their song "Round and Round" was completely overplayed but put an arrow through my heart.

Aside from Def Leppard, the other three bands I mentioned were all landing via Los Angeles. In a sense, I guess it was an iteration of the British invasion from earlier and would be followed by the grunge movement coming out of Seattle. I find it incredible how these new sounds take root in one specific area, explode out of said location, and cause everyone else to desperately try to catch up and replicate them. While I greatly respect the British rock bands, my heart is more closely tied to the LA scene. I love many bands from this era, one stands above as my favorite band of all time, and that is the bad boys from the Sunset Strip, Mötley Crüe.

We have to rewind a tad to the start of eighth grade. Remember the bravado and swagger we were carrying as we started the school year? It was September 1983, and we were still enjoying warm weather out on the playground, listening to the *Shout At the Devil* album on someone's boom box. MTV was the enterprise fueling what my generation chose to subscribe to. Mötley Crüe made their inaugural debut video with "Looks That Kill."

On rare occasions in life, you come across something and know it speaks to you on an entirely higher, ethereal level than other things. I fell head over heels in love with Mötley Crüe. For starters, all the visual components taking place before my eyes—fire, brimstone, and their signature pentagram—

became the combination of props creating their backdrop. The band rocked black and red leather, piercing spikes, head bandannas, long, flowing hair, and makeup resembling warpaint.

But when the chorus commenced, seeing the whole band together for the first time, I knew I'd found my rock tribe, fronted by shirtless Vince Neil, with perfect blonde hair and a chiseled body to match. His vocals, reverberating high out of the television, had me in a trance. Moving over to Nikki Sixx— bassist and founder of the band—the incessant thumping coming out of his guitar put me under a hex. The lead guitarist Mick Mars was maybe a bit frightening to look at, but his aggressive guitar-playing was in perfect unison to Nikki's bass. All of this fabulousness was sealed perfectly by Tommy Lee, the tall, lean maniac holding the sticks.

After seeing that video, I marched right over to Sam Goody and purchased the *Shout At The Devil* album to continue my obsession. The whole package appealed to the rebel teen surfacing. I traded in my Jordache for tight leather pants. The dawn of high hair commenced, and the young world kept Aqua Net and Stiff Stuff in business. Meanwhile, my Mom fretted over what the hairspray was doing to my beautiful cream-colored canopy bedroom set—the layer of film on my dresser was thickening daily. On trips to Spencer Gifts in the mall, I bought spike leather belts, arm bands, and thick silver dog chains. Bandannas of every color now took up residence on my canopy bed posts. Occasionally, I wore bandannas on my head and experimented with wearing them around my wrists and wrapped around my thigh over my jeans.

As my persona shifted, my bedroom got re-imagined as well. I no longer wanted a curtain on my canopy bed—the decor was now all about the bandannas, spikes, and chains.

Behind the bed hung a huge red Mötley Crüe tapestry with a black pentagram, and posters covered every inch of my walls from floor to ceiling—bigger, more formal ones purchased at record stores, but also pictures pulled out of *Hit Parader* and *Circus* magazines. I lined my ceiling with black velvet glow-in-the-dark posters, and I replaced my ceiling fan lights with blue and red bulbs, adding strobes to pulsate blindly throughout the room. When we moved to Papa Frank's house, Mom said he always kept my door closed because he was scared of the contents.

Ladies and gentlemen, welcome to my wild side . . .

# Chapter 17 - "Sister Christian"

Unlike grammar school where I went through a few cycles as a fish out of water, coming into high school with developed social skills made a huge difference. Wearing uniforms and receiving structured discipline removed a lot of unnecessary distractions. With no boys to impress at our all-girls school, we didn't have to worry about looking like fashion models, minimizing competition. We were all on equal footing—there were no gifts handed out and no favorites, and everything was objective. This created a safe, reliable, and somehow even nurturing environment.

In a class of just 69 students, appropriate attention was always provided by the faculty, meaning you couldn't disappear into the background. The teachers were a combination of nuns and lay teachers. Our nuns were Felician Sisters who all lived in a convent on-premise; the high school section of a larger college campus. A little history on Felician Sisters, refreshing some details from the internet: Their foundress was Blessed Mary Angela Truszkowska, who grew up in Poland during a period of unrest, and cared for women and orphans. She was inspired by St. Francis of Assisi and called upon her fellow sisters to live a life of simplicity, prayer, and service. Founded in 1855, the Felician Sisters profess public vows of chastity, poverty, and obedience similarly to priests. They arrived in North America in 1874 and have eight chapters across the country. Our Felician Sisters subscribed to a discipline including brown habits, scapular, headdress, veil, collar, and wooden crucifix around their neck, complemented by a ring professing their vows.

I wanted to include this information because from my point of view, nuns have gotten boxed into an unfair stereotype. Ours certainly were strict, with some of the old-school sisterhood clinging to archaic beliefs and norms. Our school librarian, Sr. Emily, insisted the chair be placed EXACTLY six inches from the desk when we left our seat, and the consequence of failing to abide was demerits. To this day, I don't need a ruler to measure a foot or less! As the primary enforcers of the rules and the demerit system, the nuns did instill, at least for me, an underlying fear of getting caught. I quickly established I did not want to be pegged as the troublemaker and get issued demerits, which led to escalating levels of detention, suspension, and eventually, expulsion. Inherently though, I enjoyed shenanigans—over the next four years, I'd master the art of "flying under the radar." Billy Joel said it best in "Only the Good Die Young"—no one was going to accuse *this* Catholic girl of starting much too late.

All this aside, the old Catholic school tales of physical punishments did not occur, at least not to me, nor did I witness anything in my time there. In fact, while they subscribed to strict vows, the nuns I dealt with were also wonderfully layered human beings. Upon researching Blessed Mary Angela and her desire to create an order caring for women and children, I believe she fully succeeded. These sisters were warm, caring, and nurturing. They smiled, laughed, joked around, played instruments, sang, danced, ran school play productions, and organized sports teams. Most of all, they cared about each one of us as individuals, putting in quality time to help us grow into adults prepared for the world ahead.

I returned to the school recently. Sr. Alicia had a positive impact on me, and although we hadn't seen each other in 35 years, she recognized me instantly—I was blown away. Her recognition meant a great deal to me and illustrates my point: We were all far more than numbers to these women, and they were all unique people who helped mold us by sharing their talents, faith, and gifts.

Back to the 69 girls in my class. We came from different towns, backgrounds, and lifestyles, and I was blessed to meet each and every one of them. To me, our diversity led to some of my strongest views about acceptance. Remember when I told you at St. Leo's I always felt different due to my parents' divorce coupled with the fact that I had no siblings? My new peers came in with a variety of circumstances, and could be me, with one major exception continuing to bubble below the surface. The irony of this is, maybe the one "exception" was mostly self-inflicted, because I'm still friendly with a number of women from my class, and they accept me fully for who I am.

Little mini groups formed based on our common interests, styles, and tastes, and a group of us became close friends over our four years together. It wasn't siloed and it never felt cliquish—we all had bonds with other friends outside the group and all got along amazingly well. But in our inaugural homeroom, my good friend Linda was seated all the way up front, while I was almost all the way in the back. Linda would turn around with her priceless stare anytime she wanted my attention; usually as a result of the sister accidentally kicking her in the leg or spitting on her (this particular nun had thick glasses and a bit of a stutter).

Linda became my partner in crime for any and all antics. These were innocent little things we concocted to keep ourselves entertained, mostly as an escape from boredom and monotony but also coupled with a bit of rebellion shining through. Like the girl in the song "Rebel Rebel" by David Bowie, we certainly had our moms in a whirl. Our brains were hardwired to focus on silliness a majority of the time. One notable antic involved accumulating an orange peel collection in bio lab. We stuffed them in a drawer, where they remained all year long (I hope someone eventually discovered and discarded them). We'd also sit on the floor in the hallway leaned up against the lockers, throw gummy bears or gum in the middle of the hall, and wait for the first person to step on it. When it got stuck on their shoe, we'd roll around chuckling. Nobody ever asked us what we were doing or what was funny— it was like we were in our own little court jester bubble.

When we didn't have the same class, Linda and I established a set time to meet in the ladies room (yeah, we managed to figure this out without cell phones). We did things like using our hall passes to play a game of toss into the toilet. We also learned where the frozen pretzels and ice cream cups were stored in the cafeteria, since we were often around after class for various activities, and helped ourselves. And shadow puppets were *always* present during Mass and assemblies, thanks to us. Our teachers tried to separate us, but most times we'd sneak back together. One of our lay teachers was onto us—we drove her crazy.

Linda grew up in Ridgefield Park. Three other girls at

Immaculate also arrived from that town, so Sandy, Dot, and Lauren formed the majority of the rest of our circle. Sandy could be equally silly, but she was usually also the one who drew the line at some point, while Linda and I crossed over it and kept sprinting. Smart and creative, Sandy worked at a tuxedo shop and had us dress up in tuxes on school spirit day our junior year. She got us all different-colored ties and cummerbunds. I've always admired Sandy for her wonderful family and the close ties she kept to her Colombian heritage. She also introduced us to *aguardiente*, a potent Colombian spirit—the stuff is no joke!

Dot subscribed to our antics as well. We busted her chops a lot, and she was the recipient of a lot of my pranks—she's a really good sport. I got in a ton of trouble one day during religion class when I decided to tie Dot's shoelaces to her desk chair. We had a surprise fire drill, and when Dot got up with the chair attached, she couldn't get them untied. My religion teacher already hated me—needless to say, this didn't go over well.

Lauren was our fun-loving Van Halen fanatic, insisting we act out all the band's videos during recess in the outside courtyard. One of my favorite classes of all time was first aid—we created what we called a "first aid diary," from which we learned way too much about each other. We had a funny inside joke involving blue school socks, so on the last day of our senior year, I had our group gather up all our blue school socks and gave them to Lauren as a gag. Classic '80s movie *The Breakfast Club* brings to mind the song "Don't You (Forget About Me)" by Simple Minds, illustrating the ties that bind you forever when you're going through these formative years.

Boyfriend activity was also aplenty during my high school

years. My grammar school romance in eighth grade had ended by the end of the school year, and my freshman year I started dating Ray, a guy introduced through Tracy's friend Karen. I'm not sure how it ended; I think it was my fault. He was a nice guy, but our interests were worlds apart. I was hanging out with Linda, Sandy, Dot, and Lauren a lot, and they were friendly with a group of guys, some of whom they were dating. It was through this channel, during Dot's birthday party my sophomore year, that I met my first true high school sweetheart.

Glenn was handsome, a football jock, and a bit of a rough and tumble boy, though he could also be sweet and mushy with me. We were on the same plane with sports and the same type of music. Collectively as a group, we all loved Bruce Springsteen (hey, remember, it's Jersey)—"Born to Run" echoes in my mind as I remember this time in my life. We were still babies, but growing up fast.

Glenn lived in Ridgefield Park and didn't have a driver's license yet, which made seeing each other challenging. We were in young love, so Glenn would do whatever needed to come see me. I remember him riding his bicycle from Ridgefield Park to Lodi, to come spend a half-hour with me before having to turn around and bike all the way back home. He'd take the public bus to come visit me in Elmwood Park.

By this point, things were getting more serious, and Mom was getting more uncomfortable with the situation. At the time, the roadblocks she tried to put up drove me crazy, yet in hindsight they were completely warranted. I have incredible respect for how she picked up on everything critical without being told anything; in this case, bringing me directly to the "woman doctor." Her intuition was spot-on. "Sister

Christian" by Night Ranger was never so on point. My time had come—no regrets.

# Chapter 18 - "This Used to Be My Playground"

*Let's hop in a time machine. We're going forward many years*: Plodding slowly back to the parking lot, Linda and I were hell bent on getting into the gym one last time. A subtle pulse of rebellion creeped back into our veins as our brains flooded with way too many memories to ignore. We had made an attempt earlier in the evening and failed, due to a guard attending the front entrance—we tried to slink by him to no avail.

We'd returned to Immaculate Conception 35 years after graduating to attend a candlelight service and commemorate the closing of our alma mater, after learning that they were permanently shutting their doors. The staggering number of RSVPs, as well as some shameful social media threats, forced the decision to hold the vigil out on the front lawn. The event was a beautiful homecoming for every graduating class—our class of '88 had the highest attendance—we shared so many memories, laughs, and tears. We looked forward to traipsing the halls once more—our hearts needed some closure.

We neared the back of the school by the cafeteria entrance and saw some folks inside. We approached the door, where our "break-in" became a non-event—they let us walk right in. As we meandered through the cafeteria and into the hall to descend down the gym stairs, everything flooded back in a tidal wave. The weight of the moment was suddenly upon me as feelings of reverence, pride, and entitlement took hold. The tears wanted to release as soon as I entered the gym, but I was too overcome to permit them to fall. Linda was egging me on to shoot a basket one last time, but I was too paralyzed in the moment to move my feet. The backdrop of Madonna's "This Used to Be My Playground" whispered in my ear—I was standing in my childhood dream for the last time.

I guess we should backpedal to where it all started. *(Time travel, here we go!)* My freshman year, I decided to try out for the basketball team. I'd played a bit in grammar school, and all those trips to the park by my apartment needed to be put to good use. Since I wasn't a naturally gifted athlete, I had work to do; plus, it was competitive, so I knew getting onto the varsity squad was a bit out of reach.

I was grateful to make the junior varsity squad, and Linda, Sandy, and Dot all made it, too, so I knew we'd have fun. The coach was Ms. Checkan, a tough cookie serious about the game who helped me learn the basics my first year. I wasn't the greatest, but I wasn't the worst either, and I got a lot of practice. As it turned out, Linda and Sandy both spent more time off the court than on with various injuries. This is how we came up with their nicknames Gimp One and Gimp Two—we all had lots of nicknames for each other, some of which are not fit to print. One of mine was Gumby, and Linda still calls me this—we probably cause a lot of confusion to others when she calls me "G"—yep, still in our bubble!

By sophomore year, I was ready to give varsity a shot. We got a new coach, and for the next three years, I'd have one of the most rewarding and positive experiences of my life. A huge part of this was our coach, Mrs. Careri (we called her "Careri"; not as a sign of disrespect, rather as an endearment showing a trust and comfort beyond formality).

During tryouts, the effort and energy I had to invest was unlike anything I'd ever encountered. The intensity of this tryout involved performing on full throttle, from beginning warm-up laps through endless sprints, suicides, and shuffles, culminating with practice drills. This period marked the beginning of my dependence on Mineral Ice, Ace bandages, Gatorade, and navel oranges.

My hard work paid off—I landed on the varsity squad as a guard. In addition to Careri, I found role models among the varsity juniors and seniors, including Liz, the team captain and Jennifer, co-captain. Some outstanding freshmen made the team, including Danielle (Cinque from here on in) and Kelly. I learned when you have a great coach and the right dynamic among players, the bond and closeness you will encounter is unmatched. We spent lots of time together, both on and off the court, and nothing could break the power hold. Sports best prepared me for the real world—both in discovering the meaning of teamwork and how to exemplify the traits of a leader.

We worked hard on the court and played hard off the court. Our division mostly matched up against other Northern New Jersey Catholic high school programs. This was at a time when parents didn't have to drive their children all over God's creation. We had a school van that Careri drove—oh my, the fun we had! Blasting music, we generated a rowdy atmosphere of yelling, laughing, and singing, and after the losing games, I'm sure a few tears fell. We played a lot of dance music. The one song I remember playing repetitively was "Because of You" by The Cover Girls, and Kelly and I would spin around in our seats while the van barreled down Route 17. Since sports build up the appetite, mine was voracious during my playing years, but with the amount of calories I burned on a daily basis, I could literally eat anything I wanted. After victorious away games we nagged Careri until she stopped at McDonald's. Cinque and I began a celebratory habit of each ordering a Big Mac, Chicken McNuggets, large fries, and chocolate shake. And during lunchtime at school, I'd scrounge all my friends' leftovers (in return I always cleaned up the table, to which they pronounced I'd make an excellent wife one day—ha!). I've always had a decent appetite, but this was another dimension.

Sophomore year flew by, and suddenly I found myself in junior year. It was sad to see Liz go, but Jen was a great captain and an outstanding athlete who taught me a lot. The bond among the whole team was something special—coach, players, cheerleaders, managers, scorers, and some standout parents. My Mom attended some home games when she could come, but I have to give a shoutout to Kelly's mom Mrs. Ivacic—she went to every game and supplied us with endless amounts of navel oranges. I was addicted, and ate several a day.

Yes, there was music on the court, too. There, we'd listen to "Wait" by White Lion on a loop to charge us up during warmups. As I progressed in my basketball career, I developed shin splints, and the bottom halves of my legs were constantly wrapped like a mummy for support. The pain could be intense, with piercing jabs like acupuncture gone badly. Relief only came when I unwrapped the sweaty, moisture-filled bandages and reapplied the welcomed Arctic Blue Goo, which left a strong minty smell wafting through the room. In addition to shin splints, I suffered two concussions during this time. This kicked off a lifelong series of unfortunate head jolts; I swear, any opportunity to hit my head will hunt me down and find me. But nothing could deter me—my love of the game was greater than any risk of injury.

When I entered my senior year, I had my eye on the role of captain. I wasn't 100 percent confident I'd succeed—Cinque was the point guard and a superior player to me. Ultimately, I worked hard to earn my spot as captain. I acknowledge Careri for both encouraging and empowering me to overachieve my original goals. I was also glad Cinque was my co-captain—I considered her my basketball soulmate, and the following year she'd go on to be captain. I would have wanted no one else by my side. The last year for me was amazing; not because of a great record or high-scoring games, but because of the love of the team and the game. It was where I felt completely comfortable in my skin at all times.

I had to practice shooting a lot due to some weird type of arc, which Careri constantly pointed out to teach me to correct it. I am 5 feet, 3 inches tall—layups were not my sweet spot. The girls we played against were massive (one of two basketball concussions resulted from getting clocked in the head by one of them.) My specialty was outside shots, and when I was on, I was on. This wasn't consistent. What I lacked on offense, I picked up on defense—I was a feisty, pesky little animal. I ultimately exited my senior year sharing the title of class athlete with one other classmate. Wait, *what*? Yes, and here is my inspirational message to anyone struggling with something that's not a natural ability: You can succeed. It requires commitment, disciplined regard, and never, ever giving up, no matter what anyone else thinks or says about you. The skeptics are envious because they see something in you that can't be taken away—your heart, spirit, and resilience.

Basketball was always my priority, but I wasn't a one-trick pony. I played softball for the first couple of seasons, sitting out the later years, when I switched to team scorer. I still enjoyed being around the game when I wasn't playing. The other big extracurricular was stage crew, which I did for three years, becoming president my senior year. The attraction was obviously ignited by the Broadway shows my Dad took me to as a young child, and my time on stage crew gave me a firsthand glimpse behind the scenes. We had some talented people both on stage and off—the song "Fame" by Irene Cara jumps through my head, reminding me what it takes to succeed. My friend Tracy was in some productions. The play *I Remember Mama* was one of them—we got Tracy's two little sisters in the mix as well. The lights were commandeered by Monica and Gina, and I'm still friends with Gina. A genuine person, she's always been one of my favorite people, and we're on the same wave length about a lot of things in life.

Lastly, I belonged to a writers' circle at school. Once a year we issued *Blazon*, a compilation of short stories, poetry, and other creative works by students. I always loved English literature and creative writing in school. One mentor was Sr. Adalbert, who was tough but gave me more constructive criticism than anyone about my writing and public speaking, always pushing me to be better.

Ms. Pfister, a great lay teacher I had my senior year, also nudged me; in fact, she made me come in after senior exams to sit in her office and finish my last assignment. I submitted a futuristic play based on my group of friends attending our

25-year reunion.

During my high school years, I wrote a ton of poetry, some of which made its way into *Blazon*. In my view, poetry and musical lyrical writing go hand in hand. For example, the songwriter Peter Gabriel created "In Your Eyes" with masterful lyrics flowing as if spoken by a muse. Poetry became a form of expression for me to release whatever was lurking deep inside, which as you will come to see, was a lot more than most anyone realized, including myself. I'm ending this chapter with a poem I wrote from the time. It's unedited and perhaps a bit simplistic, yet it clearly illustrates the internal struggle brewing.

## SECRET LOVE

Emotions hide deep within
    yearning to be known;

Secret feelings locked inside
    trying to escape my heart.

For in there I hold
    a love so strong;

Which I know I can't resist
    yet will always remain withheld.

This special love
    surrounds my heart;

Waiting for your touch

Still knowing its cry is silent.

The burning feeling
   when I look into your eyes;

Overwhelms me
   although I cannot bear to tell

I wish to express
   my feelings to you;

I would give all of my love
   and all of my heart.

I would always be true
   but I know in time;

Your heart would be tied
   to another.

I save my heart
   from feeling the pain;

Of a lost love
   unable to be saved.

Now this love remains deep inside
   and never will part from me;

At least I know, a secret love
   for you there always will be.

# Chapter 19 - "Surfin' U.S.A."

When I moved back to Elmwood Park in 1985, my bus route to and from school also covered Fair Lawn and Maywood. The bus was full, and our rides together were long ones. Through this daily trek, I became good friends with Heather and Robyn. They were both a year younger than me, but we all knew each other from St. Leo's. Turned out that Robyn's mom Sharon and my mom went to high school together, and her cousin Kelly's mom Florence went to school with Aunt Linda. Elmwood Park is that small—I went to school with a number of people whose parents went to school with Mom, Dad, or Aunt Linda. It's oddly comforting.

Heather and Robyn had also joined the basketball team as our primary scorers. The closer we grew, the rowdier the bus rides became. Most of the kids were well-mannered, but as usual I found my home intermingled with the rowdy bunch. We were loud, playing music on full blast, and we stood up or sat on top of the seats for most of our trips. I'm not sure how the bus driver could concentrate, or how we got away with all these shenanigans. Tracy was also on the bus, and while she definitely lived in the well-mannered category, she did participate in our musical escapades. We played music on one of our boom boxes and certain songs repeated daily. One of them was "I Was Made for Lovin' You" by Kiss. When the part of the song comes on with the electric shocks, we would all pretend to zap each other with our hands using the devil sign. Another popular choice was Led Zeppelin's "Stairway to Heaven," arguably one of the best-written rock songs of all time. We'd always fast-forward through the instrumental parts to get through the song in five minutes. Clocking in at 8:02, this song made our attention deficit kick in—we felt it was way too long, and we didn't want it to suck up our whole bus ride.

Our penultimate daily tradition, however, revolved around the song "Surfin' U.S.A." by The Beach Boys. On our way out of Maywood, right before getting on Route 4 to head to Fair Lawn, a mountain-sized crater in the road would launch us up and out of our seats (hey, it's Jersey—harsh winters kill our roads). It wasn't enough we were standing up or sitting on top of a seat; we decided we needed to take it a step further. One day we decided to convert the big bump into a surfing opportunity. Standing sideways as we approached the crater, we crouched our knees with arms extended as if we were about to crash into a wave in Californ-i-a.

As fun as those bus rides were, upon getting my driver's license senior year, I wanted to be a cool cat and drive to school. My September birthday proved fortunate timing with the start of the school year. I'd swing by and pick up Heather and Robyn, and away we'd go. My first car was a red '77 Chevy Nova I bought from my savings for around $1,100. I purchased it from an elderly couple who kept it well maintained. Heather, Robyn, and I named the car "Betsy." This car was worlds away from Charlie's luxurious Lincolns and Cadillacs. I had to let the car warm up for at least 10 minutes before taking off—year round. Betsy also lacked pickup, but it didn't stop me from pushing the speedometer on the highways. You always retain a certain fondness toward your first car, and we had a lot of laughs and good times. Betsy once confided in me that her favorite song was "Cars" by Gary Numan.

I put the poor girl through her paces, constantly hitting garbage cans and backing into trees and curbs. It's undocumented how many times I flattened my tailpipe and had to bring Betsy to our local mechanic Roger to get it fixed. One day, Mom and I had an argument before I left for school (though we never fight now, I was a handful back then). I stomped madly down the stairs, climbed in Betsy like the little hellion I was, and backed out of the driveway in a huff. I forgot my mom was parked on the other side of the road. As my car slammed into the side of her car, the front screen door of our house flew open, nearly off its hinges, as Mom ran onto the porch to see what the commotion was. I froze for a second, looked directly at her, honked, waved, and quickly sped away!

Sometime after turning 15, I got a job at Roy Rogers. I'm sure it barely paid over minimum wage, but any money in my back pocket in those days would have been good money. I didn't get an allowance, but Mom made sure all the main areas were covered, so I had no complaints. The funds earned at Roy's were needed for music, posters, special designer items, and makeup. The other cool thing about working at Roy's was we could eat, if I recall correctly, for free. My huge appetite was pleased.

When I worked at Roy's, generally I either opened or closed on weekends, or worked some nights during the week for a couple hours. Time to cue "Working for the Weekend" by Loverboy. Roy's taught me about the responsibilities of a job, and I learned how to do everything—run the cash register, replenish the salad bar, operate ice cream and soda machines, along with a host of other tasks. Though I did learn how to flip burgers, for the most part the guys were the cooks—I guess they wanted the cute girls up front at the register. Eventually, I got Heather, Robyn, and Kelly jobs there as well.

We worked with a great group of people, and even the managers were fun. We became friendly with a number of them and hung around outside of work. One friend, Joann, was in college at the time—she referred to us as the "bunny crew." Things going on behind the scenes would probably make you swear off fast food for good. Cockroaches were bountiful—we'd line them up and watch them race each other. Our code for a cockroach sighting was "Harry." I guess it's unavoidable, but I have learned to compartmentalize that thought, because I'd probably not eat out anywhere.

I also gained a few more boyfriends through Roy's. First was Steve. We dated for a while—a year younger than me, he was innocent and a nice guy, and I was ultimately too much of a handful for him. The funny thing is when I was dating Steve, Donna was dating Paul until we swapped mates. I'm relatively certain Donna and Steve got married—they were a more suitable pair, so I'm glad for them. Paul and I didn't date for long, though I did take him to my senior prom.

Between school, all my extracurricular activities, and work, I'd built up a decent social circle. In hindsight, I was uniquely positioned to get along with mostly everyone. As a jock, I could associate with anyone involved in sports (part of my signature look involved wearing my sweatpants inside out—not sure how I came up with this!). I also played some guitar, and music was always at the core. A rocker at heart, I hung out with a few people considered metalheads. We weren't burnouts, but our music choices aligned, so we got along with them, also. Additionally, I had friends of the quintessential big-haired urban Jersey girl variety. While I didn't consider myself one, my hair could certainly compete. The different clubs and circles brought me into many circumstances where I became friendly with all sorts of people. The one group I didn't associate with as easily were the uber-focused academic kids. In addition to having no common interests (they were seemingly singularly focused on studying and discussing classwork), I suspected that most of us were probably a bit too outlandish for them.

I share all this not to brag—it's more a precursor of sorts—it was a good time and my popularity and confidence were likely never higher. I loved my life and all of the passions I was pursuing. I was developing and feeding all the elements one could classify as the definition of fulfillment.

Still, a dominant part of who I am today was buried below all these layers. Every so often, the truth would make an attempt to come rushing to the surface, and I'd question why I was feeling what I was feeling. It became the one thing I couldn't and wouldn't reveal. I suppose it was a combination of the time I grew up, my heavy Catholic background, and a fear of not being accepted. I believed I'd never share these desires with anyone, let alone act upon them. Over time, I've come to learn stifling any part of your true self will slowly but assuredly eat away at your soul, and if you continue down the path for too long, you may never return.

# Chapter 20 - "Head Over Heels"

At first, I barely noticed her. A bit too cocky for my own good as I entered into my junior year in 1986, I was predominantly focused on *my* activities, friends, work, and school. The proportionate weighting of school to everything else generally trended lower, of course, as I continued to figure out how to get by without a huge amount of effort.

A few people in my immediate circle were somewhat friendly with her, so eventually I started taking notice. She marked the beginning of a developing pattern over the next 20 years, in which my interest would always gravitate toward someone somewhat outside the fringe of my inner circle. I guarantee this was purposeful, though I would never have recognized it at the time. I wanted nothing about any of this too closely hinged to my direct sphere of reality. In a sense, I always took interest in someone I knew deep down was a safe choice— meaning they were not going to push me beyond my comfort zone, which was out of the closet.

She was guarded and standoffish at first, with no intention of giving me the time of day. Eventually the iciness broke, and we started playing into some sort of personas—my tough, cool jock to her posh, pretty girl. Diving deeper and deeper, I was falling directly into the web, without a clue what was happening. A popular song at the time was "Head Over Heels" by Tears for Fears—I never found out until I was falling.

We both started getting more flirty as things escalated. We began talking more and more on the phone, spending hours at a time. I wasn't sure how to navigate beyond the "friend zone"; ironically, I think the true feelings started coming out in long letters we'd pass back and forth. Her perfume was intoxicating to me. She would spray it all over the notes. I kept a shoe box enveloped in the familiar aroma of white lily and hyacinth I could always dream with in the silence of my room. Still, nothing had happened between us—we were hiding in plain sight, holding hands under coats. I was aware enough to know something had to give.

One late fall Saturday evening, I invited her over my house when I knew Mom and Charlie were going out. My nerves were shot, but I was determined. Coming up with a not-so-creative plan, I literally had no idea what I was doing. I ordered a pizza from Leone's and put on a Blockbuster rental called *Silent Night, Deadly Night*, a slasher flick about Santa Claus, figuring when she got scared she'd want me to hold her close. When I write about it now, I recognize how dumb it sounds, but none of it mattered—an unstated destiny had already been created in the stars as to how this night would go. True to form, by midway through the movie, things were going exactly as expected. Don't ask me how the movie ended—my guess is lots of people got slashed and Santa bites the bullet at the end.

With the blue and red overhead lights mysteriously blanketing my room, I made a judgment call of the most romantic music viewed as intimate but not drippy, and put on Journey's new album, *Raised on Radio*. Listening now to the lyrics of "Girl Can't Help It," it winds up strongly assimilating to what became our eventual truth. That night, I understood the difference between what was happening and anything I'd previously known, entering a newfound reality—being with her was the most natural I'd ever felt with anyone. In the moment, I believed it was the same for her. Actually I still do, but I doubt she's ever acknowledged it to herself or anyone else. Doesn't matter. I was there and she was there.

We became official, but the extent of our pronouncement was kept between us. Acting like a typical teenage couple, we picked a song, which was "Human" by The Human League. How hysterical—our song was about infidelity—but she loved it, so I went with it. On Valentine's Day, I showered her with her favorite perfume, a dozen roses, and a charm bracelet. It was more than I'd ever spent on any other person on a gift. The secret romance challenged us all the time. We'd sneak off to hidden places not entirely hidden (amazingly, we never got caught). The best moments were when we'd find ourselves truly alone, which weren't often. Speaking of getting caught, remember how I told you my mom has a sixth sense when it comes to certain things when it comes to me? At one point, she confronted me and asked me if I was gay. I fully denied it. I've mentioned this to her, but I guess she somehow blocked it out. I often wonder what trajectory would have occurred if I'd just said yes.

We dated the rest of the school year. When she started working at a restaurant, she began sharing details with me about the owner, and I realized things were going on behind my back. Like Corey Hart, I was wearing my "Sunglasses at Night" while she was deceiving me, but in the moment I was holding on and hoping it would pass. It was the beginning of the end.

She seemingly decided out of nowhere what we were doing was wrong. Look, I ultimately can't blame her for this. We did think it was wrong, though deep down in my core I knew it was right. Too many things were stacked against us, and the '80s were not welcoming to alternative lifestyles.

Every summer, she went with her family down the shore. We were still talking but basically broken up by this point. In my heart, I hoped she'd return and things would go back to the way we were. I was miserable and got jealous when she'd tell me about some guy she'd met. Since I knew exactly when she was coming back, I wanted to surprise her. I rode my bicycle all the way from Elmwood Park to her house several towns away. With a giant case of the jitters, I rang the doorbell hoping "The Boys of Summer" Don Henley warned us about on the radio were a distant memory. I was wrong, and as we stood out on the porch and talked, I knew I'd be entering into my senior year single again. As I left on my bicycle with a deflated ego, a little voice inside my head said, *don't look back.*

# Chapter 21 - "Seasons Change"

As senior year began, I was still heartbroken but moved on, and the anticipatory promise of things to come helped me shut out any negative self-talk or spirals. At the same time, a wall of protection went up, refocusing my priority on basketball. Ironically, when I put up the wall, she tried to pull me back into her control. At one point, a new freshman cheerleader started doing my personal cheers when I played. Absolutely nothing was happening between us, but apparently she was a perceived threat. Talking on the phone, my ex would say things like, "It's just I had you wrapped around my finger for so long." Wait, *what*?

I realized that when she had no power over me, she'd attempt to reel me back in. The song by The Police, "Wrapped Around Your Finger," was hauntingly accurate. I mistakenly bought in, thinking maybe I'd break through again, and the servant would be her master. One night, I invited her to go dancing with me and a few of my friends—a bold move on my part since as far as I knew, they had no clue about the relationship. The song "In Too Deep" by Genesis played on the car ride over, creating such an intense vibe, one of my friends questioned why we were so quiet. *If you only knew, bud.*

On my end, I wasn't perfect. I didn't intentionally do any

of what I'm about to tell you, but what's the oldest-known weapon in the artillery to get back at an ex for hurting you? Firing back with "the rebound." I became friendly with someone she was good friends with at the time. It was platonic before things escalated into a relationship. I feel badly about this now. I did develop real feelings, but shouldn't have gone there. This person held me in high regard, and I took advantage—what a schmuck move on my part.

I don't remember if I spilled to my ex about the relationship or she figured it out on her own. My immaturely functioning brain had taken control, recognizing this was one surefire way to hurt her at a level she'd hurt me. I was oozing raw emotion like Cher in her rebound song, "I Found Someone." In any event, when the ex found out, she was furious. She told one of my close friends about me and the new girl, and my friend asked me about it as I was doing laps in the gym one day before practice. I freaked out a bit, but denied it. Here's the one thing I will never understand: She knew I could easily have outed her right back, so what possessed her to tell a good friend of mine? Did she tell anyone else? I never got the impression she did, but people are great at hiding things, as I can easily attest. I chalk it up to jealousy overruling her sense of reason in the moment. My life was rapidly turning into the song "Bizarre Love Triangle" by New Order.

As my senior year progressed, my ex and I started ignoring each other, and eventually we stopped talking altogether. My relationship with my rebound girlfriend continued for the duration of the school year, but I'm relatively certain boyfriends were sandwiched in between on both our parts. I did care about her, though. We broke up with "Seasons Change" by Exposé playing in the background, knowing it was time for both of us to move on.

We remained friends for a while after the breakup, and here's one crazy story: Turning right on red became legal in New Jersey soon after I graduated high school. Driving to visit her one Friday night after work, a car in front of me made a right while the light was still red. Hitting the gas instinctively to go through what I assumed was the green light, I realized my mistake too late once I looked up halfway through the intersection. A car driving on the cross street was speeding through the amber, and clocked me at a high speed. As I slammed my head on the steering wheel, blacking out, my car spun out and wound up on the other side of the road. The ambulance had arrived by the time I resurfaced in a state of fog and perplexity. Unfortunately, only one of us got to tell their side of the story, and I became the lucky holder of a ticket for going through the red light, along with a concussion. In the ER, I never called my Mom, calling my girlfriend instead. She drove me home and slept over to make sure I was okay. Mom still brings up the fact that I wasn't her first call. In my defense, I likely didn't want to face her—as it turned out, Betsy was totaled. And ultimately, Mom's insurance went through the roof. Sorry, Mom.

You've likely noticed my ex-girlfriends' names and descriptions have been left out of the equation. I've tried to avoid providing details that would enable anyone to figure out who they are. One reason for this—it is my story, not theirs. While they were part of my past, and I'm sharing my whole truth to help others who have struggled or are struggling with coming to terms with who they are, I am equally sensitive to divulging things others may not want shared. Being outed by someone else is not cool in any way, shape, or form. In fact, I've told only two other people about my high school girlfriends' identities, besides my spouse, who knows every single thing about me. Some of my friends may reach back and speculate who I'm talking about, but I'll never confirm their thoughts. Who knows? For all I know, everyone knew. No matter. My integrity is a vault—mostly out of respect, loyalty, and protection—and critical to my essence as a human being.

# Chapter 22 - "Caught in a Mosh"

The kindling of my love for heavy metal sparked with AC/DC. Out of Australia, they formed in 1973, and after the tragic death of their singer Bon Scott in 1980, the band replaced him with Brian Johnson and went on to release their bestselling album, *Back in Black.* I'm inspired by anyone who can rise above an unspeakable tragedy or sadness and turn it into something profound. And many of the best creative works rise above the surface from some form of strife or struggle. When the album and title track of the same name released, AC/DC was on the map. I listened to the album so frequently I'm surprised I didn't wear it out. The high and tight vocals of Brian Johnson are outstanding, and Angus Young is arguably one of the best lead guitarists of all time. Most would immediately recognize Angus and his signature look: formal jacket, shorts, necktie, and beanie. Getting the opportunity to see them live sometime in the '90s, I do believe it was, in fact, the loudest show I've ever attended .

I was listening to some other influential heavy metal bands, too. We used to have an expression, "Rock is my religion, and Judas is my priest." I know that's a little controversial coming out of a Catholic's mouth—it probably took the analogy a bit too far, but I chalk it up to us being a nutty group of kids.

Hailing from Britain, Judas Priest perfected the whole leather and spikes look, similar to some of the bands mentioned in my hair metal chapter. Bands like AC/DC and Judas Priest would likely be insulted to be referred to as a hair metal band. I acknowledge the similarities, but I think hair metal spun off from heavy metal as its own form, not the other way around. The song "You've Got Another Thing Comin'" is a great example of the addictive pulsing vibe Judas Priest music puts out. Here's a plug to lead singer Rob Halford, who came out as gay in the late '90s and smashed a stereotype to bits.

The third band influencing my interest in heavy metal was Iron Maiden, also from Britain. Their music was loud, fast, and explosive, like in the song "Run to the Hills." One notable thing about Iron Maiden is their supreme marketing ability. They created a whole image centered around their fictional creation, "Eddie." If you aren't familiar with him, type *Iron Maiden Eddie* to find out. Preying on your worst nightmares, Eddie could easily star in his own horror movie. Which is why it's genius—it capitalizes on the connection between heavy metal and the horror genre. Remember all those velvet posters on my ceiling? Most if not all of them were Eddie on different album covers. I can understand why Papa Frank was petrified of my room.

My friends Heather and Robyn were my metal companions and my introduction to the band Metallica (technically, they're considered thrash metal). They've been able to take the genre to a place no one ever dreamed of by fusing some of the loudest and hardest music—with an orchestra. Many car rides in Betsy involved popping in one of Metallica's cassette tapes and turning it way up to blast it. The pulsating energy of "Master of Puppets" trapped us in its lair. Similar to the 8-

track case my Mom carried in her car, my friends and I ensured we had a kick-ass selection of cassettes with us at all times. My case opened on the top and bottom and held 100 cassettes.

We saw Metallica multiple times in concert, and other than Mötley Crüe, I've probably seen them more than any other band. Metallica with Guns N' Roses at Giants Stadium in 1992 was one of my favorite concerts. I could probably write a whole book on concert experiences (and I guess I am), with so many I've lost count. I used to save all my ticket stubs, which are stowed away in a box—once the electronic age hit, it became impossible to keep counting. Admittedly, it's easier to get into a venue with ticketless entry, but I wish I had a proper tally—we Virgos care about our lists!

Then there was Anthrax. These guys were more fringe than Metallica, so fewer people were familiar with this hardcore music. A bit more alternative to the traditional thrash metal bands, they infused a bit of rap music into some of their songs. Heather, Robyn, and I were excited to see them at a smaller venue, the Capitol Theatre in nearby Passaic. Getting ready at Heather's, we all wanted to tie-dye our jeans, and Heather knew how to do it in the washing machine using bleach. I threw my black Levi's in there to be transformed, but something different came out than expected—they turned the most bizarre shade of brown! It was too late to run home and get a different pair. I took a WTF approach, ripped some holes in the knees, and created a fashion statement. We laughed our butts off at how funny they looked, but I wore them with pride.

When we got to the theater, I encountered my first-ever mosh pit and slam dancing—absolutely wild! Who knew that watching someone take a fast break running start and crashing violently into one or more people is such a rush? This concert became memorable for more than the brown jeans; mostly the unforgettable experience of an unhinged crowd I hadn't been part of in a larger forum such as a concert. As Anthrax sang "Caught in a Mosh," we lost ourselves in the tidal wave of frenetic madness.

# Chapter 23 - "Never Say Goodbye"

Slam dancing isn't the primary form of dance I prescribed to, though I did enjoy roughhousing in those days. But I've always loved to dance. While I wouldn't consider myself particularly fluid and have never had formal lessons, they aren't required. All you need is some courage and to allow yourself to become one with the rhythm, like the saying, "dance like no one's watching."

Immaculate hosted school dances and would invite a local Catholic boys' school, St. Joe's in Montvale; in turn, they invited us to their dances. This was a good way for girls and boys to meet, since the nature of our programs could make this otherwise challenging. I had no trouble finding boys to date (or girls for that matter) so this generally wasn't my reason for attending, though anything involving socializing was right up my alley. I always loved to dance to freestyle music, which was growing in popularity. "Can You Feel the Beat" by Lisa Lisa & Cult Jam with Full Force brought us on an electronic roller coaster of liberating expression.

Part of the fun was to engage in some pre-dance drinking activities. Immaculate had a no-drinking-on-campus policy, and getting caught could result in automatic expulsion. This didn't deter us. The school was surrounded by a cemetery, and a short trip over the bridge brought us to our meeting place of choice. Once we arrived at the dance with a little buzz, we became part of the crowd dancing freely to "Into the Groove" by Madonna. I need to give this woman some props. Always a huge fan since she exploded on to the scene with her self-titled album, I'm still in awe 40 years later as she continues to push boundaries. Seeing her perform at MSG, which I've done a few times, is an experience.

My friends and I went all-out both our junior and senior year for prom. I brought my ex Glenn to the junior prom. While we weren't dating, it felt natural and comfortable. The connection he had to my friends and their boyfriends made this a no-brainer and a safe choice, given I was hiding my relationship with my first girlfriend at the time.

I played the part well, with my frilly pale pink sleeveless dress, costume jewelry specially purchased for the occasion, and dyed heels to match. Glenn was handsome in his tux and matching pink tie and cummerbund. When I look back at those pictures, I see we looked great, though my hair was revolting— total mullet. The obligatory prom song of that year was "Never Say Goodbye" by Bon Jovi. For a moment, I forgot all about my secret truth as Glenn held me in his arms so strong. After the prom, we had our limo drive us into Manhattan, to a popular dance club called Wednesdays.

When my senior year prom came around, I was dating Paul from Roy's. My overall style choice and look was upgraded. I wore a white dress with a one-sided sleeve (in hindsight, the bow on the sleeve was a tad gaudy), and the mullet was replaced by a sleek 'do. Paul was from the rough part of town in Passaic. Though a fish out of water, he was sweet and did his best to fit in. Dancing to "Heaven" by Warrant, I realized he wasn't the king of my world, nor my superman. Linda and her boyfriend opted not to attend the prom, so the rest of us were meeting them at a club in Manhattan afterward. What a night we were about to have!

We arrived at Stringfellow's after midnight, and the club was hopping. Linda's boyfriend had secured a great table for us. Nearby, a few members of the cast of the hit show *Fame* were celebrating, including Debbie Allen and Gene Anthony Ray, after collaborating on another musical on Broadway. As we sat at our table, laughing and enjoying all the fanfare, in walked my favorite comedian of all time—the incomparable Eddie Murphy . Eddie fucking Murphy! His stand-up can't be touched, in my opinion. Anyway, Linda and I almost lost our shit. We tripped over ourselves to meet him and asked him to take a picture with us. He was so cool about it, and we got our Polaroid. Unfortunately, neither of us has been able to find it, so the experience will just have to be relegated to memory. Nonetheless, we partied all night long, and when the limo pulled into my driveway at dawn the next morning, Mom was beside herself. She blamed Paul, though the poor guy had absolutely nothing to do with it. She made him walk back home to Passaic. Bummer.

As senior year was wrapping up, my friends and I wanted to do something epic before heading off to college. One of them, I believe maybe Sandy, came up with the idea of going on an overnight cruise to nowhere. Our parents all signed off, except for one of my friends, who shall remain nameless (not sure if she ever fessed up!) She was afraid her folks wouldn't approve, so she concocted the fib that we were going to Great Adventure for the day (I never did ask her where she purported to be staying overnight). The hilarious part of all of this was we weren't allowed to take any pictures by the water, ensuring there was no evidence to get her in trouble! We partied and danced the night away as Gloria Estefan & Miami Sound Machine took us over with "Rhythm Is Gonna Get You." And we didn't care who was watching . . .

# Chapter 24 - "Goody Two Shoes"

In high school, I could be a punk at times. I looked up the word "punk," and descriptions I found were "scoundrel," "rascal," and "young troublemaker"—yep, yep, and yep. The word can also be tied to the punk rock musical genre, widely regarded as anti-establishment or anti-authoritarian.

My first encounter with punk rock and its new wave offshoot started back in grammar school. The first notable was Blondie, and Debbie Harry is still the bomb. A few years later, when *Beauty and the Beat* released, you couldn't find a girl my age who didn't like The Go-Go's. While the whole valley girl culture was not my speed, as one of the few all-female bands at the time, they earned my respect. "We Got the Beat" led me to dance around my bedroom, experiment with different shades of eye shadow, and if you can believe it, wearing miniskirts!

At the time, MTV was infusing some different talent into the mainstream. Would anyone have known Adam Ant were it not for MTV? In addition to Adam being staggeringly cute, I found his songs upbeat and infectious. I always related to the song "Goody Two Shoes," denouncing anything too stuffy. I started smoking in eighth grade, and while I now recognize it as one of the worst habits I ever had, in those days it was commonplace. On a school trip to nearby Bear Mountain, a teacher caught a bunch of us smoking. She said she was going to call our parents, so I went home and fessed up, but she never called.

I became good friends with someone who was a year older than me and introduced me to a lot of different music. One of the bands was The Ramones. "I Wanna Be Sedated" is great to dance to when you want to shake everything off. Meanwhile, in a nod to anti-authoritarian behavior, a couple of my friends and I picked up spray-painting as a pastime. We had code names—mine was "Cruiser." We mostly displayed our work on underpasses, but one time we hit up an industrial building in a non-trafficked area. We also had a strange fascination with road signs—I thought it would be cool to have a dead end sign for my never-to-be-realized band, but one of my pals took it and I never saw it again (hiding the evidence, perhaps?).

At one of our high school dances, we had a close brush with expulsion. When we arrived at the dance, someone with us who had overindulged at the cemetery admitted guilt to one of the nuns (fabricating a story that the drinking happened at someone's house), which led to a bunch of our parents getting called.

The one other time I recall my mom getting a phone call was in my sophomore year, when a bunch of us were involved in what the faculty referred to as a "faction." Some infighting was brewing, and many were guilty by association. I suppose the teachers didn't know where the trouble started and ended, so literally half our class was called into the auditorium by the principal. I never saw her so mad—she threw the letters to our parents up in the air at us, making us fish through to find the one addressed to us so our parents could sign and return it.

These few things aside, most of our escapades were innocent fun—stupid at times—yet fun nonetheless. In Lodi, we would play softball at this one field across town that required navigating around heavily trafficked Route 46 on foot. One day my friend and I were running late, and got the inane idea to cross the highway—not in a designated crosswalk. We ran across the first set of lanes, hopped over the boundary wall, and across the other side. I'd love to say we did this no more than once, but I'd probably be lying.

Getting a driver's license brought us a different level of freedom. Unfortunately, at 17, you don't fully grasp the responsibility that comes with the territory—all you care about is going wherever you want to be. In most cases, this was often nowhere in particular—my friends and I would cruise around looking for something fun. A popular approach was to drive around the Burger King parking lot in Lodi when all the slick urban Jersey dudes were driving their IROC Camaros around.

On one of these weekend evenings, we wound up on Route 46 going past our typical route. As we drove in the fast lane, a car full of boys approached us on our right. They were hoping for a speeding contest, which we obliged for a couple miles (my Chevy Nova was not going to win, so we weren't taking it too seriously). Then they rolled down their window, and my friend in the passenger seat did so, too. Only in the '80s could you engage in a full-blown conversation driving side by side on a busy NJ highway. We made a quick assessment and determined they were cool and safe enough. Did we know this for a fact? Of course we didn't, but it didn't stop us from following them to their house to hang out.

Fortunately, they turned out to be a decent group of guys,

albeit a little quirky. We wound up hanging with them on multiple occasions. I think one of my friends was flirting with one of them, but mostly we were just having fun. These guys were punk rockers through and through—bizarre but interesting characters all the same. They were fascinated with the Sex Pistols—the movie *Sid & Nancy*, which portrays the real-life story of the band's bassist Sid Vicious and girlfriend Nancy Spungen, had come out not long before. Speaking of anti-establishment, their song "Anarchy in the U.K." describes the term perfectly (Mötley Crüe made a rendition I actually like better). During this time, we also tuned into other bizarre movies, like *Attack of the Killer Tomatoes*.

One final anti-authoritarian tale before moving on: Three of us went to see Prince at MSG our senior year. We had taken a bus from Elmwood Park into Hoboken to hop on the PATH; like in the song by Berlin, we were riding on "The Metro." After an amazing concert that ended later than anticipated, we missed the PATH train to pick up the bus heading back to Elmwood Park, and our only option was a bus heading to Hackensack. The bus dropped us off in the bowels of downtown by the court house, and we instantly knew this was not a place for us to be in the middle of the night. With no cell phones or pay phones, we quickly headed up the hill on Passaic Street toward the Arena Diner.

Once we safely arrived at the diner, we shared some disco fries and discussed next steps. We were all too chicken to call any of our parents, and made the decision we'd schlep it back to Lodi on foot, go to one of their houses, and let our parents know we were sleeping over. This hike was about four miles to be exact, and we'd already walked a mile up the hill. Leaving the Arena Diner to continue our journey, we ran into a guy stopped at a light. He was definitely a slick urban Jersey dude, and we instantly knew he was from Lodi, though we didn't know him from Adam Ant. He asked us if we needed a lift—yikes, three teenage girls getting in a car with a stranger. *Hmm.* We made the flip decision and took a gamble. Dumb, absolutely. Once again though, we lucked out since he was a decent, normal guy, driving us all the way back to my car at the bus stop in Elmwood Park. At times, I wonder how I managed to escape all of these situations without a blemish. I chalk it up to at least one soul up above watching out for me.

# Chapter 25 - "Dust in the Wind"

Our life on Earth is centered around the passage of time. As we gain perspective, we begin to appreciate that everything is fleeting. Seasons come and go, life changes and evolves as we move along, and eventually, we'll face the inevitable moment of our passing (unless you're a vampire—if you're reading this and are in fact a vampire, I'd love to hear from you). As they approach, certain parts of our journey become inherently easier to understand. For example, as we go through our schooling period, we know eventually we will graduate. My point is, a definitive end date is within our grasp for these events, which allows us to adequately prepare ourselves.

I grappled with mixed feelings about graduating and moving on to my next chapter. In senior year I was soaring, ignited by a feeling that nothing is impossible, with the proverbial world at my fingertips. It also became easy to bury the part of my true self I wasn't ready to face—with so many distractions, I could stuff it down and ignore it. In a sense, I lived in an impenetrable bubble. I wasn't ready for it to come to an end. Maybe my intuition was trying to tell me something, because the bubble was about to burst.

The first disruption happened not long before graduation. After closing one evening at Roy's, I went to the Hyway

Theatre in Fair Lawn with my friend Ron to see *Rocky Horror Picture Show*, which aired after midnight on Friday or Saturday nights (going with Ron several times launched my lifelong love of the movie). Upon arriving home in the middle of the night, I was struck by panic. All the lights were on and Charlie's car was in the driveway. Not a good sign—Charlie *never* stayed overnight. Convinced I was getting in trouble for something, I quickly scanned my memory bank to guess what it could be. Was Mom finally fed up with all my antics?

I found Mom and Charlie in the living room. Charlie's head was buried deeply in both hands. When he looked up, I saw his face was beet red and crumpled up like a piece of paper. They sat me down. A momentary flashback of my encounter with Mom and Dad all those years ago came flooding in: *OH MY GOD . . . they're breaking up . . . not again . . . I can't do this again . . .*

Mom started to speak, but my processing speed was only picking up fragmented chunks: "Something to tell . . . Charlie . . . other children . . . his daughter . . . your age . . . died in her sleep."

Wait, *what*? This made no sense whatsoever. Aside from the occasional curiosity about why Charlie spent overnights and holidays away from us, I had no other clues. Eleven years after they started dating, I was to find out Charlie had been married previously and had a whole other family. I was in overload. I needed time to catch up, before I could switch gears to console the man who had become a father figure to me. This is where the introvert in me experiences an inherent disadvantage. I need processing time for any material impacts. I am sorry to say, selfishly, my focus at the time was more heavily weighted around how this was impacting *me*. I wish

I'd been more supportive to him at the time. Losing a child at any age, let alone at 17, is devastating. Life-altering. In my opinion, he was never the same again, and I could not blame him.

A big part of me wishes they would have told me from the beginning. I know they were trying to protect me, but I could have handled it. Who knows—we might have met and become friends. To Charlie's daughter Lynn, I dedicate the song "Dust in the Wind" by Kansas; a beautiful depiction of the fragility of life.

High school graduation day came and went in a flash in May 1988. My most notable recollection is Linda coming to the ceremony with platinum blonde hair; the new Linda as I know her today had arrived. My friends and I went to Bear Mountain on graduation weekend to celebrate, in addition to all our respective graduation parties with family and friends. My plan for the summer included enjoying my last months of freedom before entering my freshman year of college, preparing for an advanced level of academia, and transitioning to a more suitable job.

The summer of 1988 commenced with promise. I started a new full-time job as a bank teller at National Community Bank in Saddle Brook, so I could save up for commuting and other expenses for the fall semester. One day, Pop called me at work. Grandma and Pop were notorious for having horrible timing in dropping bad news. (On one earlier occasion, when the three of us were flying to California to see my dad, they informed me on our layover in Dallas that the reason for the trip was a family intervention. *Gee, guys, thanks for sharing this with me three hours before arriving in LA.* Dad had moved to California around 1980 and married his wife Roma; they are

142

still happily married and residing in the Sacramento area. It is a blessing Dad's intervention led to a successful outcome.)

On this particular day, Pop was calling to let me know Grandma had been diagnosed with advanced-stage pancreatic cancer. While I would have preferred not being at work for this news, I needed every possible second to prepare myself for what would come. My grandparents made the decision Grandma would undergo holistic treatment. This was a bit controversial at the time, and I respected they did what they felt was right for her. Given what we knew about the progression, I'm not sure anything would have prolonged or delayed the inevitable.

I went down the shore to my grandparents' as often as I could that summer. Although I was working full-time, I could easily drive down to Brick to spend weekends. Much like I had watched Mom care for Papa Frank during his terminal illness, I watched Pop dutifully care for my grandmother in her last months. My grandparents did not believe in sugar-coating, and it was gut-wrenching, watching Pop patiently try to get nourishment into her withering body, change her, and in the final days, feed her water through an eye dropper because she was too weak to hold a glass.

During this time, I spent a lot of time in gratitude for my family's faith. I was reminded of the times my dad took my grandparents and me to see *Godspell* on Broadway. The musical, based on the Gospel of St. Matthew, depicts Jesus and his followers relaying the teachings and parables in an unique and upbeat way. The music and lyrics to "By My Side" in the original production powerfully illustrate unconditional faith, similar to the faith my grandmother carried with her throughout her life.

The months went by quickly once we learned the diagnosis. Given Grandma's weakening condition, I was aware the end was near when I visited one weekend. On October 25, 1988, as I came home to get ready for the bank in the middle of the day, I saw Mom's car parked in the driveway. I knew before walking in the door. Grandma had passed.

The next year was one of my roughest time periods, with the weight of missing her every moment of every hour of every day. Something I've noticed about grief: It can lead a person to draw from it to rise above and get stronger, or it can break a person's spirit, stealing fragments and forcing their essence to become different than before. A beautiful song written by Asia called "Without You" has always resonated deeply with me.

One thing I've not divulged often is the otherworldly connection I experienced with both of my grandparents after their passing. I recognize the concept of communicating with souls who have moved on is not entirely understood, but based on my own personal experiences, I accept it occurs. I'm not asking you to subscribe to my beliefs about this, but since you've committed to reading my memoir, it's important to me that you know all my layers.

Grandma stayed around for the better portion of the next year. She intermittently watched over me many evenings while I silently grieved. I did not "see" her in the true sense of the word; rather, I "felt" her soul in my presence. I'm sure she wanted to move on but needed to make sure I was ready to face life without her. As soon as she got her assurance, she moved on, and I didn't encounter her again until 15 years later, when she came back to visit right before Pop passed.

Interestingly, my grandmother always subscribed to some

unconventional beliefs despite her devout Catholicism. She was interested in astrology and horoscopes. She also had a fascination with the meaning of dreams—anytime one of us shared our dream from the night before, she'd research the meaning.

I wanted to share a few of Grandma's favorite artists to end this chapter. One of them was Bobby Vinton. Known as the "Polish Prince," he sang the beautiful song, "To Know You Is to Love You." Another of her faves was Lou Rawls, with his deep, sultry voice. I've always been a fan of "You'll Never Find Another Love Like Mine." I will leave part two with a poem I wrote for this amazing woman not long after her passing.

## SINCE YOU'VE GONE

Many days
  I can't believe you're gone;

Many nights
  I've cried all alone.

Many moments
  With you I wanted to share;

Many times
  I reached out, wishing you'd be there.

Many struggles
  To fight the pain;

Many moments

I wish I could see you again.

Until I reach paradise

There will be many times

# III

# PART THREE

***AIR GUITAR RULE #3** – Practicing can happen anytime, anywhere—one of the best locations is in the car.*

# Chapter 26 - "Edge of Seventeen"

Despite the worry and uncertainty surrounding Grandma's unforeseen illness and passing, my post-high school plans were cemented. Deciding where to attend college can be an overwhelming and daunting experience; this was not the case for me.

I wanted to follow in my Dad's footsteps and attend Seton Hall, a Roman Catholic university founded in 1896 by Bishop James Roosevelt Bayley and named after his aunt Saint Elizabeth Ann Seton. It happens to be the oldest diocesan university in the United States. I applied to two other neighboring schools—Montclair State and William Paterson—and was accepted to all three. We made thorough rounds around the campuses, and while it was fun to have choices and compare programs, my mind was made up. It's a great feeling when your heart and mind connect, and you realize without hesitation that the path you're taking is going to be the right one.

I was equally steadfast about which major to declare. I knew I loved math. After looking admirably over Charlie's shoulder all those years as he worked with his 12-ruled paper, calculator, and mechanical pencils, accounting was the obvious choice. Without full awareness of this, I was emulating the two men in my life I most looked up to. Both of these decisions turned out to be excellent foundational choices, and it was nice to not have the pressure of uncertainty. I was also blessed with parents and grandparents who believed in the importance of gifting their offspring's education, as they agreed to split the cost for my tuition. Many of my friends had to take out loans and pay their education off over many years. I've tried to never forget this, as remaining grateful is important for maintaining a grounded outlook on life.

But even with all signs pointing to "this is a no-brainer," it's human to Monday-morning-quarterback any situation. I've pondered, *What if I had attended school out of state? What if I'd stayed on campus? What if I selected another major, centered around exploring my writing or philosophical passions?* All great questions. It'd be interesting to know how choosing those paths would have altered my life, but I believe the choices we make are purposeful and land us exactly where we're meant to be. It's not about one choice; it's the totality of all our choices making up the whole. We generally also have the ability to alter course at any point if we're not happy with a decision we made—let's hear it for free will.

With these items solidified, the other element was my job situation. I know I told you about my new job at the bank, but I want to share the story of how I got it and what it meant, because it was really kind of a gateway to adulthood. I was happy at Roy's because of the great crew, and it was easy money since it wasn't mentally challenging. I had no intention of moving on at the time. But my mom gave me a subtle-yet-needed nudge, cutting out an ad in the classifieds from the *Bergen Record*. National Community Bank was hiring bank tellers. I wasn't originally sold; in fact, I was clinging to

Roy's, knowing everything else in my life was changing. Mom gently suggested I at least go interview and see what it was all about. Really, this gentle nudge was parenting at its finest; much like a professional tightroper, Mom walked the fine line between giving her child the space to make her own choices, and recognizing when she needed guidance or encouragement to help her realize her potential.

Once I interviewed, I realized Mom was right. The bank would become somewhere I could apply my mathematical abilities, get a truer sense of the business world, and most importantly, grow up. The opportunity aligned perfectly with my college plans—I wasn't living on campus and would be commuting every day. The bank allowed me to work afternoons Monday through Friday and from opening to closing on Saturdays. This way, I could schedule all my classes for the mornings and work every afternoon. The bank manager was flexible and a great human, and was happy to offer me full-time work in summers and over semester breaks.

The banking world fascinated me. I started out in NCB's teller training program at their Rutherford location. After completing the training, I began as a teller in their Saddle Brook office, 10 minutes from home. Similar to Roy's, a great group of people worked at the bank, and I became friendly with most of them. Julie, a girl around my age who was also starting college shortly, started just after me. Working the same schedule, we became banking soulmates as well as good friends—she would go on to be part of my wedding party.

At work, Julie and I were a dynamic duo. In the afternoon hours, the bank lobby closed and the drive-up and walk-up windows remained open. With me manning the walk-up and Julie the drive-up, we had complete control over our domain.

We worked as a team; if one area got heavier traffic, we jumped over to assist. Our like-mindedness about ambition and motivation connected us, and over the next four years, we'd gain great experience and share some awesome times.

One of the most important things I learned at the bank was the importance of excellent customer service. It was often easy to distinguish between tellers working full-time as their permanent livelihood and Julie and me, who had our sights set toward our future. We applied our social and technical skills with a tremendous amount of vigor, to make customers feel important. They responded to us because we called them by name, took interest in their individual needs, and gave them prompt and reliable service.

Back in those days, there was usually an ATM machine in the lobby, but virtually all banking was done in person. There was an industrial area directly behind the bank, and every week the line would snake out the door with customers from those buildings waiting to cash checks and make deposits. Julie and I hustled, with a personal mission to get the customers through the line as quickly as possible.

I also encountered a hard realization: some people can be deceitful, motivated by chasing the almighty buck. We were often presented with counterfeit money and fraudulent checks. And one day when the audit team showed up unannounced, we learned our head teller was stealing money from the till. She went to jail—*no bueno.*

One customer who worked at the nearby Tommy Hilfiger factory caught me off guard. I was friendly with all my customers, but when she came to do her banking after work, she always winked at me. I wouldn't learn until many years later this is an unspoken signal between gay women. If

152

someone winks and you wink back in turn, it's a confirmation you both have the same sexual preference. I had no idea—the two girls I had relationships with were by definition straight. So when she winked, I froze up, not knowing how to react. Eventually, I decided to flirt back, assuming there must be some attraction due to the incessant winking. She was a beautiful girl, and technically, my first interaction with an actual gay person.

Her true feelings became more evident when one day, she slipped a cassette mix tape under my teller window. The music kicked ass, but more notably, every song was an irrefutable profession. One of them was "Like the Way I Do" by Melissa Etheridge—one of the most energy-fueled, heart-pumping songs I've ever heard (her first self-titled album has always been my favorite). I'd never heard Melissa until I got this tape, and wouldn't discover until later she was out, loud and proud, but the song was a clear clue about my customer's feelings for me. I wondered if "Tommy Hilfiger girl" thought I was dating Julie since we were always laughing and carrying on, but in reality, I was strictly dating boys. The two tumultuous experiences from high school were buried deeply in my subconscious, and I was doing everything in my power to erase them entirely—I kept piling more and more dirt on top, waiting for them to disappear into oblivion.

Another great song on the tape was "I Can't Hold Back" by Survivor. After listening to the words several times, it would blow some of the freshly thrown dirt off the pile, and I'd consider the possibilities after imagining a story in my eyes. One day, I left a note on her car in the Hilfiger parking lot, expressing some of my feelings to her. I know you're waiting for a great love story, but you'll have to keep waiting—we

153

never acted on it. Her sister found out I was dating someone, which put an abrupt end to the regular visits—I'd seen my last wink.

This was my second opportunity to take a different path. The first happened three years earlier when Mom asked me if I was gay. Once more, staring down the possibility to come clean and live my whole truth, I totally choked and let it pass me by. The song on the tape reverberating inside me—"Losing My Religion" by R.E.M.—epitomized the feeling of an unrequited romance, which I started to believe was my destiny.

When my first college semester began, things got real. My intense class schedule required me to cram all five classes into morning time slots so I could make the half-hour trek back to Saddle Brook by 2:00. This didn't allow for any breathing room—after getting up early, commuting, attending class, and working until 6:00, I had to go home and study. It sounds exhausting to me now—thank God I've been graced with a high energy level—so long as I keep moving, I can keep up the momentum. A great illustration of this time in my life is "Edge of Seventeen" by Stevie Nicks. This woman is one of my idols; her voice captivates and moves me, and the guitar riff throughout this song haunts me. As an adult, I've come to know the comforting sound of a white-winged dove's call, as we hear them cooing outside our home.

My accounting and business classes were eye-openers, and initially, a huge struggle for me. I was still coming to terms with the loss of my grandma, and trying to apply the same mediocre level of effort I'd expended throughout my school career—huge mistake. While I didn't fail any classes, my overall GPA wasn't up to my standard, and I was starting to question my major.

One professor was downright brutal, and he unknowingly almost forced me into changing gears. I dug deep and really thought about what I wanted. The spark in my belly that I've always been able to count on helped me pick my chin up and keep forging ahead. It was time to get serious about life, rise about the fray, and make myself and everyone I loved proud.

Fortunately, I was able to get my head on straight and power through the second semester, faring better. I loved being on campus and made some new friends I'd hang with in the cafeteria between classes. A bunch of girls from my high school attended Seton Hall, lovingly dubbed "The Hall," including Linda. She was a psych major with a completely different class schedule, but we met up on campus once in a while.

Another exciting development was unfolding: The men's basketball team was *on fire* leading up to March Madness. They made it to the Final Four and were heading to the NCAA Championship against Michigan. I made plans to cheer on with my fellow Pirates, and we watched the game from Aiello's pizza place on campus. The atmosphere was electric! The game went into overtime! Then suddenly, our dreams shattered as we lost in a buzzer beater by one point, 80-79. Leaving the campus, all we heard was silence.

Loss aside, the experience fueled my lifelong love for the Seton Hall men's basketball program. I bleed royal blue, and I'm so proud of my team—they recently won the National Invitation Tournament for the first time since 1953. A great song by U2, "Pride (In the Name of Love)" speaks to civil unrest, but I relate to the word. In fact, the amount of pride I hold for things dear to me is unmovable.

# Chapter 27 - "Welcome to the Jungle"

My sweet, reliable, four-wheeled Betsy became extremely familiar with Route 23 in the first couple of summers following high school. Heather, Robyn, and I added Kelly and Sue to our group, and we hung together often. Our rationale for traveling this particular highway was to get to Toye's campground, a camping community Heather's family had frequented for years up in rural Sussex, New Jersey. Heather's parents, Peggy and Gary, had a family-sized trailer at the campsite. We slept in tents but were invited to use their trailer for showering and toilets; otherwise, we'd have to schlep over to the public facilities on the other side of the lake (this diva isn't a fan of community showers).

Peggy and Gary always welcomed our circle into their home and hearts, and we had fun spending time with them. This may sound unusual given our age—don't kids in late teens generally want to be as far away from any parental authority as often as possible? But we could be ourselves without them passing judgment. And I looked up to them immensely. They started referring to us as their "rent-a-kids." I also became close with Heather's two younger sisters and older brother. They are a great family.

On Friday evenings after school and work, we'd pack up

Betsy for the weekend. In addition to our clothes, toiletries, and camping gear, food and beer took top priority (maybe some water and Snapple, but that was secondary). Our organized system involved chipping in for essentials and shopping in advance. We'd prepare things like macaroni and pasta salad. Other staples included the obligatory hamburgers and hot dogs, and for breakfast, we indulged our singular fascination for Taylor ham, egg, and cheese sandwiches that we'd make on the grill (such a Jersey thing—on our first trip to Rhode Island, we despaired when we couldn't find pork roll in the supermarket). We needed several coolers to hold all the food, but somehow we made it all work and became adept stowing everything in the mid-sized trunk.

Route 23 starts out as a typical NJ highway but eventually narrows to one lane with a speed limit drop, which always made the trip feel longer than it actually was. We always managed to keep things entertaining, and one of our Friday night rituals was to start the trip with Guns N' Roses' *Appetite for Destruction* in the cassette deck. One of the best albums of all time, in my opinion—the carnival ride comes off the hinges with the first track, "Welcome to the Jungle." The opening riff by Slash, followed by Axl Rose's familiar screech, begins a roller coaster of a song I never want to get off.

We usually encountered one challenge upon arrival: darkness. Typically evening by the time we got started, we had to navigate tent setup in the dark—if it happened to be raining, total disaster. Hence, nothing was more satisfying than finishing setup and cracking open that first can of cold beer around the campfire. The startup and maintenance of the campfire, as well as setting tarps over the picnic tables nearby, were always the handiwork of the guys—a fair tradeoff, since the girls took care of preparing all the food.

Oh yes, there were guys there, too. Our immediate and extended circles were growing larger. The girls had started hanging around at the Elmwood Park firehouse, where Heather's brother Gary was a volunteer, and we became attached at the hip with the whole crew. It was through these circumstances that Robyn would begin dating and marry Phil, and I would begin dating and marry Seamus. Prior to Seamus, however, I dated a number of other guys in those first couple of years after high school. I had a summer fling with one of the guys at the campground. He was a country boy and a bit older than me, so we were somewhat on the down-low due to the age difference. I think of young love similar to that of Danny and Sandy in "Summer Nights" by John Travolta and Olivia Newton-John from the *Grease* soundtrack. That movie and its songs transcend time—you always want the characters to tell you more. I miss Olivia on this Earth; she has always been one of my favorites with her sweet, angelic voice.

When we weren't camping, we were having parties at the firehouse or hanging out at Heather's house enjoying memorable times together, and through it all, I was having a blast with no serious commitments to anyone. Some of the memorable dudes I dated included an over-the-top Army brat, a goofy but lovable stoner, a steroid-fueled truck driver, a Corvette-driving slick urban Jersey dude, and an Emilio Estevez lookalike, with a few randos thrown in the mix. By reveling in this boy fest, I was shoving my true self as far out of reach as I possibly could, hell-bent on forgetting entirely.

I experienced one crossover encounter (you know, kind of like when they cross over on *Law & Order* night) between Corvette dude and Emilio Estevez. I was dating Corvette dude and was getting a little tired of his ego—I never did figure out how his head fit in that little sports car. We were still dating, but I was planning to break up with him, because who wouldn't choose Emilio Estevez? I invited the *Breakfast Club* doppelganger to Heather's house for a party one weekend, because Mr. King of the World was supposed to be going down the shore. He decided to surprise me by coming to Heather's instead, and caught me red-handed. Needless to say, it got a little messy. Oops—*so long, Captain America; I'm with Emilio now*. Something about this time reminds me of the song "I Remember You" by Skid Row, one of my crew's favorite power ballads. Sebastian Bach's vocals are off the chain in this song.

Meanwhile, back at Toye's, we had graduated to a pop-up trailer Heather's parents bought for the girls—they were *that* kind and generous. Peggy passed in recent years after a hard-fought cancer battle. I was so glad I got to visit her beforehand—what a special woman. The pop-up, while barely large enough for all of us to sleep in, was a huge upgrade from tent life. I was still at the age where I didn't mind roughing it, but it was really nice to arrive on Friday without the whole tent conundrum. We could head right over to our gathering area where the fun had already started and commence our weekend festivities.

We spent a lot of time playing drinking games at the communal picnic table, with Thumper being a popular choice. We played music constantly and repeated some favorites; one of these being Bad Company's "Rock 'n' Roll Fantasy." The song still brings me back to those carefree, endless nights.

Memorial Day weekend in 1990 was our official Toye's summer kickoff weekend, as well as our annual hometown parade on Monday. The volunteer firemen were always part of the parade, so the guys were planning to leave the campground on Sunday, and we'd make it home in time to see them on Monday. Two new entries to our Toye's group on this particular weekend were Seamus and his sister Cathy. Seamus and I were already friendly from time spent together at the firehouse. I would often find him standing out front smoking his Marlboros, and would always stop and chat, joining him for a cigarette. Seamus is four years and change older than me, but we knew of each other through St. Leo's. His sister Cathy also went to Immaculate Conception and I knew of her as well, but since she was three years ahead, we didn't really cross paths. When I think back to those days, what I remember most about Seamus is a happy-go-lucky, kind, and sweet guy—an affable, lovable 6-foot, 4-inch teddy bear towering over my petite 5-foot, 3-inch frame. And that we always enjoyed each other's company.

We all sat around the campfire that chilly Saturday evening in May, as the distinct smell of tinder wafted in the air and we huddled together to stay warm. With Steve Miller's "Serenade" playing in the background, as the wood kindled, so did my relationship with Seamus.

# Chapter 28 - "Free Fallin'"

A swarm of butterflies stirred erratically deep inside me while Seamus drove us through town in his black Ford Bronco, the decisive tempo of "Kashmir" by Led Zeppelin swirling around our heads. It was silly to feel this way—we'd been friends and knew each other well, so why these nerves? It's strange when a relationship alters course and suddenly, you mean something different to each other than the day before. Things in life can change so quickly, and if you're not paying attention, you might miss the moment.

Memorial Day weekend concluded with the girls returning to watch the guys march in the parade. Standing in front of Co #4 on the Boulevard on a promising sunny day, we were like proud mama hens as the boys approached, decked out in their formal dress uniforms and striding in perfect unison. When Seamus caught my eye, he smiled from ear to ear, and I knew in an instant a monumental shift had occurred.

We navigated the rest of the week in heavy deliberation over the nature of our relationship. Seamus wanted to take me on a date, and feeling torn, I expressed my fear that pursuing this direction might ruin our friendship. I'd come to appreciate our chats and the ease with which we related, and was afraid dating would mess up our comfortable vibe.

Still, taking the relationship in another direction made sense. We shared similar career interests, we were both raised Catholic, and we enjoyed similar pastimes: music, sports, movies, travel, and time with family and friends. Nothing was in the "watch-out" column to further dissuade me, other than the fear of losing a good friend.

As we parked by the Gilbert Avenue baseball field, Tom Petty's "Free Fallin'" played encouragingly in the background. Seamus was persuasive, insisting our friendship was solid and could withstand the shift back if a romantic relationship didn't work out. He wrote my name in the sky, and we fell out into nothin'. Our first official date was on Friday, June 1st, 1990. We went to the movies and became a couple watching *Pretty Woman (masterful choice, dude)*.

A few benefits revealed themselves early in our dating period. The initial "getting to know you" awkwardness was a non-factor because we already knew each other. Also, there was no grilling from our friends deciding if the other was going to pass muster. The one nuance we did have to navigate through was family introductions. I already knew Cathy, which was a plus, though I wasn't sure how she viewed me in those early days. Seamus and Cathy are what you'd refer to as Irish twins, born only 11 months apart. They were protective of one another, so her lens toward me seemed to be with one eyebrow raised. I understood this. For starters, Seamus was older than me and had already graduated college, while I was just starting my junior year. More notably, I had spent the last two years dating more guys than appeared on the history of *The Dating Game*. I'm sure she was thinking, *Who is this twit, and what does she want with my brother?* What started out feeling like skeptical reserve turned into an amazing sisterly bond; one I still feel for her today.

As you may have already deduced, Seamus comes from an Irish and Scottish background, and his first name is Gaelic for James. James was his official birth name, though no one ever referred to him as James, except for his Mom, who would teasingly refer to him as Jimmy when she wanted to get a rise out of him. He had his name legally changed to Seamus Francis McMurray because he wanted our marriage certificate and other legal documents to reflect who he was. There's no doubt about it; he was never anyone other than Seamus, taking on the persona of his name better than anyone I've ever known.

Seamus invited me over his house, as things were evolving at a rapid pace. Upon walking through the side kitchen entrance on the first meet and greet, I was addressed ferociously by the family dog, Smokey. This 14-pound salt-and-pepper Miniature Schnauzer with ears cropped and tail docked had me convinced I'd be leaving with one leg. Wondering if someone had put out the signal to attack, I skirted around him cautiously. I came to learn he did this to everyone except immediate family and, excuse the cliché, his bark was worse than his bite. Smokey would one day become part of my home and heart.

I became endeared to Seamus' parents the moment I met them. His dad John was Scottish and extremely proud of his heritage. Though he wasn't as tall as Seamus, John gave off the appearance of being tall, with the most amazing deep timbre in his voice. His personality matched his presence—confident, decisive, and highly opinionated, but equally soft and loving.

I found John's sense of humor infectious, though I think he got an even better kick out of himself. One of his favorite

163

quips when we asked him something was "You writing a book? Leave that chapter out," or the alternate "Make it a mystery." Which is why I'm certain he's up above laughing out loud as I write about him now.

Cathy inherited John's ballbuster qualities. Once we clicked, I was invited to bear witness to the comical torment she would prescribe on her brother. She laughed hysterically, explaining how passionately Seamus chanted "Thunderstruck" by AC/DC while headbanging around the house. Cathy's laugh would get me going, and then she would mimic Seamus' actions and we'd double over. At a wedding, Cathy ordered a tray of 20 kamikaze shots, and when Seamus walked up next to her at the bar and the bartender asked who was paying, Cathy pointed to him, took the tray, and walked away!

Seamus' mom Eileen came from a large Irish family. I marveled upon learning Seamus had 40 first cousins across the pond. Eileen was soft-spoken, kind, and loving, though she was someone you wouldn't want to cross. She had no qualms about expressing her displeasure when she was not happy about something. All those years in Catholic school had me prepped for her no-nonsense persona. Also living in the McMurray household was John's mom, Sarah, a wee woman with a thick Scottish brogue; I never could catch everything she was saying, no matter how hard I tried. I got a kick out of her mannerisms coupled with her accent—Cathy and I would try to repeat things she'd say, rolling around in chuckles.

Seamus had a similarly easy transition meeting Mom and Charlie. He quickly bonded with Charlie over the Rangers and Jets. At the time, my Mom's office was doing weekly football pools, so Seamus and I both joined in the fun. This was how we got our nicknames Big Bear and Little Bear, and I still use mine for all my pools. Over time, we met more layers of one another's extended families. The first time Seamus met some of the Battinelli clan, we went to Aunt Josie and Uncle Moe's for pasta fagioli, one of Uncle Moe's specialties. Uncle Moe kept telling Seamus he had sauce on his face, prompting Seamus to wipe repeatedly with his napkin. After a few times, I realized what Uncle Moe thought was tomato sauce was actually the prominent red birthmark Seamus had near the side of his mouth—we laughed about that one for years.

During our dating years, we were both insanely busy. Seamus had graduated from King's College in 1989 with his bachelor of arts in business administration, but decided he wanted to add a BS in accounting. He began taking classes to make this a reality. In addition to work and school, he served as a volunteer firefighter and played softball in a town men's summer league sponsored by Co #4. I became their scorer, and doubled as the eye black supplier before the games.

On my end, I was finishing my last two years of school while working at the bank. We were also socially active, and our circle of friends seemed to be ever expanding. Between my high school friends, his college friends, and our joint friends from the firehouse and softball, we enjoyed every moment of togetherness. Floating through our courtship as if on a cloud, we were "Comfortably Numb," in the words of Pink Floyd. The relationship was easy breezy and flowing as we created the foundation of our young lives.

I graduated with my bachelor of science degree in accounting from Seton Hall in May 1992 and was proud I had turned things around after that rocky start my freshman year. Mom, Dad, Pop, and Seamus all attended the ceremony at Brendan Byrne Arena in the Meadowlands. Also present was a new adornment on my ring finger—Seamus had proposed earlier in the year.

Our relationship had become one of love and commitment, but it was also a whirlwind. When Seamus nervously arrived at my house one afternoon before I got home to get Mom's permission (in his softball uniform), he said he had to ask her something, to which she replied, "What, do you want to marry me or something?" Hysterical. Mom smashed the tension of the moment and made Seamus comfortable to proceed with asking for my hand in marriage.

Mom loved Seamus, but was cautioning me to slow down, concerned I was too young and needed to focus on my advanced schooling and career. We would be studying for our CPAs, and we had our whole lives ahead of us, so why rush things? Her perspective was rooted in protectiveness and experience, but I wasn't listening. Headstrong and decisive, I believed we could have it all—a happy life together, successful careers, loving families supporting us, and of course, an exciting social life. We weren't heeding any warning signs, but as the Grateful Dead so eloquently taught us, every silver lining has a "Touch of Grey."

# Chapter 29 - "Smells Like Teen Spirit"

As someone who loves to do quick math, I'm thankful I was born at the start of a decade. It's still moderately easy to figure out how old I am (which seems to get more challenging to calculate as we get older, right?). It's also simpler to recall how old I was when . . . (fill in the blanks). In 1990, I was 20 (see how easy?), and my teen years were behind me, left back in the '80s with my cherished glam metal. I was adjusting fine to my age, but still in denial that my favorite music genre was on its way out. As a result, when I started hearing the buzz about this Seattle sound movement called grunge, I was reluctant to jump on the bandwagon. Fusing punk rock and heavy metal seemed to be right down my alley, but my Mötley Crüe boys were becoming less relevant, which I could not accept. Thank God for resurgences!

My grunge boycott ended one day in late 1991 in the parking lot of my local retail convenience center, which contained two important go-to businesses—my hair salon and Dunkin' Donuts. Having a good hairdresser and nail specialist are golden rules in a woman's life, and I've been a coffee junkie since my days working at Roy's, when I had to get up early to open the store. Starbucks was still only located in Seattle, and Dunkin' was the best coffee around. Seamus and I were obsessed and went almost daily; we both liked our coffee the same way back then—light and sweet. I ditched the sugar entirely many years ago and now prefer low-fat milk, but I still remember the first satisfying sip of a Dunkin' L&S.

I started my car after one of my regular coffee runs when a sound came out of the radio unlike anything I'd ever heard. It felt completely different—the guitar was heavy, yet slightly distorted somehow. The sound was hard but dipped into soft little pockets—fast, slow, fast, slow, fast, slow, fast. The voice was like the guitar; muffled and gritty, and so distant from the high and tight heavy metal voices I'd built my teenage years' soundtrack around. Sucked into the vortex, I sat parked in my car, waiting for the song to conclude. The radio DJ came on and informed me I was listening to Nirvana and their first single, "Smells Like Teen Spirit." That haunting voice was Kurt Cobain.

My association to grunge music ties heavily to dive bars, likely because I had just turned 21 and Seamus and I were going out with our friends every weekend. We worked hard during the week, so we needed to blow off some steam. Back in the '90s, dive bars were popular and plentiful in our area, and the good ones got packed on weekends. Our needs were simple— ice cold beer, a great bartender, a jukebox with jamming tunes, and a dartboard.

One of the first dive bars we frequented was Hobnob Pub in Garfield. The thing I most recall was how dark it was—if you've never been to a dive bar, darkness is a common theme. I've never been able to figure out if people don't want to be seen, if they don't want to see each other, or if the bar owners are trying to create an ambiance that doesn't really exist in the decor. At times I can appreciate a dark room, perhaps because things lurking under the surface automatically feel more settled and comfortable.

I can picture a moment; actually many moments, when we're all sitting in our favorite booth at the Hobnob, empty beer bottles covering the table, cigarette-filled ashtrays stationed everywhere, and Pearl Jam's "Black" enveloping the room, further darkening the space around us.

But by far, the most memorable of all the dive bars was Ed's Tavern in Saddle Brook. We spent countless weekend nights at our happy place. On any given Friday it would go something like this . . .

Seamus, Billy and I are the first to arrive at Ed's after driving over together after work. We walk into a mostly vacant room, except for a few patrons seated around the large square bar. We're greeted with a booming hello by Freddy, one of two regular bartenders on shift. Freddy and his brother John are two of the greatest guys, which keeps us coming here weekend after weekend.

Freddy drops the Ed's coasters down at our usual seats at the bar, on the side closest to the door. The coasters inform us that Ed's is "Where new friends meet," though in our case, it's definitely where old friends meet, but a catchy tagline all the same. Within seconds we have icy cold beers sitting in front of us, and we give each other cheers after surviving another long week.

My next order of business is to ask Freddy for quarters. I mosey over to the right side of the room, where beyond the booths sits a large jukebox. I light up a cigarette and hit the flip button. I'm going to play three songs for now, but I'll be back several times before the night is through. Jukebox selection G8 is appropriate given my week; that'd be "Brain Stew" by

Green Day—it captures my mental state at the moment. I scroll absentmindedly until landing on Red Hot Chili Peppers, deciding to take it on the "Otherside" and selecting K4. One more tune—flip, flip, flip . . . here's a good one . . . yeah, P9, Stone Temple Pilots' "Plush." Got time to wait for tomorrow.

I stroll back to the crew. Tommy and Kevin have arrived, and another round is already in progress. Freddy's backed us up with the next round on him, signified by a round plastic Ed's Tavern token. I ask Tommy what time Tammi and Laurie are getting here, and he says Tammi's waiting for Laurie to get to her house, so probably within an hour. I love the guys like brothers, but the girls keep it properly balanced. Linda's making an appearance later, as well.

As the music plays, I sit and stare vacantly at the bar, take a nice swig of my Coors Light, and try to wash away the stress from the last few days. It was a heavy reporting week, and yesterday we missed the FedEx drop-off and had to arrange for a special pickup at my house. They arrived at my house around 6 a.m. today and guaranteed delivery to Maryland by the end of business. It's not always pretty, but we ALWAYS make our deadlines. I'm proud under my watch we never miss, but now I'm ready to put it in the rear view.

I'm startled out of my stupor when Mike walks in. I've known this guy since kindergarten, and I'm always happy to see him because we speak a similar language. He can't stay long, he's got an early shift with the EPPD. He grabs a beer, and we head over to play a round of darts. I'm not a pro, but we enjoy playing a few rounds of cricket on the dartboard .

The evening is picking up as the crowd thickens. Over-lapping conversations, louder voices; the jubilation level heightens moment by moment. This is the most enjoyable part of the evening to me. Nobody's more than a couple drinks in, and the mood is festive. You would think we'd learn our lesson, because at some point tonight it will start getting sloppy, which is when things can easily take a bad turn.

Tammi and Laurie enter as their bubbly selves, and the party begins. Time for a round of Kamikazes . . . as we toast with our first shots of the evening, the clear, chilled liquid potion of vodka, triple sec, and lime juice drips sloppily all over the bar and floor. Away we go . . .

It's 1 a.m. The floor is sticky, the smoke has permeated our hair and clothes, and we need to start calculating an exit. Between who's mad, who's slurring, and who's crying , it's hard to determine who will get the drunk prize for the evening. The girls have left and it's down to Seamus, Tommy, Billy, and me. We lost Kevin about an hour ago, but I checked on him and he's still sleeping soundly in the back seat of our car. Billy and I are usually the strategists working on the rest of the crew to convince them it's time to go. Freddy's announcing last call. Another group of guys arrived about an hour ago, and some tensions are brewing. I'm not sure why, but things will get ugly if we don't leave now. Tommy is trying to be the pacifist he always is and befriends one of the guys in the crew, putting his arm around his shoulder. Yeah, not gonna work, but I give him kudos for trying.

We finally gather up the posse—Billy stopped drinking a while ago, so he drives us all over to the Saddle Brook Diner. Nothing like a Taylor ham, egg, and cheese on a hard roll to soak up the night.

# Chapter 30 - "Takin' Care of Business"

Let's just describe the period immediately after graduating from college as "fairly bizarre." After spending the majority of your waking days in life thus far on a structured and disciplined school journey, designed to prepare you for the "real world," upon actually arriving there, it's as if you've suddenly landed in a foreign country where no one speaks your language.

Today, more colleges and universities have programs designed around helping recent grads land their first professional gig. I also know from firsthand experience that more companies now have paid or unpaid internships; a great way to get some practical experience before graduating and potentially line up a permanent position. Maybe I missed the memo, but I don't recall these types of programs when I was graduating. I suppose I went to a job fair or two, but don't remember anything resulting from them.

Hence, after getting my degree, I continued working at the bank during the summer. NCB needed the help and I was happy to be earning a full-time income in a comfortable environment. I knew this would be temporary, while I launched a job search for my first accounting position. The feeling of not knowing what would come next was both exciting and petrifying. I knew something out there was meant for me, but had no idea what it was. To a Virgo who thrives on having a definitive plan with free reign to execute, these feelings clashed. I dug into my faith and entered into the unknown, like the song "Dreams" by Van Halen—time to spread my wings.

I employed a tried-and-true method at the time, which was to devour the classifieds, in search of my next opportunity. While I don't recall every interview, three stand out. The first was a cost accountant position at a manufacturing plant for a utility company. Interesting, but ultimately the industrial vibe didn't feel right, and I wasn't jazzed about cost accounting.

One promising prospect was with a bank (not NCB—I inquired, but nothing was available at the time). I had grown to love the banking world and understood the inner workings. This was an auditing position at a savings and loan association that had branches from Buffalo, New York all the way down to Cape May, New Jersey. It seemed like it would be right in my wheelhouse.

They offered me the job. I was thrilled. In fact, I was more delighted than The Pointer Sisters singing "I'm So Excited," and I just couldn't hide it. This was it—my first official job out of college—I was headed for a career in the banking industry! Relieved and anticipatory, all the little sugar plums were dancing around my head . . . I'd be president of the bank one day after moving up the financial institution ladder and . . . *hold on, hot shot.*

My momentary futuristic visions grinded to a halt upon hearing the compensation package. The salary was compara-ble for the time, but with a hitch: All the commuting I would need to do schlepping between Buffalo and Cape May was not reimbursable. Wait . . . *what?* This didn't seem right to me. My annual salary would be chipped away at to pay for gas, mileage, and wear and tear expenses on my vehicle. I was not nearly as pumped as I had been upon getting the offer. Ah, if only I could tell my 21-year-old self one thing, it would have been to enlist the power of negotiation, but I didn't yet possess the sort of business savvy or confidence to do so.

Despite the letdown on the traveling expenses, I planned on accepting the offer. But first, I had one more interview scheduled. I wasn't anticipating much. It was for a billing position at a company called M.A.S.I. in Hackensack. It certainly didn't grab me from the simple description—I wasn't even sure why I was going. I knew nothing about the firm and the title didn't sound luxurious.

This is where I truly believe fate, destiny, or whatever you would like to call it sometimes grabs a hold of us and pushes us in the direction we're seeking. We don't understand why or how—we just know it does.

Keep in mind this was 1992, and when interviewing in these days, you typically met one person who would be your supervisor. Unlike today, where multiple rounds of interviews occur with different stakeholders, nothing mattered but the guy in the driver's seat holding all the cards.

Upon arriving to interview, I traveled up the small elevator to the third-floor receptionist. A lovely woman named Doretta greeted me and called back for my interviewer. As I waited, I felt an unusual confidence for a new graduate trying to land their first role. I had nothing to lose, because a job was already waiting for me, literally a phone call away. Like Chrissie Hynde of The Pretenders in "Brass in Pocket," I was gonna make them notice.

A couple minutes later, I was greeted by a tall, gangly man with nerdy glasses who introduced himself as Al. Al was dressed professionally, but he looked as if he'd already worked a full day, though it was only 10 a.m. His hair was wildly unkempt, and as I followed him to his office, I noticed his untucked shirt. Did he just come out of a cyclone? I wasn't sure.

When we arrived at his office, we sat down, and Al casually kicked his feet up on the desk and began talking to me. *Here I am, dressed in my traditional navy business suit, trying to be all serious and professional, and this guy has his feet up on the desk?* I wanted to be offended, but something about him; maybe his boyishness or his odd mannerisms, made me think he might be certifiable, and I actually found myself in tune with his energy. We bonded over Seton Hall (his alma mater, too) and our mutual Polish heritage. He was direct with me: This was not an accountant position; rather, it was an entry-level role working for the accounting arm of a private real estate firm called Hampshire Management Company. While the possibility existed for advancement, I'd have to earn my stripes and start from the ground up.

It didn't sound as high profile as the auditing title the bank was offering. I knew if I got this position, I'd really have to roll up my sleeves and prove myself. We finished the interview and Al walked me out. But as I was leaving, walking through the third-floor office, I felt this indescribable energy—alive, electric—almost running through the building like a current. What was happening?

Feeling satisfied, I headed over to the bank to start my workday. I knew I'd interviewed well and we connected on all cylinders. Al said he'd get back to me shortly, which was good because I didn't plan on holding out too long—the bank was waiting for my answer. I was floored when I got a call the same afternoon. He offered me the position, for the same exact salary the bank had offered me, and I would not be commuting from Buffalo to Cape May on my own dime. Decision time. As Bachman-Turner Overdrive professed, I'd be "Takin' Care of Business" to set my course.

Even so, weighing all the pros and cons wasn't easy. The position potential at the bank had the edge, as did the comfort of the banking world I had gained a passion for. On the flip side, Hampshire was offering the same salary, and I wouldn't have a smidgen of the travel expense—the commute from Elmwood Park to Hackensack was less than 10 miles. In addition, Seamus and I were planning a wedding and studying for the CPA exam. The travel commitment for the bank job was going to add a ton of time I could better use elsewhere.

While I was completely unsure if this position was going to fulfill my needs, when I looked at everything in totality, the Hampshire position made sense, at least in the short term. Hey, if it didn't work out as expected, it was a stepping stone, and I could easily change gears whenever necessary. Thirty-two years later, I'm not sure where all the time has gone, but needless to say, it was the right choice—I'm still there!

Saying goodbye to my friends at the bank was hard, but they gave me a great sendoff. The message on the cake said, "Congratulations Cheryll! Our debit - their credit." I still find this amusing, because in banking you debit an account, which is a deduction to cash. On a general ledger when you debit cash, it's adding to the balance, not subtracting. The accountant in me wants to go back and reverse the saying on the cake. All kidding aside, once I walked out of those bank doors for the last time, I didn't look back. It was time to make a life for myself.

I started working at Hampshire on August 3, 1992. I'd come to learn this private family-owned real estate firm was in its third generation (now its fourth) and owned commercial real estate properties all over the country. The majority of the portfolio primarily encompassed retail and some industrial properties. I was green in real estate, but my position provided a super foundation to learn about the business. All the people at Hampshire were (and are) extraordinary. The culture vibes as a tight-knit community in which everyone is committed to the same goals.

Our team of four was responsible for all the tenant administration, including things like lease abstraction and billing, common area maintenance reconciliations, and calculation of leasing commissions (I know it's jargon—I won't quiz you!). I quickly fell in love with all the complexities of each property, each like its own business with multiple nuances. While I performed all these functions, I was also learning the backbone of accounting—how to read a general ledger from the ground up. Each property had its own permanent file containing all the agreements and documents. I pored over these to understand the details of each asset. My dedication and focus paid off, and I was promoted to manager of the small team.

While I was learning about the real estate world through a fire hose, things were on full throttle back at home. Wedding plans progressed, though we had a lot to get done—venue, DJ, photographer, flowers, guest list, seating, and Mass preparations, which required us to attend Pre-Cana, the premarital course required by the Catholic church.

Between my new position at Hampshire, wedding plans, and the busyness of our social circle, I'm not sure why Seamus and I thought we should study for the CPA exam at this time. I guess we wanted to get it over with as quickly upon graduating as possible. We tried to invest the required time in our classes with Becker, a popular CPA exam prep program. With four parts to the exam, the coursework and study requirements were intense. Seamus and I were trying to get it all in, but in hindsight, we should have dedicated more time to the cause. I felt like Jennifer Beals dancing to "Maniac" by Michael Sembello. I pride myself on being a masterful juggler, but this was one too many balls in the air, and something needed to drop; thus, our attempt sitting for the exam resulted in failure.

I'm not a believer in holding on to regrets, but I do have one. I wish I had the confidence to take the exam again. I was so close to passing, and if I had gone to sit for a second time, knowing myself as I do, I would have succeeded. In the last 10 years, I've passed the real estate salesperson exam and received my insurance producer license for property and casualty. While prepping for each of these was not fun and I've never considered myself the best test taker, I'm good at memorization when I apply myself. Sure, the CPA exam is hard and complex, but in the end, it's all about memorization. At the time, though, my priorities were elsewhere, and my logic was that I wasn't interested in going into public accounting anyway, so why bother going through the torture? This was the lie I told myself to excuse it away. In reality, it was the fear of failure knocking me off course.

# Chapter 31 - "That's What Friends Are For"

With my budding career in order, it was time to focus on our wedding. Seamus and I (with the assistance of our supportive parents) traveled around New Jersey to find our venue. After an exhaustive search, we landed on the Sheraton in Hasbrouck Heights, appreciating that everything for the evening other than the church was in one location. They also offered a comprehensive package, costly but not over the top—we were trying not to break our families' budgets.

I don't remember how we selected our DJ. Was the DJ part of the Sheraton? I think it's kind of ironic this is the one bit of information I can't easily recall, given my love for music. I do remember how we carefully crafted a must-play song list together; a lengthy list containing music from our respective heritages along with our personal favorites—at least the ones suitable for the event.

We met a talented photographer named David, and we liked his personality and samples. It turned out to be an easy choice for us, and later, Tracy used him for her wedding. We turned to a local florist owned by the Fuennings, longtime friends of my Aunt Josie and Uncle Moe. They put together beautiful, affordable arrangements. Once we selected a local limo company, we had all the primary services arranged.

Next came what I felt was an exhausting process of dress shopping. During this time in my life, I was actually wearing skirts and dresses. At the time, professional women did not wear pantsuits—everything was blazers and matching skirts or coat dresses, and I owned many. Seamus and I were also attending many formal parties and weddings that required us to get all gussied up. Still, finding something traditional I'd also be comfortable wearing given my personality and style proved an arduous task. I drove around to multiple bridal shops and sifted through many racks before finding my perfect choice at Mildred's Bridal Shop in Hawthorne. It was a beautiful dress; elegant and not gaudy.

Seamus and I encountered a bit of a blip regarding our bridal party. Without getting into details, some controversy ensued surrounding someone Seamus had asked to be in the party. This required reconsideration of the choices and selecting someone new to join the party. Seamus' final choices were Phil, Billy, Mike, Kevin, Cousin Christopher, and Jack. On my side were Robyn, Tracy, Sandy, Julie, Linda, and my soon-to-be sister-in-law Cathy as maid of honor. We chose raspberry-colored bridesmaids dresses. The girls organized a beautiful bridal shower—I walked into my shower carrying a tray of eggplant parmigiana I made, thinking it was for another party—duped!

We were trying to keep to a reasonable number of guests, but Seamus and I both had many friends. My family isn't huge, but Seamus has a large family in Ireland, so our invite list was going to be larger than expected. We knew we'd get a number of declines from across the pond, but even still, having to whittle down our list was not enjoyable.

The Mass would be celebrated at St. Leo's. We had a couple of special considerations; the biggest of which was that we wanted Seamus' uncle, Father Seamus, to marry us. Father Seamus was the brother of Seamus' mom, and he lived in Ireland. We planned the readings and song selections, and put together a program with the help of one of St. Leo's priests. I remembered Pat, a singer from grammar school years who had a beautiful voice, and with the help of my eighth-grade teacher, Mrs. Rubino, we were able to get in touch with Pat, who agreed to sing at our wedding. While I never got to actually hear it, one of the songs we requested be sung prior to the bridal march was "All I Ask of You" from *The Phantom of the Opera*. Seamus and I saw the show after his parents bought us tickets, and I was completely mesmerized by the soundtrack. The powerful lyrics make me feel like I'm wrapped in a safety blanket.

Our final count landed below 150 guests, within the range we were shooting for. Phew. Now to plan the final details: seating chart, marriage licenses, and last-minute honeymoon arrangements, since were flying to Aruba the day after our wedding. With all of the plans involved for an elaborate traditional wedding, is it any wonder you don't have time to enjoy it, or even consider the serious commitment you're about to make? I don't believe we had one moment to ask ourselves or each other any of the tough questions. Pre-Cana is designed to help you explore some of these items, but counseling outside of the religious realm should be considered. We were both speeding into a future without a full picture, and we didn't have a clue.

Leading up to the wedding, we did a lot of celebrating. We each had two bachelor and bachelorette nights. On the first night, the girls took me to a male burlesque show akin to Chippendale's. We sat in the front, and I wound up lying on the stage with sweaty bodies dancing over my face. Hugely embarrassing and entertaining. On the second night, we met up with the guys at a local restaurant and then went to chill and kick back with a few beers at a dive bar.

Our rehearsal and rehearsal dinner were held Friday night, the eve of the wedding. All of our out-of-town guests had arrived. After the rehearsal, our immediate family and bridal party headed over to The Cobblestone in Clifton (which was previously Villa Paisano, the restaurant my mom, Charlie, and I had frequented every Friday night). A preview of things to come was looming. Our best man had imbibed one too many, and his slurred speech offered way too many references to "the man upstairs." While I would never denounce someone expressing their faith, he was clearly smashed. *Oh, boy.*

I woke up on my wedding day to a beautifully temperate and sunny day. The morning itself was a blur, given the amount of people trafficking through our small house on Falmouth Avenue. I don't even remember getting ready. I'm assuming I went to Grace's to get my hair done in the morning; my nails were already done in a classic French manicure. Soon, David was at my house taking pictures, and every minute up to go-time was filled with some other detail.

When I climbed alone into the limo parked in front of my house, my mind started racing. The moment had arrived, and suddenly my noggin was filled with nothing but question marks. I felt panicked and had no idea why—it was as if my mind wasn't my own. *Where the heck is Dad, and why hasn't he come out of the house to join me?* I looked at my watch. *Oh my God—we're going to be late. Right now, 150 guests are waiting for me and I'm late.* I spun my head swiftly to the right in a huff and got lipstick on the shoulder of my dress. Meltdown, tears, all of it. Finally someone came out of my house and I got their attention, and they went to retrieve my father, who was apparently unaware he was supposed to be coming with me in the limo. *God help me.*

We finally left for the church at 2 p.m., and the flood of emotions had not ceased. Which is why I can't even describe how I felt walking down the aisle. Once I saw Seamus, my aura calmed. *Away we go.* The Mass was beautiful and perfect. The most amazing thing happened toward the end—suddenly we heard the faint sound of heavenly music coming from outside. Seamus' parents had arranged for a bagpiper to play for when we walked outside. What an incredible touch—I find the beautiful sounds emanating from a bagpipe to be regal, traditional, and authentic. I couldn't have asked for anything more as we said our I do's.

After the Mass, we took pictures at Saddle Brook Park with the wedding party and one of the fire trucks. We allowed plenty of time for pictures before the wedding reception, which didn't start until 6 p.m. Time flew by, and the next thing I knew we were gathered with our wedding party in our private suite while cocktail hour was underway for the remainder of our guests. When they announced the wedding party, we burst through the doors, ready to celebrate with our family and friends. All the planning joys, frustrations, tears, and anxiousness were behind us—it was time to begin our journey as man and wife.

We selected "(Everything I Do) I Do It for You" by Bryan Adams as our wedding song. We both loved *Robin Hood: Prince of Thieves* with Kevin Costner, which had come out the summer before. It was true—we were doing everything for each other. Almost to a fault. Looking back, I see both of us were already starting to ignore what we needed to do for ourselves.

The wedding day was darn near perfect until we sat down at the table with our bridal party for dinner. At this point our best man, who I'm now guessing never came off his high from the night before, continued on his mission of destruction throughout the day. I would learn later, hard liquor had started flowing at Seamus' house before the Mass. Most of the guys enjoyed one or two celebratory shots—understandable. I should mention the best man had been dating my buddy Linda for some time prior to this. Not sure exactly what set him off, but he was completely irrational by the time dinner arrived, and the profanities being hurdled across the table at my friend were unacceptable. Up to this point, everyone had done a good job keeping bride and groom out of the fray of whatever had been going on behind the scenes, but now it was all coming out to bare. We were now upset, and the rest of the party was trying to keep things under control. I was pissed. Don't fuck with my family or friends. I don't care what the circumstances—too many lines were crossed. But then I realized Linda hadn't heard anything he was muttering at the time, so I let it go in the interest of getting through the day.

Seamus and I spent a ton of time receiving our guests. Other than the unfortunate episodes caused by our best man (and wait, there's more), the one thing we both realized afterward is we spent more time greeting our guests than enjoying each other and the day. (I hear that's a common issue for newly married couples, so you readers who haven't tied the knot yet, consider this a cautionary tale—carve out specific time to enjoy each other!) At least we did dance. One of the reception highlights for me was when our friends gathered around us as we sat on the dance floor and sang the remake of "That's What Friends Are For" by Dionne Warwick & Friends. It was so heartfelt, reminding me when tension gets high, you need to keep smiling. It managed to take some of the sting away from the dinner shenanigans, as I realized how I loved each and every one of the people who we'd asked to stand up for us.

The party continued with some of our go-to songs, ones we'd go on to celebrate with time and again at our friends' and families' wedding receptions. I love "Blister in the Sun" by the Violent Femmes, especially the whispering portion as you scooch down until you're literally lying on the floor. The ultimate, though, was always "Paradise by the Dashboard Light" by Meat Loaf and Ellen Foley. In the tense moments when everyone *stops right there*, my girlfriends and I would line up one side, boys on the other, and recite our diatribes as if we were part of the play. Legendary.

Our night flew by, and for the most part all was well. The exception, of course, was our best man, who was continuing to act out. By this point our friends had him cut off from being served. In the state he was in, this didn't go well. After an altercation with one of the bartenders, he got driven home. Later in the evening, after the reception, he somehow found his way back, but we'd all had enough. Time to go to Aruba . . . *take me away.*

# Chapter 32 - "Time Warp"

My love of horror movies was instigated by my grandmother Claire. Other than the afternoon soap operas she tuned into and the news she watched with Pop, I don't recall her watching anything but horror movies. My grandparents had a full-sized television in their bedroom, and Pop would watch sports in the living room while Grandma commandeered the set in the bedroom. While you might view this as an indication of separation, in the case of my grandparents, I believe it represented something else. They were so confident in their relationship, they could respect and celebrate their differences.

Grandma and Pop taught me the way to be part of a unified, loving, and committed couple, while being able to express individuality at the same time. They aligned on all their values, worked together to create a beautiful home environment, and gave each other freedom and space to develop as humans. Don't get me wrong; their relationship wasn't perfect. I remember Pop getting gruff at times, with Grandma responding in turn with *"Cicho byc"* (Polish for "Be quiet"), and they would retreat to their separate corners until the tension blew over. These moments aside, watching them gave me the model for what a successful marriage could and should be. I have always tried to emulate these characteristics, but haven't always been as valiant in my efforts. I'm still trying, because I believe being in a committed relationship is one of the most beautiful aspects of life.

So back to the horror movies. You are probably asking yourself right now, *what on Earth do horror movies have to do with committed relationships? You just got married, Cheryll—aren't we gonna hear about what happened next?* My answer is that horror movies have nothing to do with committed relationships, unless that's how you like to spend your time together. I just need to share this as part of my history, and as I wrote this book, I had a sudden need to write this chapter.

Back in the '70s and '80s, many channels offered horror movie double features like *Chiller Theater* and *Creature Feature*. These series were so popular, they even created a *Creature Feature* board game (I know because I had it—similar to Monopoly, it contained horror movie characters instead of properties). Through these shows, I got introduced at a young age to all the classic black and white originals. For many children, this might have caused them terrifying nightmares, but for me, watching these movies always had a comforting effect. Maybe it's because with my grandmother I always felt safe, and she was able to relay these were just movies as opposed to reality. My sleeping disorders are steeped in reality, not fiction. In fact, escaping through movies, shows, and books is my form of therapy!

The black and white classics have always been most impressive to me. Today's movies are so technologically evolved, creating suspense, tension, and fear through special effects and visual elements, and going over the top is so commonplace, it's like *yeah, cool*; it almost desensitizes us . But back in the

'30s and '40s, when these early films were made, they had to create all of the emotions through their acting. When I watch these films now, it amazes me how adept the actors were in perfecting certain images on the screen. While I will buy in to a visual blockbuster laden with special effects galore, I know what those movies are going to be and set my expectations accordingly. What I most appreciate about most movies is the acting, and I'm guessing the level of my analysis points back to watching all these fabulous moments so early on in my childhood.

The ultimate horror actor was Bela Lugosi as Dracula. With his iconic mannerisms and facial expressions, he created one of the most recognizable images ever to be seen. I relate to vampires—there's something mysterious, whimsical, and romantic about them. They thrive in darkness and live most of their life in singular silence. Most of all, they are completely misunderstood, because it's difficult for us to comprehend something could never die. Could it be possible? A great song by Rob Zombie called "Dragula" has the perfect music to complement this kind of vibe. I relate to all the *Batman* movies for similar reasons, having a lot to do with the darkness and being misunderstood. Do I subscribe so well because I think I'm often misunderstood? Maybe.

In addition to the classics, Grandma and I watched horror flicks spanning later decades. Along with some good ones, an equal to greater number of cheesy ones held court on the TV. At one point, the horror movies being made were downright awful, but in some campy way I can appreciate them. I've caught a few of them from time to time on Turner Classic Movies and laugh my butt off, finding them so ridiculous they are funny. One example is *What Ever Happened to Aunt Alice?*, in which a maniacal woman clobbers people and buries them in her yard. She signifies each grave with a pine tree, and by the end of the movie, she's got a whole yard filled with pine trees.

Similar to many kids growing up in the '70s, I've watched all the reruns of *The Addams Family* and *The Munsters* multiple times. The ironic part of both of these shows is they were each on for only a couple seasons, but their characters achieved legendary status. *The Addams Family* continues its relevance with movie and series franchises that have done well, drawing in a new generations of watchers. Have you ever heard the song "Uma Thurman" by Fall Out Boy? I love it for two reasons. In the background, you can hear the theme song of *The Munsters.* Also, they cleverly use lyrics in the chorus to weave in "dance like Uma Thurman"—a nod to my all-time favorite movie, *Pulp Fiction.*

The first time I saw this movie, I went with my new Hampshire girlfriends. I was the one who selected the movie, so about a half-hour in, my friend Monica leaned over and said, "We're never letting you pick a movie again." Monica has since acknowledged it is now one of her favorites also, but we all laughed hysterically at the time. Quentin Tarantino is one of those guys—you either get him or you don't. I happen to think he is a genius.

By the '80s, I was fully entrenched in all kinds of horror movies, including the slasher genre, which was prolific at the time. The best of these is the *Halloween* series in my opinion; especially the first two. Jamie Lee Curtis does no wrong in my book! Though not a slasher film, the best movie transformation I've ever seen was from *An American Werewolf in London.* The movie itself is campy, but the first time you see David Naughton change into the monster in front of your eyes, you find yourself wanting to "Bark at the Moon" like Ozzy Osbourne. And can you agree that another impressive transformation occurs in Michael Jackson's "Thriller" video? While zombies are not my favorite horror genre, this video is a masterpiece. My grandmother loved it, too, though it may have been more because of her love for Vincent Price.

Cult classic *The Rocky Horror Picture Show* is another one of those movies you'll either relate to or won't. The first time I went to see it with my friend Ron, he explained in advance that this was an interactive movie. I wasn't sure what that meant, and as I sat in the audience, I felt out of touch, because everyone was doing all these crazy things and I had no clue. I sat and observed the madness, but by my second time I found myself doing the "Time Warp" with the rest of the audience. I don't remember all the prompts we acted out, other than maybe throwing rice when Brad and Janet get married. Now when I watch the movie, I simply enjoy it for its quirkiness and awesome soundtrack.

While my favorite movie of all time is *Pulp Fiction*, I consider the best horror movie a three-way tie, thanks to their respective stellar character acting. Let's take Jack Nicholson in *The Shining*. I've never seen someone play a psychotic maniac so well. And of course it's based on the book by Stephen King, my favorite author. Could this give you an indication of where I might head next on my writing journey? Maybe.

Then there's *Silence of the Lambs*. Anthony Hopkins reaches into this character so well—how is it we become so endeared to a cannibal? Sure, the story line is outstanding, as is Jodie Foster, but Anthony seals it for me and millions of others. The last award in my three-way tie goes to Anthony Perkins in

*Psycho*, created by the mastermind Alfred Hitchcock. Anthony is so creepy, his character still manages to scare the wits out of me.

In addition to horror, my grandma loved sci-fi, and I've come to appreciate most of it. I'm a bit of a *Twilight Zone* junkie—similar to the vampire concept, I enjoy exploring the realm of breaking barriers of what we think is possible. This is probably why I also love Stephen King's writing. They all correlate to one theme—*the mind is truly limitless*—so why can't we believe certain things can be true?

This leads me to my ultimate escape into the unknown: it began on May 25, 1977, when my grandparents took me to the movies. They were going on and on about this movie we had to go see. The movie was *Star Wars*. If I go on in excess about this franchise, my absolute nerdiness will pierce through and you may abandon ship (the Millennium Falcon, perhaps?). What I will say is this movie and all of its prequels, sequels, and series following have impacted me more than I can put into words.

I love when the good guys win, but I'm also drawn to the dark side. In a similar way, Darth Vader is misunderstood. The best moment in Star Wars history may be when Anakin Skywalker is transformed into Darth Vader in *Star Wars: Episode III - Revenge of the Sith.* It all collides so beautifully, and you finally have the full picture to explain everything we didn't know as an audience watching for the first time in 1977. I've seen every *Star Wars* movie multiple times and have watched them all in succession when a new triad is about to commence. If you're curious, I always start with *Star Wars: Episode I - The Phantom Menace* because it is chronologically the first in the storyline for all the movies made. This may be debatable with some fans who believe you should start chronologically by when the movie was released, but to me that no longer makes sense. I think I'll end on this note before you lose me (or I may lose you)! I will say I also love all the *Star Wars* spinoffs created under the Disney domain. I am especially endeared to Grogu from *The Mandalorian* series. Everyone who knows me knows this, which is why I've been gifted a growing number of Grogu tschotskes! I believe the franchise can go on endlessly, as far as the mind can go. *May the force be with you.*

# Chapter 33 - "Hold My Hand"

Okay, back to real life.

Prior to getting married, we also had to find a place to live together, since both of us had been living with our parents. We knew putting a down payment on a house was out of reach in those lean early days, so we felt a house rental would suit us best. We needed to stay in Elmwood Park due to Seamus' volunteer fire duties, and we wanted to be close to family and friends. Finding a nice rental wasn't easy—there just weren't many houses available. We had gone to see a newly updated two-family home that we liked, but the rent was out of our range.

After this, we found out through word of mouth about another rental—an apartment on Orchard Street owned by one of the local post office employees. We went to look at it and determined it was everything we were looking for. A first-floor dwelling with the entrance around the side, the apartment contained two bedrooms, a nice-sized living room, decent-sized kitchen, full bathroom, and our own washer and dryer. It was perfect for our first living arrangements. The landlord, a single, middle-aged guy, lived upstairs. He didn't seem like a nosybody or give the impression he'd be up in our grill. The rent was more affordable than the other rental a few houses down, so we grabbed it.

He turned out to be a great landlord, with the exception of a couple of incidents. He had a habit of falling asleep late at night while cooking, which resulted in activated smoke alarms followed by a visit from the fire department. Speaking of which, nothing is more unsettling to me than the scanner going off in the middle of the night and a loved one running out to fight a fire. A feeling of helplessness ensues, and I never got used to it. One time, we were all hanging out at Heather's on a Friday night when the guys got called out. After they didn't return, we got nervous and started driving around, following the direction of the smoke. Here's the crazy thing—it turned out to be the company my mom worked for, Olympic Glove & Safety, burning to blazes after being struck by lightning. The building behind Olympic contained cosmetics, which turned out to be highly flammable. All of us stood witness, watching them fight the fire—the guys were so brave. Olympic had to completely rebuild.

After the wedding, we were starting to adjust to being a married couple when life came in and threw us a big-time curve ball. Seamus' mom Eileen had type 2 diabetes for many years, but now the disease was progressing, and she was undergoing dialysis treatments. As the condition turned more serious, we tried to remain hopeful. Unfortunately, Eileen was diagnosed with cancer as a secondary illness brought on by diabetes. Things were progressing rapidly, and none of us had time to comprehend what was happening.

Eileen McMurray passed with all of us present in March 1994. She was just 52 years old. We were all despondent and inconsolable, with a lot to come to grips with. Similar to my grandmother five years before, I watched a woman so strong in faith and conviction go gently into the Lord's hands. I'm reminded of The Beatles' "Let It Be"—we all searched for words of wisdom but had none.

During the wake and funeral, I was trying to dig into my own faith and experiences with loss, so I could be a source of support for my husband, sister-in-law, and father-in-law. This was when I learned how differently people respond to the death of a loved one and determined there is no right or wrong way to grieve. Seamus was dealing with everything inwardly. I tried to get him to discuss it, and he seemed to retreat more deeply.

Hootie & The Blowfish had recently exploded on to the scene. I was doing anything to get Seamus to "Hold My Hand" and rise above the mess. Nothing I did seemed to help. It was a dark time in our young lives. It's difficult enough dealing with death on an individual level, but when you're part of a couple, things can get more complex. I can't say why, but something shifted during this time, and I believe our strength as a couple took a downturn. Seamus was creating his own coping mechanisms to deal with the loss of his mom, not all of which were good for him. Truth be told, I was probably creating some of my own. I now wonder what I could have done differently during this time period, though I'm not sure I have any answers. As Paula Abdul sang, I felt I was "Blowing Kisses In the Wind." I guess I was too young and not fully developed as a person to succeed in being the support he needed at the time.

As it does, life continued to go on around us—careers, family commitments, and social lives carried on without regard for the loss we'd encountered as we attempted to climb back into normalcy. Outwardly, we made the best of it, but something was off. It was warm outside, but the temperature was "Cold," as eloquently illustrated by Annie Lennox—cold, cold, cold.

Sometime later, we finally had a breakthrough. Seamus opened up to me one night, and I think it was what he needed in that moment. The beautiful song by Bonnie Raitt, "I Can't Make You Love Me," had come out around this time—we turned down the lights and went back to bed. But the ties that bind had already started fraying around the edges.

# Chapter 34 - "Roam"

Throughout my marriage to Seamus, we had a lot of good times between the rough patches. At the prime of our lives, we had huge social circles and made the most of every moment. Both of us enjoyed traveling, which we did often. We traded in our camping gear, favoring trips to Narragansett, Rhode Island, where Seamus' family had inherited a small beach house a couple of blocks from the beach.

We made many fond memories during our trips to the area. The house was small, but we'd always bring our entourage of friends and squeeze in—when you're younger, you don't care about privacy. It was usually a three-hour road trip to get there, but in the summer months; particularly on holiday weekends, you could get stuck in bad traffic. I remember one trip took us seven hours. Once we arrived at our destination, though, it was all worth it.

We came to appreciate how clean the beaches were compared to popular spots at the Jersey shore. At the time, places like Point Pleasant and Seaside Heights had become overpopulated and people were trashing the beaches. While you could drive down further to places such as Wildwood or Cape May, where the crowds were a little less rowdy and beaches cleaner, the traffic was horrendous getting there. And the prices for everything—to stay, to eat, to drink—had also climbed to the point that you could take a trip to an island for less. We preferred the chill, quaint vibe of Rhode Island to the rowdy, over-the-top antics happening "down south" in our home state.

In addition to the Narragansett beaches, we discovered many great restaurants, and certain spots became our favorites. You could order some of the freshest seafood at Champlin's, a typical New England lobster shack. For a more upscale dining experience, we'd go to The Coast Guard House and enjoy a few summer cocktails and a great meal. I remember sitting, relaxing, and laughing in the salt sea air, while a song like Don Henley's "Sunset Grill" provided melodic accompaniment in the background.

We regularly took trips to popular places surrounding the area. One of our favorite places was Newport, which we could drive to in under 30 minutes. Compared to sleepy little Narragansett, Newport bustled with tourists and a ton of restaurants, bars, shops, and things to do. I became fascinated with the Newport mansions. These historic houses built by the ultra-rich during the Gilded Age served as summer homes for the likes of the Astors, Vanderbilts, and Rockefellers—their escape from New York City. I fell in love with these houses constructed with such detail, precision, and opulence. They truly are amazing.

In addition to having access to a summer house in Rhode Island, we also lucked out that Seamus' Aunt Helen and Uncle Chris lived in Nassau, Bahamas with their two sons, Christopher and William. It was our first trip after we got engaged—I was beyond excited; I'd never been outside of the United States. We hopped on a plane to "Fly Away," as Lenny

Kravitz encouraged. Once we arrived, we headed directly to the bar with Cousin Christopher. Unfortunately, it rained the whole week, and the sun didn't come out until (of course) the day we were leaving. We spent a lot of time in Nassau bars. I don't think we were too upset—it was just fun taking in the Bahamas vibe. I got turned on to conch fritters when I visited, and now I order them anytime I see them on an island menu.

Now that we were married, we also started expanding our travel horizons. A group of us began going on cruises—our favorite cruise line was Royal Caribbean. If you've never been on one, you may be concerned about getting seasick. I recognize some are prone to this, but so many effective aids are available to prevent nausea and keep your trip enjoyable. People wonder if you feel the rocking all week—we never had any issues. The first day we got our sea legs and adjusted, and after that, we could hardly feel the ship moving. I love how a large cruise line is almost like a little town with so many things to do, places to eat, and opportunities to gamble if you're so inclined. The part we most enjoyed was exploring different islands, and getting a feel for where we'd like to travel in the future. We'd take a flight down to Miami to embark, and get ready to "Roam" for the week like the B-52s.

Some of the more remarkable places we visited included St. Thomas (I always managed to leave the island with a new piece of jewelry). We had a great day navigating Dunn's River Falls in Ocho Rios, Jamaica. In Grand Cayman, I felt like one with the ocean as we swam with sting rays. I love water creatures; in fact, I'm not afraid of any sea life, even species considered dangerous. I am, however, afraid of the sea; more specifically, deep water. Though I learned how to swim, as an adult I've reverted to my fear of drowning, stemming from

199

that traumatic pool experience when I was a young girl. I've tried to get over it but have not been successful. If I can't touch bottom, I freak out. It's bizarre, because I know how to swim. It goes to show sometimes your oldest traumas never go away. And it's too bad, because I think I'd enjoy deep-sea diving and snorkeling. That's what I liked about Sting Ray City in Grand Cayman—you can touch ground!

We visited so many different places through cruising, but we also enjoyed our time on the ship. We spent hours lying out in the sun, hanging out at pool bars, and playing Bingo. As Janet Jackson urged us to get away, we'd go on an "Escapade." We looked forward to the dinner experiences on the cruise ships, always opting for the formal dinner—we'd dress up for the evening like we were going to a wedding, take fancy pictures, and experiment with exotic foods we didn't normally try at home.

When Seamus and I weren't traveling, we continued to spend a lot of time with family and friends. Many weekend outings revolved around sports. Seamus and the guys loved sports equally to Dad and Pop, so I was used to this. I've been a Cowboys fan since I was about seven. I'm awaiting the rise similar to when they established their last dynasty in the early '90s. (Fun fact: I got my first tattoo at age 35, a Dallas Cowboys star, on my upper thigh. For my second tattoo, I decided on a "tramp stamp" containing a cross and banner with my school motto *"Hazard Zet Forward."*)

Ever since my freshman year at Seton Hall, when the Pirates went to the championship game, March Madness became an important annual event to me. Aside from rooting for my team when we get into the tourney, I love doing bracket pools. These games are ripe for some of the most exciting moments in sports television. When Seton Hall makes it back to the Final Four, I want to be present. Also on my bucket list is going to the Super Bowl to root on the Cowboys when they resume their greatness.

I typically pick up baseball during the playoffs (the season is so long) and cheer on my Yankees. I watch the Rangers throughout the season, but especially in the playoffs. (They broke my heart during the 2024 playoffs—I was convinced they would bring the Stanley Cup back home for the first time since 1994.) I vividly recall watching those games with Seamus and his dad, both big-time Rangers fans. I guess you can say I bleed various shades of blue. For the teams I'm passionate about, I get a bit overexcited watching the games—standing, pacing, swearing, yelling—all of it. I transform into another person—when the alter ego arrives, watch out!

Seamus and I got season tickets for the New York Jets. I will always root for them as long as they aren't playing the Cowboys. Our friends, Tom and Mary Ann (parents of our friends Tommy and Tammi), had been regular season ticket holders for years. We wound up getting season tickets as well—Seamus and I got two, and our friend Billy got two. The Jets have been breaking fans' hearts around the New York metropolitan area for years (for those who don't know, the New York Jets and Giants actually play in New Jersey, at the same stadium), but we had some of the best times tailgating. We'd order sub sandwiches, pack our coolers with beer, and head to Giants Stadium early, spending hours in the parking lot, listening to all types of music.

Everything was designed around our entertainment for the day and having some fun, just like Sheryl Crow said in "All I Wanna Do." We were kind of like a community. We usually had more fun in the parking lot—once inside the stadium, we typically suffered through a losing game in adverse weather, inclusive of snow, rain, wind, and bitter cold. Linda and I recently went to a Cowboys-Giants game at what is now MetLife Stadium. It was pouring buckets, and I realized I'm not sure how we managed through all those games in such horrendous weather. I now prefer to watch in the comfort of my home; just one of many things to change since those days.

# Chapter 35 - "Dancing Queen"

After acquiring a solid real estate foundation in my first position, I was ready for a new challenge. The opportunity presented itself when Hampshire entered into a joint venture with CB Richard Ellis, one of the largest commercial real estate brokers and management firms in the country. The purpose of the partnership was to manage office and industrial properties for large institutional clients. Jimmy (the CEO and son of the founder of Hampshire) was assembling a team, and I was selected to be a portfolio accountant. It was exciting for me to finally put my degree to the test.

This period of time put the rest of the picture together for me as it related to managing an asset. We started with a smaller team, but as our asset management count grew, so did our staff. I soaked up information like a sponge, digging in deep to understand the business. The institutional clients were mega players, and we had a responsibility to meet whatever the requirements per the management agreement. This included putting together detailed financial reporting packages thoroughly and accurately with input from property management. Everything was assembled by the accounting department, a strong team working together and employing quality control via reporting checklists. Sending out these packages timely as well as accurately meant everything to ensuring excellent service to our clients, and I still look back with pride. We did whatever it took.

This new position also involved learning the ins and outs of some of the biggest real estate accounting systems. We were obligated to utilize whatever software the client requested, and as a result, were running four different real estate accounting software systems at once. Initially, it was overwhelming, but it created a depth in understanding I couldn't have otherwise achieved. I also found once you start getting an appreciation for how the systems operate, the elements become similar. Without getting too technical, various sub modules (like accounts payable, for example) feed into the main general ledger module. The trick is to understand the underlying tables across all the modules and connect where pieces of information feed from and to.

As we grew, so did my position and scope of responsibility. By the time we were running at full throttle, I was promoted to portfolio controller, responsible for a team of property accountants, accounts payable, accounts receivable, billing staff, and admins. I was able to take what I'd learned and apply it to managing others, which comes naturally to me. I've continued to recognize how closely the teamwork I learned in my basketball days correlates to life, and have been able to keep reapplying the threads of knowledge I picked up long ago.

Along with the rewards of promotions and raises comes a higher bar. Driven by our clients' high expectations, everyone was committed. We worked long hours, especially during reporting periods. The clients all had different due date requirements, which was good because they were staggered, but it also meant we never truly got out of a cycle because we had to report every month. My friends and I definitely picked up the "work hard, play hard" motto during this time.

On Friday night, it was finally time to play hard. Infrequently, we'd go to Ed's and meet up with the guys, but generally we went out closer to Hackensack. We'd start our weekend relaxing with a cocktail and listening to music, and then head somewhere where we could dance. One popular place, Rosie's in Little Ferry, offered a huge bar, DJ, and dance floor.

Kim, Maria, and I were the recurring ringleaders of our Friday night fun, but we brought along other work and non-work friends wherever we went. Our friends Kathy, Monica, Darcelle, and Ivette would sometimes join us in the fun. Certain Fridays we'd meet at Kim's house after work, where some of her friends would come as well, and we'd go to a real dance club. I remember us waiting for everyone to arrive in Kim's massive living room, and getting our feet ready for the evening with a little "Dancing Queen" by ABBA. We would put a finger on top of each other's heads and spin around. Our favorite dance club was Boomer's, which was on the top floor of a cylinder-shaped hotel in Saddle Brook. We danced the night away to songs like "It's Raining Men" by The Weather Girls. Ironic song choice—great tune all the same! We usually worked on Saturdays, so after a long night out, getting up wasn't always fun. But we were troopers and still young, so nothing a ball cap, sunglasses, and a strong cup of Dunkin' couldn't fix.

On occasion, we'd also get invited into Manhattan for an outing or event thrown by the CBRE brokers. One place had a great bar, and we played music out of the jukebox.

Some of our broker friends were big Barry White fans, and I remember us playing songs like "You're The First, The Last, My Everything." We got it together, baby.

In addition to all the club-hopping, our friend Monica's husband Emmett was big on karaoke. Every year, they hosted a big bash at their house in Garfield, and we'd karaoke the night away. A few of us actually loved to sing, and the more liquid courage we had, the more interesting the night became. One popular choice we'd sing as a group was "Love Shack" by the B-52s. It's such a fun song—*tin roof, rusted!* Some of Emmett's friends who frequented all the popular karaoke places would always come to their parties. This dude who called himself Shadow asked Kim, Maria, and me to perform backup to his lead in Foreigner's "I Want to Know What Love Is." We had fun going along with it for the evening, but he took our newly formed group seriously. He apparently got this vision we would follow him on his circuit and become his permanent backup. *Umm, negative, but thanks for the offer, Shadow. You rock on, man.*

Between long hours spent building a career and the Friday night partying, the frayed edges in my marriage were slowly getting more noticeable. Things were way out of balance, and I was prioritizing my career over my husband, though I didn't recognize it at the time. Some of our rough patches had started a trajectory for me, which was to sink my focus into work instead of working on strengthening my marriage. Mom's cautionary words after I got engaged stomped around in the back of my head. *Oh, crap.*

# Chapter 36 - "River Deep, Mountain High"

It is hard to wrap my head around the concept of slavery and subsequently racial segregation, and how anyone ever decided that was okay. I continue to witness many forms of inequality in the world we live in today, and it deeply saddens me. I don't understand why some people view themselves as better because of their skin color, race, religion, sexual preference, fill in the blanks, and continue to persecute those who are not like them.

I know this is a topic likely to be viewed as controversial. Respectfully, I feel strongly compelled to write about it. If I don't, I'm not speaking my full truth. It's something I consider often, and it troubles me to my core, and if I don't speak my mind, I'm choosing to ignore the problem. How will we ever evolve if we don't talk about this?

I am nervous attempting to put this into words. I want to be sensitive and don't want to offend anyone. Most importantly, I haven't filled everyone's shoes and can't adequately speak for everyone. It would be impossible for me to attempt to say I can understand what it was like to be discriminated against in the way a Black person was during slavery or racial segregation, or even is today. I won't try, but the mere thought of it makes my heart shatter into a million little pieces. Any form of inequality is morally and ethically wrong. Period. No reason or excuse can justify it. Further, religious protections do not provide the right to discriminate, and I believe anyone using religion or any other excuse as a shield or badge has lost the message somewhere along the way, or never got it in the first place.

Fundamentally, I've come to believe a space exists above religion, and that is humanity. These two elements should be able to work in perfect harmony with one another. As a lifelong Roman Catholic, I believe the primary message Jesus was trying to teach was to love one another above all things. In the proper context, all religions bubble up to the same universal message, and the theory behind them isn't all too different. What makes us unique in our religious beliefs should be celebrated while maintaining our passion and conviction toward them. These foundations are meant to create a basis of goodwill toward one another. Where I think we've gone off the script is when we try to demonize someone who doesn't see it the way we do. Who are we to say their belief is right or not right?

I am not formally educated in the history of our country regarding inequality to start spewing out myriad examples. Oh sure, I can cite the horrible atrocities creating the path to where we are today, as well as things going on in our country currently where I feel we're getting it wrong and taking backward steps. Instead, I am turning to music. Why? Because it unites us as a human race. I've been to all types of concerts and shows, and at times I've taken a step back in the moment to bear witness to the humanity around me. Here are all these people, coming from all walks of life, unified peacefully, and enjoying being in the same space for a few short hours. I've felt positive global energy in a crowd like this. It doesn't happen at every concert I attend, but when it does, I can feel it coursing through my bones. If we can come together so beautifully in these moments and forget about all the things making us different, why not always?

One of the defining trajectories in music history began with the Motown era, originating in Detroit in 1960 with one record label founded by Berry Gordy Jr.—Motown Records. I've often thought about how important this was, because it was a catalyst to better integrate the types of music we listened to as Americans. The Motown sound combined soul with popular music to create its own definition. I've created a fictional vignette and some songs to invoke some further reflection . . .

I was excited for the evening. The Swinging Starlights, a band I'd been following since they exploded out of Detroit several years ago, was coming to perform at Jazzie's nightclub, a small venue in Manhattan. I wanted to arrive early to get a good seat and took the train in, since the station was just a few short blocks from the venue. Unfortunately, the train was delayed, so by the time I arrived at the club, there were just a few seats left. The hostess escorted me to a small round table near the back of the venue.

As I sat waiting for my whiskey sour to arrive, I looked around the audience. Given this was an all-Black singing group, I was a little surprised by the audience composition, which was predominantly white. I was hoping for more of a mixed crowd, which would be a welcome change from the unspoken separation we often fell into as a society. In fact, the only Black people in the room were a couple seated at the table immediately to my right. As I looked toward them, they both smiled brightly, and I smiled and said hello. We engaged in small talk sharing our excitement for the act to arrive. I learned the couple, Jeanette and Gordon, were the parents of one of the band members. They were beaming and so proud of their son. He was on his way to the big time.

I asked why they weren't seated up front, near the stage. They explained that they had asked to sit up closer after arriving early, when it appeared plenty of open seating remained, but the hostess told them those tables had all been reserved and the only available seating was in the back. My guard automatically went up, because when I had arrived, I saw a large sign stating, "First come, first served. No advance reservations accepted."

I thought about it and responded, "Gee, maybe you could speak to the owner, and perhaps they can accommodate you since your son is one of the band members?" They looked at me strangely and replied, "Have you taken a look around this place? We would get laughed straight to our seats in the back. There's no point in trying." Something twisted inside my gut. I shook my head and sat with the unsettled feeling in silence.

The Swinging Starlights finally came on, and they didn't disappoint. Comprised of four men and one woman, the group performed a blending of some of the popular hits at the time. They opened with "Reach Out (I'll Be There)" originally sung by The Four Tops. The woman singer unleashed her vocal range in "You Keep Me Hangin' On" by The Supremes. The biggest stunner was the finale, which was "River Deep, Mountain High" by Ike and Tina Turner. I was thrilled I got to see this group perform, and it was fun to watch Jeanette and Gordon respond so excitedly to their son's presence on stage. But a pall remained on the evening. My conversation with them was troublesome. I was disturbed by how they had been so obviously discriminated against, but what bothered me more was that I had failed to do anything about it. Instead I accepted it as it was, saying nothing. They seemed like such lovely people. Before leaving, they gave me their number and invited me to look them up if I was ever in the Detroit area. I thanked them, and we said our goodbyes.

Several years later, I was heading to Detroit for a business trip and decided to call Jeanette and Gordon to see if we could meet up. When I called, they remembered me right away. I mentioned I was heading their way for a few days, and they told me The Swinging Starlights would be performing at a small venue in Detroit, and asked me if I'd be interested in attending. I was delighted to accept the invitation, and we made arrangements to meet.

On the night of the show, I got ready early so I had plenty of travel time. I hopped in a cab and drove across town to The Soul Lounge, the nightclub where they were performing. Upon entering, I found the overwhelming majority of the attendees were Black; in fact, I might have been the only white person in the club. I was met with the warmest greeting by the hostess. She said "You must be Cheryll? Please follow me—we've got your table all set up for you." *Hmm.* I hadn't called in advance, and was a little surprised at the reception. I followed her to the one empty cocktail table with a reserved sign, all the way in the front. I looked to my right and saw Jeanette and Gordon at the next tiny table, beaming brightly at me. I thanked them profusely for arranging the great table, to which they replied, "You're a guest in our hometown, and we wanted to make sure you got to see the band up close."

Sitting so close, I almost felt like part of the act. The

Swinging Starlights had beefed up their cover list to include some more recent hits. My two favorites were "Could It Be I'm Falling In Love" by The Spinners and "You Make Me Feel Brand New" by The Stylistics. It was a spectacular night, and I was so happy to see my friends again. I also felt completely welcomed and was grateful and humbled for their hospitality. The irony of it all did not escape me.

# Chapter 37 - "Love Is"

I doubt anyone who knows me would consider me super affectionate or mushy. I know I've revealed some of this here, but I don't tend to do so in everyday life. This is one of the hidden aspects of my persona, because in truth, I'm extremely sentimental. My emotions remain locked deeply in my core and throughout my internal network, as opposed to through outward expression.

It may be because I'm not always sure how to share emotions of the heart without them coming off sounding clinical or detached. In these situations, the things going on inside of me don't readily match what comes out of my mouth. I can't say for sure why this is, but I've determined it's part of my composition and learned to accept it for what it is. It's also probably another reason why I started writing to express myself. I've always been clearer and more succinct that way, and it's usually how my strongest emotional convictions manage to get released and out into the world.

Another surprising fact might be how a Mötley Crüe fangirl can appreciate a good love song. These tunes manage to capture the essence of heartfelt emotions better than trying to speak them. I'm not a crier by nature, but many songs move me to tears. Most of this happens in my car when I'm by myself, though I'm thinking someone is definitely on to me! No better type of love song exists than a duet, because you get to hear both sides and feel the outpouring of love between two people. Some of the greatest singers and songwriters have come together and created the most beautiful music.

Duets remind me of Mom and Charlie. The influence of easy listening tunes comes from both of them. I was so happy when, in 1995, they shared with me that they were getting married after being together for 19 years. In my view, they were finally allowing themselves to be happy and live their lives instead of worrying about what everyone else needed or wanted. As Barbra Streisand and Barry Gibb so beautifully captured, they certainly had nothing to be "Guilty" of. My Mom had worked so hard and endured a lot of heartbreak throughout her life. I was relieved, thinking maybe she wouldn't have to sacrifice her happiness any longer.

They chose to get married on The Binghamton, a boat converted to a restaurant in Edgewater with spectacular views overlooking the Hudson River and the New York City skyscape. It was a small wedding attended by Mom and Charlie's children and their spouses. It was so surreal to meet Charlie's family after all those years, and felt like a new beginning, where all slates were wiped clean. It reminds me of the song "With You I'm Born Again" by Billy Preston and Syreeta Wright. Everyone deserves a second chance at love if the first time around doesn't turn out as you initially thought it would.

Speaking of second chances at love, Seamus and I witnessed Seamus' dad being able to experience the same. A while after Seamus' mom passed, their neighbor and longtime friend told John she wanted him to meet someone she worked with at the bank. Kathy had also lost her husband at a young age, leaving behind daughter Kristen and son Bobby. The stars aligned perfectly. John and Kathy went on a blind date and realized they shared the same values of family, faith, and love. After a short time, we all aligned as one big family unit. Similar to the song "Suddenly" by Olivia Newton-John and Cliff Richard, the wheels were in motion.

When Mom and Charlie got married, Mom moved into Charlie's townhouse in nearby Saddle Brook. To date, Mom had lived in our home on Falmouth Avenue, which led to a discussion regarding the house. Aunt Millie still lived upstairs, so selling the home was not a consideration. Mom would need to rent out the first floor, and we all agreed the best course would be for Seamus and me to move in and pay rent to Mom. We were able to pay a lot less than we would anywhere else; enough for her to cover the mortgage, taxes, and utilities, which would also allow us to save money for a house of our own. The situation worked out well for all parties, and we were excited about the prospects.

When Seamus and I moved into the house on Falmouth Avenue, it was with an addition to our family. Remember Smokey, the McMurray family's miniature schnauzer? We agreed he would come live with us. Schnauzers are extremely protective and loyal and attach primarily to the master of their domain. I had not previously occupied this space, so I didn't feel he wasn't particularly warm to me. Once he moved in, the dynamic shifted and we grew very close. Smokey and I started our own courtship like Roberta Flack and Donny Hathaway in "The Closer I Get to You"—his love captured me.

As our parents settled into their newlywed situations and we into our new dwelling (which for me wasn't new at all), we resumed normal day-to-day life. This is one of the curious and tricky things about life. When we're in a steady state and things are going relatively well, we start to convince ourselves it will stay as is with no disruption. In 1999 and 2000, however, my mom was diagnosed with stage 2 breast cancer on both sides, and Charlie was diagnosed with prostate cancer. This was a lot to process all at once, and I wasn't sure how to respond, especially as it related to Mom. The situation was serious, and she'd need to undergo a lumpectomy, radiation, and chemotherapy. After watching the destructive progression cancer took on other people in my life, I related to this disease as many others do—with abject fear and contempt. In fact, I hadn't witnessed anyone coming out a survivor. I was terrified. What happens when your one constant rock goes through a period of vulnerability? I was about to find out.

At first glance, the prognosis didn't seem too encouraging. Despite this, I learned through this experience that my mom is one of the most resilient people I've ever known. She managed all of it—the surgery, the radiation, the chemo—like a champ. I know the chemo in particular knocked her on her ass, making her physically ill, but she never let it deter her. She continued working throughout the whole treatment program, and unless you knew her you wouldn't have known she was battling cancer. Twenty-four years later, she's still thriving—I'm blessed to know and love this cancer survivor.

During their respective journeys, I also watched Charlie and Mom support each other unconditionally. What started as an incredibly frightening proposition turned into one of profound inspiration. I believed the strength gained during this encounter inexplicably bound them together in such a way nothing could destroy. I guess I never learn. As Vanessa

Williams & Brian McKnight captured in the song "Love Is"—it breaks your heart.

# Chapter 38 - "Wicked Game"

Years ago, a few of us started a running joke at Hampshire, coining the company as "Hotel California," based off the legendary song by the Eagles. Throughout Hampshire's history, multiple employees have left, only to mysteriously return at some juncture. We seem to fit the philosophy that you can check out anytime you'd like, but you can never leave. I am proud to consider myself part of this club, given I've technically left Hampshire twice to work for CBRE and returned both times.

The first of these returns happened in 2000. I was working for CBRE under the joint venture arrangement, and it was coming to an end. CBRE offered me a position as a property manager for assets in New Jersey, working out of their Teaneck location. I was originally planning to take it, figuring I'd branch out into something different. As we neared the end of the joint venture, I began a conversation with Hampshire, and after traveling to their primary office in Morristown, I was offered a position as an accounting manager.

I faced an interesting choice. Did I want to focus on breadth and go wide, or reach for further depth into the accounting world that I was originally trained for and accustomed to? I needed to consider the big difference between CBRE, a national real estate brokerage and management firm, and Hampshire, a successful private owner and operator. The thought of doing something different at CBRE was intriguing, but I'd be spending a lot of time on the road at my properties. I drove to all the locations to get a feel for the routes and what it might be like, and wasn't exactly jazzed about the prospects.

With the Hampshire position, I'd be commuting to Morristown every day and be able to apply my skills to dive deeper into my accounting role. Similar to my current situation, I'd have a number of reports and expand my management skills. Another huge factor was the travel. While my commute from Elmwood Park to Morristown would be longer, it was consistent. I've never minded traveling for work on occasion, but my personality thrives when I have a reliable routine. The combination of continued depth and growth in a technical and management capacity, coupled with the familial vibe at Hampshire that I wouldn't be able to replicate at CBRE, helped me make my decision. *Morristown, here I come.*

I settled into the new role easily, due to my familiarity with the Hampshire business and people I had already worked with. One of the biggest lessons I learned was the nuance of managing different personality styles. Due to my comfort at Hampshire, I may have come in with a bit of a chip on my shoulder. I was confident, which was a plus, but not too humble back then. A few of my new reports likely felt intimidated by this vibe, so it took some time for us to click, but we ultimately did.

At 30, I was still enjoying my work hard, play hard motto. Friday happy hours continued closer to home base, but I found a lot of fun places in Morristown to explore, as well. Bonding with co-workers outside the office, I strengthened relationships I'd had for years and formed new ones, too. One of our favorite places to go was Jimmy's Haunt, a huge bar and club in town. It had multiple musical genre rooms, and we'd make our way around and eventually hit the dance floor late in the evening. Personally, I liked the vibe of the alternative rock room the best. One of my go-to groups at the time was the Goo Goo Dolls. I related to the song "Iris"—buried deep were parts of me I didn't want the world to see.

Another highlight of the year was a trip I took to New Orleans with Linda, Tammi, and Laurie after we decided a girls' trip was in order. This was right after the Yankees beat the Mets in the Subway Series (triumphantly awesome). We decided to go for Halloween, as we'd learned it was one of the most festive times of year. New Orleans is such a special place. Rooted in a deep, rich history of so many blended and diverse walks of life, NOLA exudes a vibe unlike anywhere else. I immediately felt an energy throughout, connected at some higher level I can't describe. The architecture is awe-inspiring; I particularly enjoyed walking through the historic Lafayette Cemetery and the Garden District, and participating in a ghost tour. My friends got freaked during the tour and abandoned ship, but I was mesmerized. I'm always intrigued by the supernatural and it doesn't "scare" me in the typical sense of the word.

Naturally, we immersed ourselves in the debauchery taking place on Bourbon Street. Wall-to-wall people packed the street where anything goes, and we moved from bar to bar with sensational music spilling out of each entryway and bleeding into a cacophony as you're strolling along. The concept of open carry was both crazy and awesome, and we filled up at a popular pizza place (which doubled as a quick eatery to soak up the booze). We frequented one place with a band playing spectacular rock and blues music, and when they asked for a request, we opted for Steely Dan. They played "FM" for us, and there was no static at all.

At one point, Laurie and Linda were feeling under the weather, so they returned to the room early, leaving Tammi and me to continue partying into the wee hours of morning. We still laugh about our eventual crawl back to home base, and while we thought we were being quiet, in reality, were far from using our inside voices.

I was so saddened to hear of the devastation brought to the area by Hurricane Katrina in 2005. I hope to return someday, and I'm happy I got the bar hopping out of my system while I was still young.

Back on the home front, things weren't going so well. The spatial rift between Seamus and I was becoming a crater, and I continued down my path focused on career and partying with my friends, escaping from all reality. A marriage requires both parties' unwavering trust, commitment, and compromise. I will not get into details of where I feel Seamus went off the track on his part. Some things had occurred over the course of time stemming back at least five years, and my trust in the relationship had dissipated. I was trying my best to recover from them. Additionally, in considering those three critical values, I admit I was not holding up my end of the bargain. Seamus and I finally separated and lived apart for a while. We went through counseling, attempting to rebound from the wrong turns we'd taken. I believed in the vows we'd professed and was not going to just walk away.

On September 11, 2001, Seamus and I were still living apart, and the world was going about its business as if it would be same as the day before. I drove down Route 287 South heading into Morristown on the most beautifully sunny day, feeling energized for a great day. When I arrived at the office, everyone was buzzing and I couldn't piece together the commotion. Once we started hearing and discussing the reports, we all went upstairs to the executive offices and stood in front of the television in absolute horror as the events of 9/11 unfolded before our eyes.

People, already rattled and incredulous, started experiencing varying levels of panic as we heard reports of Picatinny Arsenal being targeted for attack, and folks living in that general direction wanted to go swipe up their children. We didn't know what would come next—we were scared. All we wanted was to get home to our loved ones. Like so many others, I had friends working in Manhattan and had a hole in my gut thinking of them until I found out they were safe. Though we were living apart, Seamus and I drove to Falmouth Avenue to be together and continued to watch the devastation unfold on television. In a "New York Minute," as Don Henley warned us, everything had changed. It certainly put a lot in perspective, and Seamus and I decided to try to break through our challenges. He came back home.

It got better for a while, and we were going to therapy, but the sessions eventually stopped. I didn't necessarily think stopping therapy was a good move and am not sure why I wasn't pushing harder to continue. Maybe deep down I already knew the answer. Somewhere amidst the roller coaster ride Seamus and I were on, the part of me I'd fought for years to bury was starting to bubble up once again.

Someone I'd met recently was causing me to once again examine the direction my life was taking. I don't think I recognized at the time what the new relationship meant or was based upon, being so nondescript with no clear definition. I now realize it was meant as a catalyst, and so the one thing I can definitively say is were it not for it, in some strange way I know I'd not be where I am today. As Chris Isaak so hauntingly sang, what a "Wicked Game" life sometimes plays.

# Chapter 39 - "Sometimes Love Just Ain't Enough"

I can't tell you exactly the moment I decided to end my marriage. After Seamus moved back in, we intended to make it work. For over a decade, our lives had been inextricably linked. We earned degrees, started and developed careers, built a home life, and surrounded ourselves with loving family and friends. In the words of Fleetwood Mac, we'd hoped "The Chain" would keep us together—a lot was at stake. I remained hurt by some of Seamus' actions, which were now blanketed around and choking my trust in him. I wasn't entirely sure how to move past.

In a lot of respects, I was in a state of cloudiness during the time between Seamus moving back in the fourth quarter of 2001 through the first quarter of 2003. I spent a lot of time in deep reflection, weighing all the options and assessing which path to take. It was murky, confusing, and unsettling. My loyalty typically overrules everything else, and it became the thread holding me to him. Still, the wedge between us had snapped my internal system into deep analysis and soul-searching mode.

On the one hand, when I looked at everything in totality, life was good—great fulfilling career; stable, comfortable home environment in the town I grew up; and an amazing, loving family and longtime friends. Seamus and I, aside from the challenges that had broken my trust, were in most respects a cohesive couple. He was my husband and I loved him—that never wavered. But it's true when Patty Smyth and Don Henley express "Sometimes Love Just Ain't Enough"—the heart can't always be fully trusted.

In a deep, unspoken place, I wasn't happy. I knew intuitively I wasn't exploring pieces of myself that I'd disregarded along the way. Everything I focused on involved something or someone else—husband, family, friends, career. All incredibly important to me, but they left no time to focus on other vital things—health, fitness, spirituality, personal passions. I wasn't necessarily calling these things out or citing them as problems, but I knew elements were missing. At the time, I'm not sure I had evolved enough to know these pieces were necessary to make up the whole of me. I carried on with a level of emptiness and didn't know why. Instead of filling the emptiness with new, positive things, I would try to fill them with existing things, not all of which were healthy. In some regards I can be a person of extremes and excess, having an addictive personality. The emptiness would be filled with one more drink or one more dinner helping. Neither of those was doing anything to fill a permanent void; it only helped to fill a moment.

Larger than the imbalance, I was still living an inherent lie with the world, the people I love, and myself. Though I was not yet acknowledging it to myself or anyone, it was there and hung over me, weighing me down like an anchor stuck in the mud at the bottom of the ocean. Not living as your authentic self is, in my opinion, the most damaging thing you can do to yourself. The interference hovering around my marriage was entirely dysfunctional, and was not based in any fundamental measures of the word "relationship." All of it, on top of everything else, was muddling my mind, heart, and decision-making. My life had gone way off course. In the song "November Rain" by Guns N' Roses, Axl Rose relayed what I needed—some time on my own—to figure it all out. But I wasn't alone, which was making clarity difficult, if not impossible, to achieve.

It took every ounce of courage to have the conversation with Seamus I'd been avoiding for far too long. While I knew both our lives would be completely upended, in my heart, mind, and gut, I knew the right thing for both of us was to part ways. The challenge with all of this was that Seamus and I had completely different viewpoints, so naturally we couldn't see things the same. As Dave Mason sings in the old song, it was clear there were no good guys or bad guys—"We Just Disagree."

That conversation, and the next year to follow, marked one of the hardest times I've ever been through in my life. I can't speak for Seamus, but his resentment and pain were clear, and it was brutal. When I told him I wanted a divorce, it was met with all the things you would imagine, but I stood firm. We needed to move on for both of our sakes. A new version of the song "Free Bird," recently released by Dolly Parton featuring Lynyrd Skynyrd, captured what I knew was long overdue. *Time to fly.*

# Chapter 40 - "Shadow of the Day"

During our year-long separation, Seamus and I continued to live under the same roof, which made a difficult situation more complicated. What I learned most about separation and divorce is that the two people involved are seeing everything from their own angle, and those perspectives are usually vastly different. One may believe the other is more at fault; or one wants the divorce less than the other—this and more causing debate at every turn. It's a painful, sad, and demoralizing attempt to unwind something two people spent years creating and building up.

From my vantage point, I was feeling all these emotions and an abundance more. I was losing a whole family whom I loved dearly, in addition to my husband. We also had a lot of shared friends in our lives, which presented an uncomfortable situation for them. While everyone tried hard to not pick a "side," inevitably it shakes out that way through natural order. The friends who were mine first leaned toward me, and Seamus' friends leaned toward him. All of this was a lot emotionally. I'm a creature of longevity in my relationships, and this situation disrupted that. I was "Barely Breathing," as Duncan Sheik claims in a song from around the time—I couldn't find any air.

Beyond the emotional components, the legality of divorce is hugely unpleasant. This is a person you married and committed your life to, so bringing lawyers into your personal mix is a bizarre concept to me. I realize it's a necessity, but it makes things so clinical and formal. I don't prescribe to using lawyers in personal or civil situations unless absolutely necessary—they complicate things greatly and make the relationship completely adversarial. If instead the two parties could take a step back, sit down, and compromise, I believe attorneys wouldn't be needed in most situations. Seamus and I didn't have the complexity of children, but everything else we possessed was jointly owned. The process to sort it all out was tedious and tiring. I was doing my best to rise above the situation and recognize it was part of a process I didn't want to delay any further. We needed closure as quickly as possible so we could both move on.

While all this was going on, Pop wound up at a cardiovascular hospital in Camden. He underwent a quadruple bypass a few years earlier, so I was concerned, but I didn't consider the situation dire. Pop was otherwise healthy; always on the go, fishing and finding activities around the house and community every day. Unlike his granddaughter, who has never been particularly handy around the house, Pop did everything himself. I'm not sure he ever hired a contractor for anything. At 82, the guy was up on a ladder cleaning his gutters! The only time I ever saw him sitting around was when he rested after dinner, watching Jeopardy and whatever sports were on. Still, it was clear he was going to be hospitalized for a while, and since he lived alone, I needed to take care of his home and financial affairs while he was in the hospital. It was a lot to manage while working full time. I spent a lot of time traveling back and forth to Camden and going to his house in Brick to get the mail, pay bills, and tidy up the home. During this time, I was also going through mediation with Seamus in an attempt to finalize everything. My faith was testing me, but I'm reminded now of the uplifting song by Simon & Garfunkel, "Bridge Over Troubled Water"—in moments I would rise above, which would serve to ease my mind.

After a lengthy stay at the Camden hospital, Pop was transferred to Ocean Medical Center. They felt his situation was improving and he was ready to finish healing and come back home. It was the Christmas season, and I was sad he'd be spending the holidays at the hospital. We usually spent all our holidays together at Mom's, including Pop and his lady friend Kay, all the remaining Battinelli aunts and uncles, and of course Seamus and me. Instead, Mom and I ate dinner in a local Japanese hibachi restaurant and visited Pop in the hospital.

At times I'd stay the night at Pop's house in Brick, since it was so close to the hospital. This gave me an opportunity to catch up on his financial matters, straighten up the house, and visit with him. The first Friday after Christmas, I arrived at Pop's house after work, planning to take care of house business and visit him before leaving Saturday night. As I slept, I was abruptly awakened by my grandmother's voice, whose spirit arrived in a hurry to tell me something. I couldn't make out what she was saying; her voice was distant and garbled, almost like someone with their hand over the speaker of a phone. Aloud I said, "What is it Grandma, what do you need to tell me?" She kept trying, but I couldn't make it out, and the connection eventually broke. I was comforted to hear her voice but also frustrated. She was trying to give me a message, and I couldn't receive it. I stayed awake hoping for her return, but she never came back that night.

On Saturday night I returned to my home in Elmwood Park to prepare for the week ahead. Pop had been in good spirits on Saturday but was starting to get anxious—he was ready to come home. On Sunday evening, I called him to see how thing were going. He seemed fine, but with so much static on the call, it was hard to hear him. His words and voice were so muffled and distant. I didn't piece the irony together at the time. Due to the bad connection, we quickly said our I love yous and goodbyes and hung up.

At around 4 a.m. on Monday, the phone jolted me awake. It was a doctor from the hospital, telling me Pop had suffered a major heart attack—they'd done everything they could but couldn't bring him back. I sat down on the couch where Seamus was sleeping and wailed in agony, "Pop, my Pop is gone."

In the moment, our friendship took precedence over all the nonsense we were going through, and Seamus comforted me. He loved Pop, too, and in reflection, I greatly appreciate how he was there for me during Pop's passing. I attempted to get my shit together and jumped in the car alone to make the trip to the hospital. I had to see him and gather his personal effects. I couldn't believe what was happening and was going into a state of shock after my initial outburst. The indications were all so promising, and I didn't expect this. On the drive to the hospital, I listened to some tunes to reflect my mood. One of the most haunting songs ever written is "Fade to Black" by Metallica. *Goodbye, Pop.*

The week was a blur. I made funeral arrangements through Weatherhead Young in Brick, where Grandma's services had been held. Allowing for the New Year holiday and travel time for my Dad and Roma, as well as Aunt Carol, we arranged the wake for Friday, January 2, 2004, and the funeral for the following day. I find it chilling yet appropriate that the funeral arrangements coincided with my grandparents' wedding anniversary, as they were clearly ready to be reunited. I was going to miss Pop terribly, but was comforted knowing they'd finally be together again.

One night that week, as I slept on the couch in my living room, Pop came to visit to let me know he was okay. He left as quickly as he came. I also now knew what Grandma was trying to tell me—it was Pop's time, and she was coming to reassure me he was going into God's loving hands and to be with her. The bond I had with the two of them transcends this lifetime, and I still come to tears anytime I think about them. That hole has never been filled, but I know they watch over me and protect me, my two special angels. In "Shadow of the Day" by Linkin Park, I can apply the lyrics to Pop in the moment he came to me. It was our closure to make up for the last phone call we had. The next morning, the sun set for Pop and he floated away, up into Heaven.

The year 2004 was a big transition year to resolve the open matters in my life. Seamus and I were divorced on April 29, 2004, and he moved out of the house. Things were uncomfortable and awkward between us—we both needed space to figure out how to move on. The one time we came together was in June 2004, when we made the decision it was time to say goodbye to Smokey, our beloved companion. We drove Smokey over to Dr. Cataldi's office to be with him as he got put to sleep. Heartbreaking.

I also spent a lot of time settling Pop's estate. I was named executrix, which made sense due to my proximity, since Dad lived out of state. Pop's house wasn't huge, but he was always a bit of a pack rat and never threw anything away. He'd left enough food to feed an army in two packed refrigerators, and his basement shelves were stocked with canned goods. His garage was jammed with fishing gear and various workshop items. His financial paperwork was well organized, but outside of that, he saved literally everything—miscellaneous collections of "stuff" throughout the main floor, basement, and attic required multiple dumpster hauls to get down to manageable basics.

I was also debating whether to keep the house or sell it. Having a shore house seemed like a great idea as a summer getaway, but I wasn't in a position to maintain two households on one income. Logical sense overruled the luxury of having a second home and the emotional ties I felt. Grappling with the decision to hold or sell probably took longer than actually selling the house. I priced Pop's house to sell, and a nice young couple just starting out came through. I knew the house would be left in the proper hands and felt at peace with the decision.

We also planned an estate sale with the furniture and other belongings, but had to sift through everything first. It was a lot to organize, and it was difficult parting with some things, but I didn't have space for extra furniture. One day, I was rooting around in Pop's pull-down attic, trying to organize Christmas decorations and other old trinkets no one had seen in years. When finished, I made my way slowly backward down the stairs with a little package in one hand. As my foot hit the second stair going down, I felt someone firmly grasp onto my waist as if they were concerned I was falling. My friend was helping me in the house, so assuming it was her, I said, "I'm okay." After another stair, the person was still holding on, and I said louder, "I'm okay." When they didn't let go, I turned around, but no one was there. I hurried down the stairs, closed the attic, went to my friend, and asked her if she had been the one holding on to me—I was momentarily questioning my sanity, but also knew it wasn't physically possible it could be her. She confirmed she was in the kitchen the whole time and asked me what the heck I was talking about. It cemented what I knew—it was one of my grandparents, my guess Pop, as the hands felt so strong and sturdy.

Again, I'm not asking you to prescribe to my belief about these things. To the events I've borne witness to, I am steadfast—and no—it wasn't a coping mechanism or some other scientifically plausible explanation. Other than with my grandparents, I haven't had any other encounters like this, though I believe the possibility exists for it to happen again. People have varying levels of sensitivities to these types of connections, and I don't consider mine particularly strong, but the bond with my grandparents was so powerful, these encounters had space to occur.

The closing took place in January 2005. This would allow me to settle and bring closure to Pop's estate. In between dealing with the house, I was sifting through financial accounts, providing documentation, and managing the accounting of the estate. Pop loved collecting coins, and he had safes throughout the house to hold them. He had provided me instructions on many things preparing for this time, including telling me where all the safes were. What he didn't share was where the passwords were. As I went through Pop's possessions, I started finding these teeny tiny pieces of paper with code combinations, with absolutely no indication of what they were for. They were hidden everywhere, so it was like going on an Easter egg hunt, but not nearly as fun. I eventually matched everything up except for the master safe in his living room closet. I searched to no avail, and wound up having to hire someone to crack it open. I think Pop was messing with me as one final goof. He was funny. One Halloween when I was young, he dressed completely in black and put black face makeup on, and came to our window to spook us. He scared the crap out of us—what a randomly nutty sense of humor! Thanks for the last joke, Pop, as if I wasn't "Unwell" enough, like Matchbox 20 told us. I was just a little impaired. As with Grandma's passing, I wrote a poem in honor of Pop the following Christmas.

## THE LAST KNOCK

My heart is waiting for the knock, though my head acknowledges it can never be heard again.

Like clockwork every Christmas morning, I anticipated the moment.

When I'd open my kitchen door there you stood, eyes beaming with the fervor of a man who truly knew what it meant to live, to love, and to lose.

There you were, with your old suit jacket and clip-on tie which made me chuckle to myself . . . and would amaze me in the same breath because by your example I learned what's inside of a person is what really matters.

You'd kiss me hello and bellow out "Merry Christmas, Sweetheart," accompanied by the safest hug I've ever known.

In every instance I knew your silent partner who left us years before was following gently behind in your footsteps . . . and so began another holiday filled with family and joy.

Last year we had to break the tradition, unaware it wasn't a temporary lapse in our routine.

Here I remain in my ponderous state, fighting to maintain the memories you both helped to create.

Your precious ornaments on my tree–

The cuckoo clock chirping out the time to my empty walls–

Pictures capturing happy moments from long ago–

The Book solidifying your essence–

A lonely statue waiting to hear your prayers.

All of them reminding me of what once was and the legacy you've granted me to complete.

They are all here, as I know are both of you when I need you. These truths make me feel better.

But they just can't compare to the knock at my door.

My head acknowledges, but my heart needs to hear it once again.

# Chapter 41 - "Blurry"

With both Grandma and Pop gone, the glue holding the Turoff family together had disintegrated. In a way, I think Dad and I both came to rely upon this glue so heavily that we weren't sure how to navigate forward as a family—as a result, the gap between us felt larger than before. It's taken us years to close it, and we're still working on it.

My relationship with my Dad is different than I would envision it to be. On the parental similarity scale, I am more like my dad than my mom. I've joked with her, questioning if I was switched with another baby in the hospital, given how different we are from each other. Let's say I possess the attributes of my father and have picked up some habits from my mother. Given this, on paper you'd assume Dad and I would have a relatively easy time figuring out how to be father and daughter to each other. It's not so simple, but I know we both work on it in the way we know how, and we'll keep trying.

With my divorce and the closure of Pop's estate in the rear view, it was time to forge ahead and rebuild my life. In a lot of ways I felt as if I was starting from square one. I found myself staring at a figurative disassembled Lego set with thousands of pieces in front of me, and wasn't sure where to begin. Life was "Blurry," as Puddle of Mudd described in their song—*how would I make up my own ending?* I honestly didn't have a clue.

I started by taking some small steps forward to make my space my own. With the support of my mom, we applied some fresh paint and ripped carpet out of the hallway floor and put down tile. I also purchased some new furniture, including a living room set. I focused on the spare bedroom, which had been my room growing up, and decided to transform it into my comfort zone, serving as my home office and tranquility room. I wanted to do something bold, so I painted the walls Pepto-Bismol pink and added a raspberry-colored couch to the design. It looked a little wild, and pink isn't typically in my color palette, but it was a statement piece (for what I'm not sure). The freshened-up digs helped me to visually signify a new path forward.

I also decided I needed to get away after the trying past few years. I treated myself to a vacation and invited a friend who had helped me during this time. After extensive research, we decided on French Polynesia. We flew to Tahiti and stayed the night, took a puddle jumper to Moorea, where we stayed for four nights, and on to Bora-Bora for four more nights before returning to Tahiti for the last night. It was the most extravagant trip I've ever splurged on and worth every penny—the islands are absolutely breathtaking.

The connection we made to nature and wildlife was a treasure I will never forget. We walked out of our over-water bungalow onto our own private deck and stairs leading to crystal clear bath water. The living room contained a glass floor where we could sit and gaze at the beautifully colored tropical fish swimming in unison. In Moorea, we swam with the dolphins. In Bora-Bora, we chartered an excursion with four others plus a guide, and swam with stingrays and sharks, and headed back to the bungalow on cloud nine. The next morning we turned on the television and learned that Steve Irwin had been killed by a stingray. I felt awful for him and his family, and it was so ironic that one of the best experiences of my life with these beautiful creatures had caused tragedy for another.

During this period of time, the relationship I mentioned in an earlier chapter which had been one catalyst responsible for the last straw in my marriage was still hanging around, loosely dangling by a thread. I was trying to latch onto it with both hands, mistakenly thinking I could make it something it was not and would never be. All it became was a distraction from evolving into my full truth. *What was I thinking? Did I believe it would pacify me, or be the easy way out of revealing my whole self?* I don't know. Like The Killers exclaimed in "Mr. Brightside," I needed to open up my eager eyes and see the whole picture, but wasn't there yet.

As part of the surface-level world I was beginning to con-struct for myself, somewhere along the line I decided it was time to fully leave the nest. I'd lived in Elmwood Park my whole life, and was living under Mom's roof continuing to pay rent at age 35. My mom would have allowed me to continue in the same fashion forever, and in some ways it would have been comforting, but I realized I might never fully become a responsible adult until I did my own thing.

The cloudy part was where I should plant my roots. I was trying to get closer to the office in Morristown, and also not be too far from my mom, while trying to anchor myself to a new location where I thought the "non-relationship" relationship I was in could develop into something clearer. The last part is where I went astray, causing me to make a decision I wouldn't have otherwise made. I'm sure of it now, but had no idea at the time.

I purchased my first home in Succasunna, New Jersey in December 2005; a four-bedroom, three-bathroom bi-level on a decent piece of land in a nice community. It was 12 miles from my office, which sounded great in theory. In reality, what I found was an unfathomable number of people wishing to escape the higher cost of living had gone in the same direction as far as Pennsylvania, and all the traffic was heading east. The ride down Sussex Turnpike or Route 10 could take a half-hour on a good day, but most days was closer to 45 minutes to an hour.

I found myself completely alone for the first time. In some regards this was positive. I learned the definition of true independence, established routines, and did what I wished with my time and energy. The challenge became the thing I was holding on to that was not right for me, causing continued confusion and emotional baggage. It became the darkest period of my life. I filled my time in Morristown bars with co-workers and friends, drinking more than I should have and making not-so-great choices as a result. Three out of four grandparents had an alcohol problem at some point in their lives, and the other one had a mental issue. The alcohol issue had extended to my dad, and fortunately he beat it down.

I'm not embarrassed by any of this, but because of the facts at hand, I knew I had an addictive personality and needed to keep it in check. No one or nothing was present at this time to keep me honest, and coupled with all of the grappling to discover who I was, I let myself get reckless. I'm not proud of this, but it illustrates the damage not living your truth will ultimately do if you're not careful. It was the biggest life lesson

I've ever had to learn. I thank God and my two angels for watching over me up in Heaven. The song by the mastermind Elton John, "Someone Saved My Life Tonight," has always resonated with me—it almost had its hooks in me, but didn't win. It surely tried, though.

Internally, I was in a lot of pain. I wanted to love and be loved, but wasn't doing the right things to find it. When I was home alone, I'd have a couple drinks to try to forget how alone I was and all the baggage I was carrying. I slept most nights on my couch in my family room in front of the television. The "non-relationship" relationship was also crumbling, and out at bars, I'd hook on to people and situations in desperate attempts to grasp at straws. Yikes. As Duran Duran sang, "Save A Prayer"—things appearing completely acceptable in the dark weren't so the morning after.

A few other events along the way didn't help me come out the other side so quickly. We lost Aunt Millie and Uncle Moe within two weeks of each other in early 2006, and around Easter another painful realization came to light. My mom discovered Charlie was having an affair. I was angered and confused. The man who had been such a father figure to me had hurt the one person I loved more than anyone, and I was totally resentful. I did everything I could to help her through, but all I could do was be present and listen. Charlie was not someone I ever wanted to see again—I couldn't consider having any kind of relationship with him based on what he'd done to her. He made his bed and now he'd have to lie in it. What a dumb-ass move on his part. You may think I'm biased, but honestly, they did have it all. Jerk.

A couple of things finally enabled me to find my path to truth. The first of these was a complete end to the confusing and unhelpful "non-relationship" relationship. It was painful, but it needed to conclude for me to have any shot at happiness. I took one more dip into the abyss, and suddenly in true Genesis fashion, one day I decided "Tonight, Tonight, Tonight"—I'm gonna make it right.

# IV

# PART FOUR

***AIR GUITAR RULE #4*** - *Diversity is encouraged—nothing wrong with mixing in some air guitar drums every so often!*

# Chapter 42 - "True Colors"

The process of coming out was a slow and methodical one for me. There was no *Time* magazine issued pronouncing to the world, "Yep, I'm Gay." No photo shoots were taken with *Out* or *Curve*, two prominent LGBTQIA+ magazines, to alert the community a new member had entered their club. Everyone's journey is different, and in my case I'd spent the last 37 years of my life with a secret I'd hidden from everyone, including myself. The first step I took in the early spring of 2008 was to come out to, well, me.

After getting some distance from the "non-relationship" relationship, I started thinking more clearly. I was still feeling unhappy with how the situation had turned out, but it forced me to evaluate the totality of my life. I began to look at myself in the mirror through a different lens and came to the realization I couldn't continue to live like this anymore. I had to convince myself that the benefits of coming out would be worth any price I might potentially pay, and I wasn't completely sure what ramifications might occur. In the worst-case scenario, I could lose any number of relationships with loved ones, career reputation, or an element of my safety. I asked myself, *Would losing any one or perhaps all of those things be worth it? What would I gain in return?*

After reflecting, it boiled down to two primary benefits: The first was the ability to live authentically and be completely comfortable in my own skin. The second was the chance to find love with another person who was like me—not secretly like me, not questioning if they should be like me—LIKE ME. I'd never had a relationship with another woman who was comfortable with living their truth, or even sure if it was their truth. But I knew it was mine, and I couldn't spend the rest of eternity holding this in any longer. I believe it was slowly killing me inside, tearing up my spirit and rotting in my gut. Amy Lee from Evanescence powerfully expresses my truth in the song "Bring Me to Life"—I was living a lie and needed to be saved.

The floodgates first broke open with my two friends Deb and Deb. They already had some insight into who I might be, because when we were out and about in Morristown, some of my "True Colors" would surface, as Cyndi Lauper belted out in her words of empowerment to an entire LGBTQIA+ community. So one night at Sushi Lounge, a deep conversation took place, and they encouraged me to start exploring who I was. It was a small but major step forward, as I suddenly felt like I had some support behind this. I was no longer completely alone with my thoughts and this decision.

While I recognize everyone's circumstances are different, if you are reading this and struggling with how to come out or if you should, I offer you one piece of advice: Find one person with whom you feel safe enough to share your true self. It's enough for right now. It's so important to pick one person you trust unconditionally to bounce this around with and get your confidence behind you. If you're not sure who to turn to, talk to a professional. If you can't afford a professional, find a local

LGBTQIA+ community center so you won't have to go through this alone. The main thing is to find someone, because talking about it out loud does make it possible. Please don't continue to live in agony. You are a human being deserving of being your true self and worthy of finding happiness and peace.

As I confided in my friends, I also began trying to educate myself. I knew nothing about the LGBTQIA+ community. I lived in a straight world. I tried going out to the internet to find community groups or support networks; *anything* to connect me with my people. Though this was just 16 years ago, the internet wasn't what it is today, and it was difficult to find much information, or learn the places to go and people with whom I could connect. I discovered a community center in Morristown, but I wasn't ready for a public pronouncement; I saved the info, thinking it might eventually come in handy.

I learned about a gay bar in Boonton called Switch, and one Friday night after being at happy hour with a couple of co-workers, I decided to go check out the place by myself, looking for an opportunity to connect with anyone in the community. Here's another word of advice: Don't do this. What I found was the patrons were all traveling in a pack, and I was the odd man out. I guess I assumed more people might be flying solo, which wasn't the case, so it was hard to break into any meaningful conversations. I tried approaching a few groups of women to strike up a dialogue, maybe get added into their crew, but they must have recognized I wasn't sure how to act or what to do—such a fish out of water.

For the most part I sat at the bar, and ironically, I connected with the gay guys better than the girls. Women can come across as standoffish and guarded upon approach, whereas a gay guy will throw everything including the kitchen sink into a conversation—they are just easier to talk to. The one thing that night did prove, though, was that other gay people were in fact living and breathing out there somewhere, so it wasn't a total loss. Like Lady Gaga claimed, I found I wasn't the only one "Born this Way," and it put a little notch in my belt.

After realizing the vibe of the nightclub experience wasn't for me, I decided to alter course. Something I've learned about myself as I've gotten more adept in understanding who I am, is I thrive in a social setting when I know a majority of people. The introvert in me is not as comfortable heading into a group of strangers. I have evolved over the years to try to focus more on the element of small talk, but I don't prefer it. My strongest conversations occur when I'm talking to a person one on one. Following this logic, I decided I needed to try to make one friend at a time, which was how I arrived at the conclusion to join Match.com. I looked forward to meeting other women, and this seemed to be my best entry point.

I created a profile. I was a little nervous because I hadn't told anyone about my discovery at this point other than the two Debs. I wasn't too concerned, as I figured the people searching my profile would be other women who were gay, and I didn't know any gay people anyway. Or so I thought—I actually found a couple of people I did know from my past, and connected with one of them as a friend. After putting up some of my more flattering pictures (I hate photos of myself; can you relate?) and describing more about myself, I chose to end my profile with the beginning of a corny joke, to encourage anyone interested to reach out to me for the punchline. The beginning of the joke is, "This mushroom walks into a bar and asks for a drink. The bartender tells the mushroom they don't serve mushrooms here . . . "

I started conversing with several women quickly, and more than anything I got acclimated to having dialogue and figuring out how this all worked. It had been 18 years since I'd dated anyone, and I knew the landscape had changed. When I was younger, there was no systemized internet dating, and fortunately, I had no challenges with finding people to date when I was younger. I learned that on a dating site, results varied greatly in how people responded and communicated.

For me, having conversations in writing first was advantageous, since writing is my preferred form of communication. Also, since it's a strong suit of mine, I could read a lot into the person before talking to them on the phone or meeting them in person. If they couldn't spell, write a proper sentence, or capture my attention with their words, I moved on quickly. I'm sorry if it sounds a little snobbish, but having an educated partner was important to me. I was open to diverse opportunities, but this was a point of admission for me.

It didn't take long for me to meet a few people in person. As an icebreaker, I had dinner with someone I was friendly with who lived in my hometown who I learned was gay by discovering her on Match. We had been friends years ago, so I thought it would be good to catch up, but after meeting, it was clear we were in the "friend zone." I also went on a date with a girl much younger than me. When we were speaking online, everything went smoothly, and when I talked to her on the phone initially, things seemed promising. She lived in Cranford, but her family had a house down in South Jersey, where she spent her weekends. I picked her up on a Friday night, and we went to a bar.

The bar was loud and had a collegiate feel. I instantly

recognized this was not a great place for a first date, but I wasn't familiar with the area and she had picked the place. The age difference was deeply felt through this one selection. I was still up for a bar with co-workers and friends, but it wasn't what I was looking for in a partner. I was so tired of the bar scene and wanted to create a different life for myself. In addition to this, the girl's communication style was unusual. She was hot and cold, and it was impossible to get an accurate read. Was she nervous? Admittedly I was—this was all completely new territory for me. I may have tried to suggest we go somewhere quieter to have a real conversation to see if any connection was present, but we stayed at this loud, obnoxious place instead. This didn't lead to any meaningful conversation, and I dropped her off home, not too encouraged about how the night had gone.

Despite this less-than-stellar first date, we kept talking on the phone and via text, but the communication was so choppy and inconsistent. She'd go from barely showing interest to seeming like she couldn't live another moment without me. Was this an age gap thing or was she just certifiable? It became too much of a roller coaster for me, so I got off the ride and continued my search. I had been chatting with another woman who was a little closer to my age. We made arrangements for her to come to my house on a Friday night and we'd go to dinner (this time at a place I selected—wasn't going to make that mistake again!).

When she arrived at my house, she showed up with ice pops. I thought this was strange, but she explained she thought we might watch a movie after dinner at my house, and she liked having ice pops for dessert. *Umm, okay.* When she arrived, I brought her to the family room on the lower level, which also had a cool bar area where we could hang out. She proceeded to take off her sneakers and put her feet up on my coffee table. Since I was barely out of the closet, I hadn't yet learned about the U-Haul lesbian stereotype, a term for those who tend to move quickly after the first date. Yeah, this definitely appeared to be her approach. I might have been able to deal with this woman's level of comfort, but her feet smelled horrendous. So before she pitched her tent for the night or God knows what else, I brought her to the restaurant.

I'd picked a popular sports pub with great food. It was an open atmosphere, with a lot of TVs and a nicely blended crowd. After the fancy footwork, I wasn't anticipating much, but was trying to be open-minded. I think she had come right from work, so maybe her feet just sweat a lot. The conversation wasn't too stimulating, but I forged ahead. At some point in the middle of dinner she told me she was going out for a cigarette and insisted I come with her. I had quit smoking within the last year, so this was not a plus in my book. I was already way past the initial withdrawals and urges and had no desire to be around smokers—truthfully, it was a turn-off. I said no, I was watching the game on TV. I tried to divert my attention toward the Yankees as a coping mechanism to get through the evening. The sports bar was a glass building so you could see outside. I was paying no mind, investing myself in the game, when all of a sudden, someone starts banging on the glass from outside. Umm, yeah, of course it was her. *OMG, she's a fruitcake. Three strikes; you're out, lady.*

As I navigated the trials and tribulations of the gay dating world, somewhere around the time I was conversing with Smelly Feet, I decided it was time to come clean with Mom. This was by far going to be the toughest for me. I sat at her kitchen table with enough jitters to rival a jumping bean. I'm not exactly sure what I said, maybe something like I figured out I was gay and had started dating women? Her knee-jerk response was "Are you sure?" to which I replied, "Yes, I'm sure." She was trying to process, but it was a lot for her in the moment. My takeaway was she loved me no matter what, but she didn't grow up with this type of diversity and was concerned the road ahead would be too difficult for me as a gay person. She, too, was concerned for my reputation, career, and safety. I tried to reassure her things were different now and all would be fine, but she needed time to see for herself. I was gentle but firm as I tried to "Catch My Breath"—like Kelly Clarkson, I didn't have time for anyone to hold me back any longer.

I also told several of my close friends in person or on the phone, typically in a one-on-one setting. Everyone was supportive, and not many people were too surprised if at all, other than my mom. Every time I told another person, I'd get a little stronger and more bullish in my conviction. It was time to live while I was still alive, as Bon Jovi pridefully stated in "It's My Life." The layers of years and years of fear, shame, and regret were lifting and getting replaced by confidence and self-assured determination. As Frankie Boy said, *time to do it my way.*

# Chapter 43 - "Booty"

First came Demi Moore. Truth be told, I was outwardly obsessed with Rob Lowe around this time as well. I watched every one of his movies multiple times, and in my closet, I had a huge poster of him wearing a white t-shirt and a chic linen suit with a dog tag dangling sexily around his neck. His tanned body and meticulously coiffed hair created "Centerfold" quality, as the J. Geils Band sang about back in the '80s. That chiseled face could stop anyone in their tracks. I don't care if you're straight, gay, bi, trans, or queer, he contains something for everyone to enjoy. At 60 years old, he's maintained his charm and appeal better than anyone else in our age category. Anyway, the point is my celebrity crush for him was real, and I *liked* him a lot, but secretly I *loved* Demi Moore. Her raspy voice was totally sexy, and she was so beautiful with those piercing doe eyes pulling me in through the screen. She earned her fame in the '80s as a member of the Brat Pack, and those movies transcend the era. After the staggering popularity of *Ghost*, she got somewhat demolished by critics for a few movies, including *G.I. Jane* and *Striptease*. I have to admit, I love both of these flicks; especially the latter, which I've watched multiple times. As Billy Joel jazzily pointed out, she looked so good in her "Stiletto" heels dancing around her living room. As an adult, I've always loved movies dripping with sexual innuendo and forward expression, maybe because outwardly as a person I am far from these things.

As Demi's popularity waned, Angelina Jolie arrived on the scene. I believe her breakout role may have been in *Gia*, in which she portrayed the model Gia Carangi, but I became fascinated by her during *Girl, Interrupted*. She was so wild and unhinged in the movie, and afterward, I followed her regularly along with the rest of the world, seeing her through her relationships with Billy Bob Thornton and Brad Pitt. The vial of blood threw me a bit, but I remained steadfast in my crush. She had the "it" factor, much like a magnet you couldn't separate from.

A few honorable mentions in my history of girl celebrity crushes. I have always loved Drew Barrymore, but the movie displaying her sex appeal the best was *Poison Ivy*. It wasn't a huge hit, but the scenes between her and Sara Gilbert as well as Tom Skerritt were hot. One other flick that garnered notoriety at the time was *Wild Things* with Neve Campbell and Denise Richards—the pool scene is truly wild. I also loved *Cruel Intentions* (based on *Dangerous Liaisons*) with Ryan Phillippe, Sarah Michelle Gellar, Reese Witherspoon, and Selma Blair—so dark and twisted. But the ultimate steamy movie goddess award goes to Gina Gershon. She managed to pull off not one but two movies—*Showgirls* with Elizabeth Berkley and *Bound* with Jennifer Tilly. As my boys in Mötley Crüe belted out proudly in "Girls, Girls, Girls," so many choices!

Around the time I was getting divorced from Seamus, a new series started on Showtime that I think was greatly responsible for making lesbians part of the cool crowd. The outward lifestyle had been expressed thus far by a handful such as

Ellen DeGeneres, and in lesser respects, Rosie O' Donnell and Melissa Etheridge. When the series *The L Word* arrived, it began to challenge the norm and boundaries, making alternative lifestyles a part of popular culture. On the boys' side, they also had *Queer as Folk* around the same time, which was equally groundbreaking. I was more interested in tuning in to the amazing creation by Ilene Chaiken, and watched the series religiously. This was one way I was able to learn about the LGBTQIA+ culture; more importantly, it began to normalize being gay and had kick-ass music to boot.

Music was also helping to put gayness into the mainstream. Katy Perry exploded when "I Kissed A Girl" got released, with all her talk about tasting cherry ChapStick. In a lot of respects, I chose a great time to come out of the closet!

My current and most longstanding celebrity crush is Jennifer Lopez. I always liked her but I think *American Idol* solidified it for me when I realized she could do it all—sing, act, dance, and all-around entertain. I saw her in concert at MSG in August 2019 as she defiantly shook her "Booty," the song featuring Iggy Azalea. The night of the concert, the power grid went down in Manhattan, and she had to stop performing after just four songs. She returned to perform the show for us the following Monday night after performing in Boston on Sunday. What a class act. To me, she is the epitome of sexiness, and I think she'll hold the crown in my book for a long time to come.

Ah, it's been so fun to escape reality for a moment and share my celebrity crushes with you —but now let's move on to my ultimate real-life crush of all time.

# Chapter 44 - "Michelle"

All she said in her initial post to me was "What's the punch-line?" to which I replied . . . wait for it . . . "Why not? I'm a fungi!" Actually, she may have been the only person to bother asking me that question, and I immediately knew she pays close attention to things. This simple one line back and forth started our dialogue. It's crazy how a simple random connection can literally change your life.

I would find out later, Michele was getting egged on by her friends to write me. Michele Elizabeth Travis was born on December 20, 1965 in Franklin Borough, New Jersey. You'll note Michele has one "L" in her name (I like to kid her that I stole her extra "L"). Still, the famous song "Michelle" by The Beatles holds water, and my Mom has been calling her "Michele *ma belle*" for years now.

Michele had recently come off a breakup and was treading gingerly back into the dating world. Were it not for her friends, we likely would have never crossed paths. I had set a radius in Match of 50 miles or less, and the distance between our two houses at the time was 53.1 miles. Can you believe it? I almost missed meeting the love of my life over 3.1 miles. Additionally, Michele had been seriously considering moving to Florida up until the point we met. You already know how I feel about fate and things meant to happen—it was clearly meant to be.

We spent a lot of time getting to know each other before we met in person. When we started communicating, I was a bit unsure about meeting up because she lived so far away, in Otisville, New York. *Where?* I'd never heard of it before. But as we continued to write each other, I found I enjoyed the easy flow of our dialogue—natural, based on mutual curiosity, on similar wavelengths. She was well-written, clear, and articulate—all critical to me. Eventually, we began talking on the phone.

The conversations went on for hours at night, with as much to talk about the next night. Michele was interesting, unique, and the perfect smidgen of crazy thrown in for good measure. Despite the perception people who know me professionally might have, I'm not as straitlaced as I appear to be (I'm actually the opposite). My career life and home life are separately owned and operated independent entities, and in my personal life, I like diversity and the element of surprise once in a while. I need a partner who is open and grounded but ready for a little adventure. Michele met all of these "qualifications" easily, but I also came to learn she's got one twisted sense of humor and I never know what might come out of her mouth.

The other thing I loved about talking to Michele was her voice—it soothed and captivated me. She speaks softly, and I often have to ask her to repeat herself, but I love her softness. Even so, every once in a while she'll break into her signature high-pitched laugh that could get me through the worst day imaginable.

Michele and I are different people in many respects. We came from different circumstances and walks of life. She

257

comes from a family comprised of four sisters and one brother who have a wide age gap, compared to my only-child existence. She lost her Dad when she was two years old, and her Mom passed away in 2000 when Michele was 35. She also covered more ground geographically than me, living in various locations throughout New Jersey, New York, and Florida. Most of all, though, I admire the way she owned her independence early in life and lived her truth from a younger age.

When we met, Michele was working for the Orange County Health Department and at a local veterinarian's office at night, in stark contrast to my white-collar real estate world. As we continued our talks, I realized we had similar views about all the important "stuff," sharing middle-of-the-road opinions about most topics and shying away from radical thoughts or behaviors.

One of the most refreshing aspects of this whole relationship was the openness with which Michele lived her life. She was comfortable in her own skin, unconcerned with what anyone thought about her lifestyle—not in your face about any of it, but not about to waste energy on someone who doesn't accept who she is. Coming from the sheltered way in which I'd lived the majority of my life (as it relates to my sexual preference, anyway), this was a welcome aspect. Michele had been out as gay from her early twenties, which I find courageous, considering the time frame.

I found myself in territory I'd never actually taken residence in before—spending time with a woman looking for a relationship built on open transparency as opposed to the secretive unavailability I'd previously experienced. In addition to her openness, the more compelling factor was what an amazingly good human being I discovered Michele to be. This caring, genuine, and wholesome soul wouldn't harm another living thing. I would later discover she is the rare person who will relocate a bug found inside the house to safety outdoors.

It was Fourth of July weekend in 2008, and I was taking care of my friend Deb's pooches so I'd be staying local. My mom was coming over to spend the day and help me garden on the fifth, but otherwise nothing else was happening. I woke up on the fourth feeling like it was time to take the next step and see where this was heading. I called Michele in the early afternoon and asked her what she was up to for the weekend. She was having a few friends over for a barbecue, and after I did some not-so-subtle hinting around, she asked me if I'd like to join them. I didn't hesitate—like Sugarland says in their song "Want To," it was time to jump in.

After taking care of the dogs, I made my trek into the unknown. I pulled up MapQuest but Michele also explained directions to me (I now find it kind of humorous and amazing, given her lack of aptitude with directions, that they were actually correct!). I was familiar with all the roads to a point— I found myself driving on the infamous Route 23 I'd traveled to Toye's Campground all those years ago, but this Otisville place was far beyond where I'd gone before. The hustle and bustle urban landscape I was used to was replaced by cow pastures and horse farms splashed in glorious shades of green.

I called her about 10 minutes before I arrived, as she said it would be better if we were on the phone so she could explain where she lived. *Huh?* Yep, I was in the sticks. As the anticipation continued to build, I thought I might explode right out of my Infiniti. *Location aside, where were we headed?* As I rounded the corner to her street and slowly pulled closer to the house, suddenly I saw her waiting for me in the driveway.

My heart skipped several beats, and as I pulled in and we locked eyes for the first time, I knew in an instant. I got out of the car, and as Lifehouse sings in "First Time," I held my breath. We embraced after a kiss hello. I knew I was home.

Our first in-person meeting was interesting. I met her friends Terry and Elaine, who were the chief "egger-oners" responsible for our meeting in the first place. I got a chuckle over their dog, nestled comfortably in a baby carriage. *Whoa dude, so this is what lesbian life is like!* We had a fun time talking and eating all the great food Michele had prepared. She is a great cook, and she loves picnic food, so I got spoiled from day one. Later that evening, we sat quietly and watched the town fireworks right from her backyard. Given the late hour and the couple of beers imbibed, I stayed the night. The next morning, I got up early but elated. I had to take care of the dogs and meet my mom at the house. Needless to say she was already busy in the yard, pulling weeds. *Oops.*

Michele and I initially spent time together on the weekends. We soaked in every moment of our time together. Things felt so free and easy, and we greatly enjoyed each other's company. We spent quality time lazing around in bed and listening to tunes. The song "Crush" by Dave Matthews Band is so reminiscent of those early days—was I dreaming?

Eventually, the weekends were not enough, and we began driving to each other's houses some nights during the week. The long distance was tough at times on top of our work commutes. We were both exhausted, but our relationship was blossoming. One of our early songs was Mary J. Blige "Be Without You." We didn't build it overnight—love like this takes some time.

As opportunities arose naturally, we started introducing

each other to friends and family. One person I hadn't broken the news to yet was Linda. I met up with her separately so I could share the news with my best friend. She's responsible for, by far, the funniest of my coming-out stories. When I told her I was dating someone, she said, "That's great!" and I said, "Yeah, her name is Michele." Completely unaware, she responded, "Michele? Is he French?" OMG.

## THE STAY

Where is the person who understands me;
    The one who yearns to live and brand me.

I like who I am and won't again be sold;
    Yearning for true love before I get old.

No longer complicated but the fear is still there;
    They'll pass me by in the moment I go unaware.

Open to the future yet still tripping on the past;
    Can I shatter the hourglass to make it last?

Power me to move forward for only a day;
    To find what I seek and know it will stay.

# Chapter 45 - "Lean on Me"

Not too long after we started dating, I got my formal indoctrination to Michele's family. We were invited to Aunt Pat and Uncle Hank's 60th wedding anniversary party at the Old Erie in Middletown, New York. Michele's mom was one of 9 siblings, and as you could imagine, meeting everyone at once was like drinking through a fire hose. Everyone was warm and friendly, especially a number of Michele's cousins. I also got to meet Michele's only (and older by 14 years) brother John.

We sat with John and his wife Di, while Michele and her brother caught up on life. John and Di lived in Connecticut, and the siblings didn't get to see each other frequently. I'll never forget how comfortable those two made me feel; it was as if I was getting a warm, welcoming embrace into the family. Though it took me time to get familiar with who was who and how everyone fit into the family, the relevant takeaway was the feeling that I was being accepted right into the bunch.

Michele's three sisters, Kathi, Lisa, and Melissa, all live in Bradenton, Florida and weren't at the anniversary party, but I got to meet them for the first time when we traveled down on vacation later in the year. I received the same welcoming vibe from all of them. We stayed at Melissa's, the youngest of the siblings and two years younger than Michele. Melissa has a busy life and is always on the go, but something which stood out to me was how thoughtful she is. I found I can engage in conversation with her at a deeper level than I can with most people. I'm not being critical toward other people about this. I find many people get uncomfortable when I start delving into deep territory, but not Melissa—she's typically open to discuss mostly anything, which I greatly appreciate.

At the time, Melissa and her husband Lewis had a son, Trey, and she was pregnant. We felt right at home staying with them, and Trey got comfortable around me quickly. One day soon after we arrived, I was sitting outside in a lounge chair reading at their pool when Trey came out with his towel and a book and perched right next to me. It's hard to believe how time has flown—he's now a grown man at 21, but to me sometimes he's still the little boy who sat next to me reading that day.

Ava came into the world shortly thereafter in February 2009, and we got to meet her for the first time in June. I have pictures of holding her in my lap and remember playing with her and the faux kitchen set she loved when she was a toddler. No matter how old she gets, I will always remember this one time when she was still a little girl and we were driving around Florida in Melissa's van. Tailored children's tunes were repeating on a loop in the car where all the songs mentioned her by name. "Ava, has good manners, and that's what matters . . . " OMG, so funny. Ava is now 15 years old. I love Trey and Ava a ton, and "My Wish" for both of them is their dreams stay big and worries stay small, as Rascal Flatts described.

Every year, the family spends time on vacation together in Fort Myers, where several family members have timeshares at one of the resorts. The first time we went down, we stayed with Melissa and Lewis for the weekend and switched to Kathi and Ken's place during the week. Kathi is Michele's oldest sister by 18 years, and she and her husband Ken have four sons, K.C., Kevin, Kyle, and Kristofer. They all have lovely families of their own whom we've gotten to spend time with over the years. I clicked with Kathi automatically, as she's got similar values to my mom, which I relate to. She's also an awesome cook. The weekends in Fort Myers are typically chaotic, but it's great when everyone has dinner together in Kathi and Ken's larger unit (though we're still packed in like sardines). It was hugely upsetting when Hurricane Ian caused such widespread devastation to the area in September 2022. Looking forward for the area to come back, and as Capital Cities sang, glad we're "Safe and Sound."

Rounding out the siblings is Lisa, who is somewhere in the middle of the pack but older than Michele by about 10 years. Lisa and her husband Bob shared an unwavering love of sports. I connect with Lisa because we can talk smack when the Yankees are playing the Tampa Bay Rays, her favorite baseball team, or when the Rangers are playing the Lightning. Lisa also has a deep appreciation for music and often goes to concerts at Hard Rock. We've stayed with her at Hard Rock Tampa and had a blast. Her interests are varied and similar to mine, which I don't come across too often.

Michele's family has gone through some hard times since I've been in the fold. John's wife Di passed away after a battle with lung cancer in 2012. I'll never forget that during this sad time, John pulled me aside during the repast to tell me what a positive addition I was to the family (and for his sister) from his perspective. It meant a lot to hear him say those words. John was diagnosed with throat cancer within six months of Di's diagnosis, but went into remission. Michele and I made it a point to spend time with John after Di passed, taking trips to Connecticut including Mystic Seaport and Foxwoods, where we saw Cyndi Lauper. He moved down to Florida to start rebuilding his life, but soon his cancer returned, and it had spread. We tried to hold out hope, but sadly it was too far progressed. John passed in January 2015. Lisa also lost her husband Bob during the pandemic, which was devastating, and what made it even more so was the inability to gather as a family to mourn. One thing I'll say is when the going gets tough, these guys bond together. I'm reminded of the song "Lean on Me" by Bill Withers—they help each other carry on.

Since we live so far apart from the other three sisters, we cherish the time we spend together. It's not as often as we'd like, but we make the most of it. In addition to Fort Myers (which is on a pause at the moment), we've tried to go down for holidays, notably Thanksgiving. Kathi always hosts a crowd and does all finishing touches with fervor. We're also excited when one of the siblings comes up to stay by us. Kathi has spent time here, and we've had some fun trips when her and dear family friend Wanda have come to stay. Likewise, we also had a great trip to Kathi and Ken's cabin in North Carolina, and once went with Kathi and Wanda to Nashville, a first time for all of us. Attending the *Grand Ole Opry* was an amazing experience, and at the Country Music Hall of Fame and Museum, we paid extra to go to RCA Studio B, where the legendary Elvis recorded a number of his songs. I swear you can still feel his presence within those walls—it was eerie yet comforting to me.

Our trips with Melissa, Lewis, and the kids have also been memorable, and we've had several opportunities to go on adventures with them. When they came as a family a few years ago, we took them into New York City to do all of the typical sightseeing. We also went together to see *Wicked*. The song "For Good" most reminds me of my feeling about the Osborne family—because I know them, I've been changed for the better.

One thing I've found remarkable about the four sisters is how notably different they are; each has such a unique persona unlike the others. And somehow, when you put them all together, it's like putting together a perfect puzzle. I also know in a millisecond's notice, they would be there for each other. I love each of them for the amazing women they are, and they each treat me like the fifth sister, which makes me feel blessed. Kind of reminds me of the song "Hey, Soul Sister" by Train—they're all one of my kind!

Over the years, Michele and I have enjoyed spending time with her siblings, aunts, uncles, and cousins. The last of Michele's mom's siblings, Aunt Lois is 93 and going strong. We love spending time visiting with her and her family. I'm so thankful I was able to find my tribe.

# Chapter 46 - "Roll With the Changes"

By the time I met Michele in 2008, my career was shaping up nicely as well. A lot had happened since I returned to Hampshire in 2000. The decision had been made to outsource our accounting platform in early 2004, and while this was a huge adjustment philosophically and emotionally, it also laid the foundation for the next 20 years of growth for me personally. As REO Speedwagon encouragingly sang, I needed to "Roll With the Changes," because that's what it takes to succeed in business.

On the first outsourcing of our accounting operation, I served as a key person on the project team. We were also migrating to a different real estate accounting system; one I hadn't used previously. With a combination of my accounting system and procedural depth, this project gave me the ability to develop my strength around platform transition.

Learning this skill came in handy, as we would ultimately go through several property management and accounting platform shifts in the years to come. The driver of this was to match the enterprise's needs to the provider, ensuring quality service and efficiency at the best price point. In our business, the main expense is payroll, so this element becomes critical in our decision-making.

Remember when I left CB Richard Ellis back in 2000 to rejoin Hampshire? Well, ironically, we wound up outsourcing our property management platform to them in 2006, and guess what? I became a CBRE employee again as a result, when once again I found myself a key member of the transition team, and it seemed appropriate for me to oversee the operation under the account director. My career came back full circle as I got the chance to grow some roots in property management after all. Another lesson learned over the years is that the commercial real estate industry is a small one, and you never want to burn your bridges. Kansas said it best: You gotta "Play the Game Tonight." I've done a good job remembering this, and it's been helpful.

In 2005, as this transition was in progress, I also met the guy who would become one of the most significant mentors in my career. Bob had worked for Hampshire years before I ever arrived, then left to launch a successful tax partnership, and eventually came back as our head of finance. He ultimately brought me back to Hampshire in 2008 to become their operations and business process manager. On the movie soundtrack from *The Devil Wears Prada* is a great song by Madonna called "Jump," and this would be my most success-ful one. The layers of property management and accounting were all culminating into my trajectory toward what I'm most passionate about—connecting people, systems, and process to improve productivity and profitability. It was a huge move for me toward this. As Tom Petty sang with charged-up emotion, I was "Runnin' Down A Dream."

Through this move, I began to absorb additional facets of the business and, under Bob's guidance, I learned more about the Hampshire business as a corporate entity; the umbrella above the properties we own and operate. By working on making improvements to various business processes, I began to connect all the dots between departments. I also took on oversight of the administration, which further lodged my understanding from the ground up of the rest of the business. Another big learning experience came when we became a regulated adviser and had to put a number of new governance compliance practices in place.

Around the time I came back to Hampshire, our CEO Jimmy started working with a leadership coach, Erica. This part-nering was also an important element in re-branding the Hampshire culture we have today, and the leadership team has worked with Erica the last 15 years. Erica has also been an important coach in my development from a manager to a leader, which I greatly appreciate.

In addition to Jimmy, Bob, and Erica, I've learned and worked with so many great people over the years who have had a positive impact on my growth and development. I've noticed my biggest opportunities have surfaced when someone is willing to provide me with honest and direct constructive feedback, continuously pushing me out of my comfort zone. The three people I've mentioned have provided this more than anyone, and it's enabled me to recognize blind spots, an important aspect of becoming a good leader.

I've always had the internal motivation to learn, grow, and develop, but we all fail to recognize at times the importance of encouraging coaches and guides and how they can accelerate you beyond your own expectations. It's reminiscent of my younger years, when I had mentors in school who did the same. I'm grateful for anyone who has helped me learn and grow.

I also feel strongly that living my truth and coming out fully at work helped me become comfortable in my own skin in my career. To be an effective leader requires transparency and vulnerability, and this personal shift bred a higher level of confidence in all areas, removing the invisible barriers I'd created over the years. As Prince said in "Let's Go Crazy," let's push a higher floor—ready to keep going up!

# Chapter 47 - "Pocketful of Sunshine"

The initial predictability of the evening was countered with a big splash of unknown, leading to a romantic moment you could easily envision appearing in one of those corny-but-addictive Hallmark Channel Christmas movies. Michele and I had been dating since July 2008, and after a deepening romance that had us spending more time together than apart, our conversation turned to consideration of a more formal commitment. Neither one of us took this subject lightly, of course. We'd both been in serious relationships before, but the beauty of this one is that both of us had learned, lost, and evolved through each one. By the time we met we both knew what we were looking for and were fully grounded in who we are as individuals. At times, we've discussed how we wish we had a head start by a few more years, because if we had been a little younger, children might have been part of our story in addition to the fur babies we adore. I'm not sure I'd consider it a regret necessarily; it's more wondering how life may have been with some offspring. Still, we are content with the life we've built together and are thankful daily we were able to find each other.

We'd been discussing getting engagement rings, and on one of our jaunts into Manhattan, we found ourselves in the diamond district on 47th Street. As fate would have it, we stepped into a family-run jewelry business and ordered our engagement rings, which we'd pick up on a date certain in the future. I planned a romantic evening for the day of pickup, which was in December 2009. The plan was to go pick up our rings and head over to Toloache, a Mexican restaurant we both loved, then go see the *Christmas Spectacular* at Radio City Music Hall. I'd also decided *what better place to officially get engaged than at Rockefeller Center by the tree?* so after the show we'd take a walk over and put on our rings. The Virgo in me was content I'd coordinated the perfect plan.

The first snafu was the jeweler was running late with finishing up our rings and had to go pick them up from their other location, which would take some time and make us late for dinner. They told us to go ahead, and they'd deliver our rings to us! This is why we loved them—they are so attentive and warm. We had a beautiful dinner and made our way to Radio City. Some snow had started falling, and fortunately we were appropriately bundled up in our winter coats, scarves, gloves, and hats. One of Michele's cousin's kids had asked us to bring a "Flat Stacy" with us for the evening, and we obliged with a picture in front of the *Christmas Spectacular* sign looking like snow bunnies.

When the show was over, we exited the building to face a full-on blizzard. The snow was accumulating at a rapid pace, and we would have to drive home in treacherous conditions, as we hadn't planned to stay the night. For a moment I considered getting in the car and abandoning the rest of the mission, but as Tom Cruise said in *Risky Business*, sometimes you gotta say, "what the fuck."

We slipped our way over to Rockefeller Center in chilling

temperatures. Not surprisingly, yet jaw-droppingly at the same time, when we arrived, we found ourselves completely alone with the heavily falling snow swirling around the majestic and beautifully lighted tree. I got down on one knee, snow beating down on our faces, surrounded by utter silence, and popped the question. I looked around, half expecting a camera crew to shout, "Cut!" After Michele accepted and gave me my ring in turn, we kissed and embraced and left quickly without waiting for the final credits. We walked back to our car holding each other tightly, and as we did and continue to do, similar to the beautifully written song for the Broadway smash *Rent*, committed to each other "I'll Cover You."

Same-sex marriage was not yet legal in 2010 in New York or New Jersey, so we planned to get married in Provincetown, Massachusetts. Michele and I had vacationed in the area a couple times when we were dating and thought it would be the ideal place for us to commit our lives to one another. For anyone not familiar, Provincetown (called P-Town by regulars) is located at the tip of Cape Cod. It's a beautiful but lengthy trip for us, clocking in at about five and a half hours. This doesn't sound like a lot until you've been in a car with someone who suffers from extreme motion sickness. Thus, on any car excursion over an hour, we are both beyond ready to exit by the time we arrive!

P-Town is not your typical Cape Cod beach town. Sure, it's got beautifully clean beaches and breathtaking sand dunes, a vibrant boating community, and anticipatory whale-watching excursions. Excellent seafood restaurants, exquisite art galleries, and typical tourist souvenir shops abound. It also happens to be the first official place the pilgrims set foot in America, and hence worth a trip to the Pilgrim Monument, the tallest all-granite tower in the United States, standing at 252 feet.

P-Town is an excellent choice for a summer family vacation. It also happens to be the gayest place in America, or at least as I've come across so far. Most people would probably guess the number-one location would be San Francisco, and in fairness I've never been there. P-Town is the most openly welcoming environment toward the LGBTQIA+ community I've ever been, though plenty of other places exist where Michele and I feel comfortable about being open, including nearby Manhattan, Key West, and St. Pete's, Florida. P-Town has become our home away from home over the years, and now we're even more endeared to it because it's where we said, "I do."

We planned an intimate ceremony for Fourth of July in 2010. You probably don't need to ask; yes, the date was purposeful—we wanted the same date as when we began dating two years earlier. We didn't want a big lavish affair, most desiring a few close friends, my mom, and a tastefully arranged ceremony. Planning my second wedding was a completely different experience than my first, and the pressures were more contained and simplistic. The one major difference was we didn't live in P-Town, and had to arrange everything from a distance, as this would be considered a destination wedding.

The most important decision was where to hold the ceremony, and we had a number of choices, but knew we wanted to get married outdoors. The beach was an obvious location, but then we remembered the small, tranquil garden path at Gabriel's hotel, where we'd stayed previously. All the hotels and restaurants are gay-friendly, but we knew we'd be completely welcomed at this women-owned resort. We inquired further, and they were happy to accommodate us and our guests. The added benefit was our guests could all stay as well, which made it the ideal location.

The next decision was where to have our reception. We love many of the popular restaurants in P-Town but wanted something a bit more refined. We chose The Red Inn, an old establishment with a modern vibe on the waterfront. We'd order off the menu versus a fixed meal so we'd have nothing else to worry about other than making reservations. Arrangements we needed to make from afar included hair, nails, and flowers. We found a great salon called West End Salon where we could get hair and nails done, and I'm relatively certain we used Provincetown Florist, which all worked out nicely.

Michele and I both shopped for our outfits. We knew we wanted a summery, beachy, outdoorsy look. What's better than linen? Michele got a beautiful sleeveless linen summer dress, and I got flowing relaxed linen pants with a V-neck long-sleeve tunic with simple but elegant white canvas shoes. We chose our birthstones as our wedding color theme; a perfect combination of sapphire and blue topaz, and got matching jewelry to complement our outfits and our wedding bands, also matching diamond and sapphire.

With those items settled, I was able to spend the majority of the time focused on the ceremony. We found a local woman officiant online. I wanted to create a program fusing together my Catholic upbringing and my love of poetry with Michele's love of nature and tribal elements. I wanted a vibe as diverse and open as our loving relationship. We selected a couple of traditional Catholic psalms and a couple of poems about love and commitment, and asked our friends to do some of the readings. We carefully put together our vows by mixing and matching samples of ideas we'd gotten online.

For the tribal aspect, we decided upon a sand ceremony and purchased sand in the two shades of blue and different size vases. During the ceremony, we'd each have our birthstone color in a separate vase and blend them together in a larger vessel, signifying two becoming one. We also got smaller vases to do the same and give to our guests as a wedding favor. The other nature element was live butterflies, which we received through the mail at Gabriel's and planned to release at the end of the ceremony.

The final layer of the ceremony was the music. Michele and I wanted songs describing our commitment to one another. We had to select our wedding song, which probably took the most time of our considerations. We landed on a song Michele suggested, "I Could Not Ask for More" by Sara Evans. I was familiar with the song but had only heard the original by Edwin McCain, so I was originally a bit partial to his version, until I realized Sara beautifully redid the song with exquisite vocals. The words of the song fit our story perfectly—we had both found what we were waiting for.

We needed to layer in three other songs to match the length of the ceremony for the pockets we needed to fill. Of course it was hard for me to reel myself in, but I managed. One no-brainer was "Pocketful of Sunshine" by Natasha Bedingfield. This was actually our song as a couple, and it couldn't be more perfect because she mentions butterflies, so we'd use it to release them—*take me away!* For the other two songs, we each got a selection matching our feelings. Michele's song choice was Keith Urban's "Only You Can Love Me This Way." Keith is one of her favorites, and I've come to appreciate his guitar playing over the years. I landed on Alicia Keys' "If I

Ain't Got You," because nothing in the world means anything without her.

We arrived in P-Town a couple of days before the wedding day. We needed to get our marriage license and firm up final arrangements. Once our party arrived, we spent time with them walking Commercial Street, enjoying good food and company and getting massages. The night before the wedding, we all went to our first drag show at The Art House. Here I was, sitting next to my mom at a drag show—she was having a great time! I have to give my mom some kudos. While she was slow to come around, she's completely embraced and welcomed us as a couple. Michele has become her other daughter, and I'm so thankful. God, I wasted ridiculous amounts of time hiding in shame instead of living my truth, but at least I got here.

Our wedding day was picture-perfect, though it was extremely hot, leading to a bit of dehydration. Other than that, perfect. We shared a champagne toast in Gabriel's common room and had a fabulous meal with our party. All in all, it was true—we could not ask for more.

# Chapter 48 - "Home"

Michele and I settled as newlyweds at her home in Otisville, the obvious choice because Michele works for Orange County, requiring her to be a resident. Additionally, I'm more comfortable driving distances and was used to commutes during heavy traffic rush hours. I packed up my Succasunna home, sent my furniture to storage, and rented out my house as an investment property. What I remember most about these times is the simplicity. Michele's house was small but cute, and we were truly living in our remote little love bubble. I remember many a weekend, chilling at home with the fur babies, taking it slow on "Sunday Morning" as Maroon 5 played soothingly in the background.

We probably would have remained content, because both of us would be okay "Forever in Blue Jeans," similar to Neil Diamond. But the commute for me was a bit longer than I wanted. It was 150 miles roundtrip, times a five-day workweek commute. I don't get fazed by mileage, but the length of the commute was tiring. Also, I wanted us to live in a larger space since we loved our time together at home. We wanted to create something new to both of us, and with that, we began our search.

The amount of time we spent looking for a new home

was laughable (and not in a funny way). We sought the ideal location for my commute and also wanted a desirable Orange County location, and looked in multiple towns. I liked Warwick, but Michele wasn't a fan of the winding, one-lane journeys I'd have to make to get to Morristown. We scoured multiple locations and hired an agent who wasn't helping us narrow the playing field. This led to multiple nights and weekends touring homes not close to a perfect fit.

We eventually hired Michele's cousin Heather as our realtor after running into her at a family picnic. Thank God, because she is amazing (and I'm not saying it because she's our cousin—she knows her stuff, including residential real estate as well as the area). This helped us greatly in matching our criteria to locations that met our overall needs. It still took some time, but at least we were on the right track. We were interested in several houses in Goshen, which was how we started searching more specifically in this area. Heather found a house on the outskirts of town, and on our first drive over, I wasn't sure this was going to turn into anything fruitful. It wasn't a bad location; it was country-forward and remote, but I almost felt too remote. We were driving through more greenery than houses. *Hmm.*

We made a left into our development for the first time. *Whoa, wait a second.* Great curb appeal, beautiful expansive houses and lawns. Winding around and up into a secluded and serene, idyllic neighborhood, we pulled up to a house with an immaculately kept exterior. I wasn't a huge fan of the yellow aluminum siding, but everything else looked amazing. We stepped foot into our "Home" for the first time. I could hear Phillip Phillips rattling around in my brain—*I'm gonna make this place your home.*

It was everything we were looking for. While the interior had not been modernized, it was an immaculate split level with four bedrooms and three bathrooms. We loved the layout, which included a large kitchen, awesome family room, formal living room, and an additional room that eventually became our library.

From the outside, our house is deceiving, appearing smaller than it actually is, and it's not until you walk through that you realize how spacious it is. Still, the clincher for us was the backyard. Resting on one full, level acre, this house featured a backyard that might be the most tranquil place we could have asked for, with a sprawling deck, Olympic-sized pool, and trees backing the property at a ridge line. Nature abounds and thrives here because we have great privacy with high shrubbery protecting us from the rest of the world.

Our closing took place in August 2011, about a year after we got married. Moving was an undertaking, because we had the Otisville house as well as a packed storage unit in New Jersey and had to arrange for a mover to transport items from two locations to our new home. Naturally, it rained. Exhausting, but we managed.

Less than a week after closing, we returned to the Otisville house to pick up some boxes, trying to clear it out for the rental, when a tornado hit a main artery close to our new house. The tornado had wreaked complete havoc, and all the roads were closed. We couldn't get to our street, and were petrified not knowing what we'd find. After a substantial amount of time driving around, we finally arrived and found our house intact. Phew. The power was out, but we didn't care. We hunkered down in our family room and thanked God, and prayed for our surrounding neighbors, some of whom weren't as lucky.

One thing I've learned is your circumstances don't matter once you've found your person; your soulmate. Oh sure, we have our moments—can any married couple honestly say it's perfect? But like Jim Croce so expertly sang in "Time In A Bottle," I'd looked around enough to know I was in exactly the right place for me.

We've been in our home for 13 years now, and love it equally to when we moved in. It's a large house for two people with a lot of maintenance, but it's worth every penny. After the closing, we upgraded the electrical components and purchased new hardware that matched our style. We've prioritized different projects each year to continue to update the house, but certain things we've left in place. Right now we're deciding where my perfect permanent writing space will be, and we're bouncing around ideas. We're always discussing something about the house, and certainly we'll never run out of things to keep us busy—that's just home ownership.

Before I move on I want to tell you (in case it's not obvious already) how greatly I love doing life with this woman. I probably don't express it often enough, and at times I drive her crazy, usually because I'm in one of my only-child-on-my-own-planet modes, or being OCD about something not nearly important enough to warrant such scrutiny. The main thing I know is we're better as a couple than apart. While I know we are both independent and could survive life alone, we don't want to. She has made me a better and more complete person than I ever was before. When I think back to the dark path I was traveling before I met her, I know she was responsible for grounding me, which is why I have been able to exceed in other areas of my life. I owe her my world, and it is hers. Gerry Rafferty's old '70s tune, "Right Down the Line," perfectly illustrates this. To me, Michele is the brightest light that shines.

# Chapter 49 - "Unforgettable"

The crazy cat lady jokes are kind of funny, and they don't bother us. We have five. I suppose if you dig down under the surface about the nature of the jokes and think about it too much, you could find it offensive. I mean, why does the association between the female gender and felines automatically imply a person is crazy if they have a multiple (or even just one) cat in their household? It's kind of like the stereotype about lesbians and U-Hauls right? Why isn't there a matching association about people having multiple dogs? It all seems a tad short-sighted, if you ask me. As I get older, I am more aware of stereotypes and try not to box someone in, though I know we all have certain impressions which have been drilled into us over the years. I'm trying to be more mindful. Everyone who knows me personally is at this moment trying to recall if they've ever busted my chops about our cats—don't worry, I still think it's funny and you're not in trouble. Five cats in one house does get a little nuts sometimes. In those moments, the stereotype may be closer to reality than we'd like to admit!

Prior to meeting Michele, I hadn't been around cats often, and I operated squarely in the dog camp. I've always subscribed to the man's-best-friend hype, and I still feel the same way. Dogs are amazing animals and wonderful companions, and I can see a time in life where a dog addition to our household will make sense. We've discussed it multiple times, and I'm guessing when our circumstances are properly aligned with the responsibility, it will happen. We almost got a French bulldog puppy several years ago. A breeder Michele knows brought the puppy over to our house as an introduction to see how it would go with the cats. Disastrous. While I'm sure the puppy and cats would have figured it out eventually, the bigger issue became the extreme allergic reaction coming over me like wildfire. I'm technically allergic to cats and dogs, but only a small handful cause this type of reaction. In any case it was the start and end of having a Frenchie!

Back to cats, I didn't have an extensive history with them. My friend Tracy had Whiskers when we were younger, but I didn't understand the fascination. I kept trying to disprove the theory a cat will always land on all four feet—darn cat always did! My Aunt Elsie and Aunt Winnie always had cats, and one called Misty would hiss at everyone when they came over, which wasn't encouraging. One time I slept over my friend Monica's house, and woke up to a cat above my head staring at me in the night's glow. I thought it was creepy and weird. But the closest cat relationship I had prior to meeting Michele was with Mom and Charlie's cat, Sammy. He was a cool cat, but the first time I took care of him, he had a hair ball attack—I thought he was croaking. Yeah, feline behaviors seemed so bizarre to me.

When I started dating Michele, her cats (Scooter, Chibi, and Oreo) somewhat blended into the background—they didn't show their presence too often, or if they did, I don't remember much. Oreo the tuxedo was a true scaredy-cat, and she may not have come out to approach me for months. Chibi, the little Persian, had one of those penetrating stares certain cat breeds seem to possess, and every once in a while she'd meow loudly at me. I think she was the first to warm up to me, and after some time, she began curling up next to me in bed. Scooter, the cool, chill cat, was Michele's first cat and had an air of confidence that made her the alpha female of the pack. The bond between Scoot and I took hold when I started spending more time at Michele's—she would stretch out and wrap herself around my neck like an airplane pillow, where she'd hang out for hours.

One indication of Michele's goodness was gleaned early on due to the circumstances surrounding these three cats. They all had special needs; specifically FIV, or feline immunodeficiency virus, further described as the feline form of HIV. I didn't know anything about FIV, but what I learned is it's not transmittable to humans (it's a different strain of the virus). It can be transferred to a non-FIV cat, but generally the likelihood is low and would only occur through open wounds. Still, Michele was overly cautious after getting Scooter, and chose to adopt other FIV cats. Generally they go through stages of the disease similar to HIV, and the life span of an FIV cat is generally not as long as the typical lifespan of a healthy feline.

Despite this prognosis, Scooter lived until the fine old age of 17. Once Scoot passed, Oreo succumbed to cancer quickly thereafter; she was only about eight. Chibi was the only one of Michele's originals to ever see our home in Goshen, and she wasn't in the home too long before also passing at a young age. All three were special in their own way, and our friend Deb got us a beautiful set of chimes after Scoot and Oreo died.

We have them outside in our pool area, and every time they ring we acknowledge their hello to us from over the rainbow bridge. As Nat King Cole and Natalie Cole sang in the lovely virtual duet, all of them are "Unforgettable."

After we lost Scoot and Oreo, we went to the Pets Alive shelter on a search to give Chibi a friend. Another thing about our cats is they all come from shelters. The number of abandoned cats looking for good homes is staggering, and we feel strongly they should have the priority after enduring whatever tough road they previously faced in their lives. We adopted two males—Simka and Jeremy—and immediately witnessed the dichotomy about cat personality and behavior, which was never more evident than with these two. When we brought them home, we set them down in their carriers in the kitchen and let them out. Simka strode right out and laid down in the middle of the room like he owned the place. Jeremy skittered off in a mad dash and dove behind the living room couch as if his life was in jeopardy.

Michele worked with Jeremy every day for a month to coax him out among the rest of the household. Don't tell her I said so, but she impressed me—I never thought we'd actually see Jeremy again. She is so patient with all our cats, and devotes endless amounts of time to socialize all of them. I'm reminded of the song "Not While I'm Around" from *Sweeney Todd: The Demon Barber of Fleet Street*. Michele's mentality begins and ends with "no one's going to harm my cats; not while I'm around." Any cat entering our household is treated like royalty and spoiled beyond imagining. Sadly, Simka and Jeremy (also both FIV cats) had cancer when we got them, and they were with us for only a brief time.

Down to Chibi again, we didn't go running out to the shelter right away. We were pretty devastated by the quick loss of Simka and Jeremy. About a month before we were getting married, Michele went to her night job at the local vet. A male kitten had come in from Middletown Animal Shelter to get neutered and would be sent back afterward for adoption. When they did the neuter and obligatory disease testing, the kitten tested positive for FIV. Since Middletown was not a no-kill shelter, he would be going back to the shelter to be euthanized. Once Michele's co-workers shared this with her, I got a frantic call at work from Michele, telling me the whole story and asking if we could adopt him. How could I allow him to go back to be killed, especially when we had the capacity to take him in? I came home that evening to our first-ever official kitten, our boy Jake (aka Jakey or Jakebear).

You wanna hear the clincher? On a whim, we had Jake tested again later, and he turned out not to be an FIV cat after all. Oftentimes, a young kitten can yield a false positive FIV result. The deduction? Millions of perfectly healthy kittens get euthanized for no good reason. It sickens me to think about this, and I'm so grateful we got to save this one. He's our first cat together, and at 14, Jake is still our pride and joy. Beautifully orange with long, flowing hair and tons of "floof," Jake is a long and lean loveball machine. He's such a warm and friendly soul, and also happens to be the best hugger in the world. When he was a kitten, every night he'd lay on my lap and sprawl out when we watched TV. He still does this but takes up a lot more room. He's got thyroid disease, but Michele gives him his pills twice a day and he's stable. Can you tell we love him to death?

A year later, the itch was back, and one weekend Michele asked me if we could go to Port Jervis Animal Shelter. They had a lot of kittens, and we walked around, checking them all out. I spotted a tiny little girl kitten, but around the corner Michele was getting bamboozled by a scrappy, snotty-nosed little boy kitten who grabbed her attention. When she opened the cage, he leapt into her arms like he was trying out for a scene in *Gone With the Wind.* She summoned me over and asked, "Can I have him?" Ugh. He wouldn't have been my first choice, but admittedly I have a hard time saying no to Michele (don't tell her this, either). "Umm, okay."

We named him Duncan (aka Duncan Heinz or Dunc) which means brown warrior. Well, he's not really brown (he's buff), but he certainly is a warrior. He came home with some sort of cold, and I refused to let him sleep with us because I didn't want Jake to contract whatever crud he'd picked up at the shelter. Michele slept on the couch with him on her chest for the first couple of nights until he got better. Duncan is a sleek, muscular cat and part Devon Rex. When we got him his coat was like straw—today, he's got the most unique and wonderful pattern and the softest fur, you'd almost think someone imprinted waves with a hot iron. Duncan is the alpha male in our household, and everyone knows it. He walks with a swagger, and is not one to be messed with—he will kick ass and take names. He is one feisty boy, but he's also got a sweet spot for us, and in some weird way, the other cats, too. He's more lenient with girl cats than boy cats, and when Chibi died, he desperately searched for her for weeks, walking around somberly and crying out loud. When he got a hold of one of her favorite blankets, he started dragging it around the house with him. What a softie, but shh, don't tell anyone. Duncan is 13 and recently diagnosed with IBD, though we're not sure about the diagnosis. Michele gives him steroids every day in a syringe, and he is stable and has actually gained back most of the weight he lost.

After Chibi passed, we were down to two with Jake and Duncan. They've grown up together, and it's been amazing watching them bond over the years. When they were younger, they'd tear ass around the house chasing each other and mixing it up, but as they've gotten older, we'll often find them in the same room, lounging on a bed together, sometimes even snuggling each other up. It wasn't until May 2017, when Michele started frequenting Woodbury Animal Shelter, the number of cats in our household mysteriously doubled—was Barbara Eden hiding behind one of our curtains blinking?

Michele wanted a little girl kitten, and a fresh litter had recently arrived at Woodbury. The cat she had her eye on was an orange and white tabby, and we were going to name her Henrietta. Michele's sister Kathi and our friend Wanda were at our house for the week, and we had just gotten home from a night in Connecticut after seeing Barry Manilow. We were all planning to go over to the shelter together, but Kathi wasn't feeling well. I thought it was best I take Kathi to urgent care, and Michele could pick up Henrietta. Here was my mistake and the lesson I've learned—NEVER let Michele go to the shelter alone!

As Kathi and I sat waiting in urgent care, I got the call. Michele informed me of two things. First, Henrietta was not a girl, and so we'd need to change his name to Henri (aka Henrick). Also, he didn't pay much attention to Michele, but his buff white brother was all over her. She asked me if we could have both. I said yes, but as soon as I hung up, I regretted my impulsive answer. I called back and told her four cats is a lot and we should discuss it further. "Too late, I'm already in the car," she said. She later admitted she lied about this—she was not in fact in the car yet. Sneaky.

Kathi actually named him for us. Archi (aka Archibald) made four. And we are certain these two new adoptees had different fathers—did you know it's possible for a female cat to get impregnated by more than one male cat in the same litter? We didn't. Anyway, today they are both sweet seven-year-old boys. Henri is one massive cat—part Maine Coon, with multiple layers of thick, gorgeous fur that he leaves behind in trails everywhere he goes. He's not a lap cat but has warmed up over the years. He loves lazing on his back in the sun in the picture window, which is where you'll typically find him on a sunny day. Henri's song is "Lovely Day" by Bill Withers—the sunlight doesn't bother his eyes. Archi is a short-haired buff and white handsome prince, and he's definitely a mama's boy, clingy beyond belief.

After hearing about how we arrived at four cats and my reservations about having so many, perhaps you're a little curious how we wound up with five. You may be assuming Michele convinced me on one of our trips back to Woodbury Animal Shelter. Your supposition would be good and completely logical, but you would be wrong. Well, at least partially. In a rare twist of events, I was the one who had a spell cast, as Etta James sang in "At Last."

It was August 2020, during the pandemic. We were dropping off donations of food and towels—with no further intentions. As we talked to the manager, my attention became suddenly transfixed on a little baby kitten crying her eyes out for me to come see her. My heart was captured, like Cupid shot his arrow through my chest. I asked the manager about her and received a hard no: "Not up for adoption." She told us Annie's story—

someone found her abandoned in a pile of leaves with a broken pelvis. She would need to be cage-bound for six weeks in an attempt to heal, and if it failed, complex surgery would be required.

We went home, and I couldn't get little Annie out of my mind. All I could hear was her trailing cry of agony as we walked out the door. Within a couple of weeks, the manager entrusted us to keep Annie in a cage at our home for the remainder of her time to heal. The manager had a spare dog cage we were able to borrow, and we set her up in my office. We renamed her, and this is where our love story with Cali (aka Calliope, which means "beautiful voice") began, as we nursed our first baby girl back to health for the next six weeks. I was working from home, so Cali had lots of company. Michele claims Cali got smarter than the average cat due to all the Zoom calls she participated in. Naturally, she was not happy about being in the cage and didn't understand why she couldn't be out playing with her brothers. The good news is the cats all adjusted to her, as she wasn't a threat to them under lock and key. We took her out of the cage twice a day during her healing process to clean the cage and let her run around in the bathroom a bit (she was under strict orders not to jump).

Finally the day arrived when Cali could be free. I was so nervous—I wasn't sure how she'd act or what trouble she'd get into in our large house unattended. We had nothing to worry about. No sooner did we open her cage than she followed us straight to our bedroom for the evening, and jumped (for the first time) onto the bed. She slept between us without moving the whole night, happy to be out of her prison. Cali is now a fully healed, bouncing, vibrant little four-year-old. The little princess of the household, she rules over her brothers and is the most special cat I've ever encountered.

How exactly does it feel to have five cats? In a word, chaotic. The cats own the place, and we just live here. I like to say the inmates are running the asylum. Would I change a thing? Absolutely never. I have found our cats to be the opposite of their stereotype. They are friendly and run to the door to greet us when we come home. They are typically loving, affectionate, and social. They're also comical, acrobatic, and fun to have around—our little Cali can fetch as well as any dog. Each has their own unique personality similar to siblings. They truly make our lives brighter, as Stevie Wonder would sing in "You Are the Sunshine of My Life." More than anything, they are part of our family, and we love them like our kids.

Oh by the way, did I mention we also have a bird? Yeah, just to keep things interesting.

# Chapter 50 - "Wonderful Tonight"

Earlier, I mentioned my youthful mantra of "work hard, play hard." I worked long hours, believing this was an effective strategy for gaining traction on the corporate ladder. In theory, I still buy in to this premise and subscribe to a time in life when you need to invest significant energy if you want to evolve in title and compensation. Coasting through the workweek works for some; it's just not in my DNA. I will always strive to give more than I get, because it goes beyond title or money—it results in fulfillment as well as a little (okay, maybe a lot of) pride. Still, I recognize I can't go at the same dogged pace I used to, and I've had to learn how to reel myself in so as not to burn out.

A time and place existed for the "play hard" side as well, and I have no regrets. I have wonderful memories and times to look back on; exciting and adventurous moments that have resulted in an endless sound bite of laughs. These memories come in handy on those not-so-easy days, and ultimately we should be able to enjoy the fruits of our labor, right? Michele and I have always liked to go on adventures and have fun. We have also come to love our home life together, and we've created a balance over the years. Recognizing that extremes begin to block out other important facets, I see how it's important to create space to explore other parts of our life and ourselves.

Travel is a constant on our priority list. In addition to the islands already mentioned, we've thoroughly enjoyed our trips to Aruba, Turks and Caicos, Bermuda, and the Dominican Republic. Both of us are fond of tropical weather, white sand beaches, and azure seas. Our favorite is Aruba, where we've vacationed a number of times. We've come to prefer the low-rise section as opposed to the crowd-filled buzziness of the high-rise area, and love our stays at Manchebo Beach Resort with its excellent service, great food, and chill vibe. Nothing like living under a palapa on Eagle Beach for a week with a bucket of Balashis by your side!

For anyone who hasn't been to Aruba, I'll share why we've tagged it as our favorite. The weather is consistently hot, but there's always a breeze by the water, which provides some respite. It's one of the few tropical islands where you don't have to wrangle around hurricane season—something about the location keeps the island at relatively low risk of extreme weather conditions. It does rain at times, but it's rarely abundant or even distracting. The island as a whole is safe, and we feel comfortable taking public transportation and car service anywhere on the island. Aruba has one of the lowest crime rates, unlike places we've traveled where tourists are strongly discouraged from going places on their own. Interesting places to explore occupy the island, and the tax-free jewelry stores are an added plus. Most of all, it's the warm and hospitable Aruban people who make us want to return.

On our last trip in late 2023, I surprised Michele with a sunset dinner for two on the beach at Matthew's, a restaurant a short walk from the resort. Moments like these I cherish most—spending quality time with the woman I love, away from the busyness of everyday life. My wife is a beautiful person inside and out, and I'm reminded of the love poem by Eric Clapton, "Wonderful Tonight"—I'm in constant fascination by this beautiful lady walking around with me.

In addition to our island trips, we've made it a habit to return to our wedding destination. P-Town is the most comfortable place for us as a couple. I'm not insinuating we don't feel comfortable or safe other places, and we certainly don't go walking around in life constantly looking over our shoulders. For the most part, we go about life much like any heterosexual couple, which is all we want to do. Whether or not someone understands or agrees with our lifestyle is their decision; we are simply seeking the same comfort and rights as everyone else. What P-Town offers is a greater-than-average level of acceptance. You can feel it as you stroll down the street, enter a restaurant, or walk into a bar. I can't recall ONE time someone gave Michele and me a second glance, which is the progress we are looking for everywhere else. We want to blend in—we're not trying to stand out.

We live for certain aspects of P-Town when we go. While we've stayed at several places, our go-to resort is The Boatslip. It's right on the water and offers a waterfront view of their sprawling deck. During the summer, we sometimes rent a cabana and hang there for the day, eventually making our way up to our room in the late afternoon. Several times each week, The Boatslip's deck gets converted into a massive party extravaganza, where their legendary tea dance takes place. According to Wikipedia, tea dances originated in New York in the '50s and '60s. The events, held on Sunday afternoons, catered to the gay population as an opportunity for singles to meet. At the time, it was a safe, alternative place to meet where the patrons would not be subject to raids or arrest. They served tea because it was illegal at the time for a gay person to be served alcohol (I know, right?). At today's tea dances, they are obviously different, with more being served than tea. The nod to our past certainly shows how far we've come, and I appreciate the tradition. Michele and I love observing the whole affair from our balcony, where we can look over all the festivities and take in the sounds, sights, and spectacles. The vibe is palpable as DJ Maryalice spins her tunes like a plate-juggling acrobat.

On most evenings in P-Town, we enjoy a superb meal at one of several restaurants we frequent. After dinner, we typically partake in one of the many drag shows taking place at popular venues like The Art House, Post Office Café & Cabaret, Crown & Anchor, or Pilgrim House. Since attending our first drag show the year we wed, we've seen several shows. I've gained a strong affinity for how these entertainers transform themselves; they're some of the most talented professionals I've ever seen. I need to give appropriate mention to the catalyst who brought the drag queen population and culture into the mainstream: the iconic RuPaul. Another prominent influence was the show *Pose*, created by Ryan Murphy, which explores the ball culture and drag houses. The level of admiration I have toward the population is one of the highest of respect and gratitude. I love the freedom of expression realized through these fabulous individuals—we always have a blast attending the shows and being around the welcoming culture. As RuPaul sang in "Supermodel (You Better Work)," sashay, shantay.

Of course we've also traveled to Florida a fair amount, with the primary purpose of spending time with Michele's family. We've parlayed these trips into multiple adventures to Disney as well as Key West. One year we attended Gay Days at Disney, welcomed by a sea of red shirts making us feel completely at home (it didn't hurt that it was also Star Wars weekend at Hollywood Studios!). At Key West we had our first encounter with polydactyls, the legendary six-toed cats at The Hemingway Home. We also attended our first gay pride event in St. Pete's, which was a lot of fun and gave us a chance to unite with our community. St. Pete's has gone through substantial development in recent years, and we've enjoyed walking around the area and having dinner on the pier—just "Give Me the Night," sang George Benson. A place to dine, a glass of wine, perfection!

Finding excitement doesn't always require getting on a plane or traveling out of the state. Michele and I have made multiple trips into New York City to soak in the city that never sleeps. When our out-of-town family visits, we take them in to see the sights that never get old for us, either. When it's just the two of us, we typically go to dinner and a fabulous Broadway show or concert at our favorite venue, MSG . The Bee Gees sang it best in "Nights on Broadway"—I can't stay away. MSG simply possesses an indescribable energy and vibe unlike any other venue. Like Joe Jackson's "Steppin' Out," we love to get into a car and drive to the other side.

We also enjoy equal periods of quiet and tranquility at home, especially in our backyard. We've continued to create a place where we feel we can escape the monotony without getting in a car. Our home has given us refuge during illness, a pandemic, and times when we just need to unplug from the level of crazy going on in this world. It's all about the balance.

# Chapter 51 - "Roar"

I have a great deal of admiration for divas. According to Wikipedia, "diva" is the Latin word for goddess, often used to refer to a celebrated woman of outstanding talent in opera, theater, cinema, fashion, or popular music. A negative connotation can get attached to a diva as well, for being demanding or temperamental. I see the diva as a fierce, bold, ambitious woman who knows what she wants and goes after it. While I do not consider myself a diva, over the course of my life I've looked to certain celebrity figures to draw inspiration from, watching from afar in wonderment at their achievements. I could cite many, but for brevity I'll focus on two.

The first is Aretha Franklin. The "Queen of Soul" had an instantly recognizable gospel-driven quality to her voice matched by no one. While many of her attributes are worth admiring, nothing greater exists in my opinion than the movement she created with the song "Respect." With a singular song, she carved a path for millions of women to find and hold their space in the world. For years and years, women have had to fight and climb mightily toward being viewed equal to men. I'm about to piss off a whole boatload of fellow Catholics, but it probably started with the story of Adam and Eve. Woman was supposedly created in man's likeness with a rib, and we have been playing second fiddle ever since. The thing is, how do we know for certain God is a man? We may all be in for a huge surprise! Either way, I can't come up with one legitimate reason why a woman (or anyone) should not have a chance for an equal path in this world. R-E-S-P-E-C-T, baby. Even more admirable than her heavenly voice was her advocacy for civil and women's rights. Rest in peace, dear woman—you were and always will be a legend.

The second mention should be no surprise—my awe for Barbra Streisand continues to be unparalleled. Beyond her immense talent, how she projects and carries herself within the world impresses me most. Similar to Aretha, she has been an advocate and philanthropist toward many important causes, including equality, civil rights, women's rights, and the environment, and made a huge impact by using her grandstand to effect positive change. Most of us may have a whole bunch of opinions about a lot of things (including me), but if we believe strongly in something, what are we doing about it? I'm trying to evolve myself to make the smallest difference while I still have an opportunity. I guess in some ways this book may be my initiation. Let's see what I can tackle, and it's okay if someone doesn't agree—I only request they "Don't Rain on my Parade."

I still have a long way to go, so reaching diva status may take some time, but as it relates to my career, I feel I've accomplished a lot. As Chrissie Hynde sang in The Pretenders song, "Middle of the Road," it's trying to find me. When I reflect back over the genesis of my career and growing the foundations, I recognize where and how all the hard work paid off. I got promoted to director of operations in 2015, and spent the next year plus as the lead facilitator of the Hampshire organization's integrated business operation project. We performed a wholesale evaluation of our structure, process, and people to meet the needs of our strategy. My experiences from the years before put me in the position to take this on, and it became the biggest project I'd ever faced. It was massive and intimidating at times, but I learned a lot about myself. Certain aspects I wish I'd handled differently, but it became a building block of growth, and the organization was able to march on with the structure needed.

Over the next several years, I focused on operational excellence, continuing to evolve efficiencies around the company. Actually at its core, that's my career mission, and it always will be. It is never a complete work because strategy shifts, external conditions change, and we need to bend, flex, and adapt. The work done starting in 2015 led to the rise to the role I'm currently in. In 2018, I became a member of the senior leadership team, and in 2022 was promoted to chief administrative officer and EVP of operations. As No Doubt sang in the upbeat song, these advances were "Hella Good." But I've also learned as a person ascends in title, so grows the associated responsibility, and we need to accept the whole package with open arms to have any credibility. It requires asking ourselves, *A title or chance at advancement in compensation sounds great on the surface, but am I willing to accept what comes with the territory?*

Circling back to equality between men and women, I consider myself fortunate I work for a company that is equality-forward; as a matter of fact, more women sit around our senior leadership table than men. People I've interviewed have commented on this as something refreshing, especially compared to what they typically encounter. This makes me proud, and I'm glad to be a part of it. It aligns perfectly with who I am as a person—the core values of this company match with those I seek to embody.

In this current chapter of my career, my focus has been around growing and coaching the next generation of leadership, instilling the culture, advancing operational efficiency, and leaving the imprint of my legacy. I'm incredibly proud of the teams I work with most closely, and they are the best part of my workday. I've also enjoyed joining Chief, a powerful network of executive women. Everyone needs peers to lean on and seek counsel from, and I've found in my core group, a peer board of advisors, we give this gift to one another. Over the last couple of months, I've also taken on an interim assignment of chief financial officer while we go through a transition. This has led to further growth, stretch, and opportunity, and I will never turn away a chance to do so. I can't sit back and stay idle. I'm reminded of the great tune by Katy Perry—times like this require me to be louder than a lion—hear me "Roar!"

# Chapter 52 - "Roadhouse Blues"

Since Betsy, the combination of my car and music has continued breeding perfect harmony in my world. While I can enjoy
music anywhere, in my wheels I experience an otherworldly
presence. It's my private sanctuary. I'm reminded of the song
"Synchronicity II" by The Police—it feels as if this unintended
connection occurred by happenstance, for me. Initially, my
car meant freedom, signifying a rite of passage to adulthood.
Those first years driving in Betsy were legendary and will
never be forgotten. As mentioned, I eventually totaled the
poor girl, which left me in a bit of a conundrum since I needed
to commute to Seton Hall five days a week. As Kenny Loggins
nailed in the movie *Top Gun*, I had fallen right into the "Danger
Zone." Thankfully, Pop sprang into action and bought me my
first new car. He had a method to his madness, and he taught
me about financial responsibility at the same time. The deal
was, he'd pay for half the car outright, but for the other half
I'd need to get a loan and pay it off myself. Friggin' genius. He
offered me a critical glimpse into adult issues while displaying
the power of giving at the same time.

For my first new car, I decided upon a Toyota Celica. It was
the first year of the infamous bubble shape redesign and had
recently emerged onto the auto scene. I am not a mechanical

person—I can't even pump my own gas, since I grew up in NJ and we are spoiled pooches. Thank God there's an old-time gas station in Goshen with employees who pump or I'd be screwed (guess I could learn). Lack of mechanical ability aside, I do consider myself a car person, and it started with my Celica. Black, sleek, and fast, the little car made a statement. Cue the heart-pounding, fist-pumping song, "Kickstart My Heart," by my boys in Mötley Crüe—I get high on speed. It was the one time I got personalized plates. CHER 90 was a force to be reckoned with out on the road.

My obsession grew into wanting something better every time, and I still always go for the shiniest penny on the lot. Practical safety considerations and reliability with the amount of miles I travel are important, but I have to be honest: I've turned into a car snob. Look, my styles are typically basic. I like LL Bean, Lands' End, Eddie Bauer, and a comfy pair of HEYDUDES. But when it comes to my ride, I want what I want. As George Thorogood twanged, "Move It On Over" so I can zip on by in the fast lane.

The Toyota Celica is a great car; especially great for a 19-year-old, but it didn't have all the bells and whistles I seek out today. I have a long commute, so my list of desired features is long to match: all-wheel drive, power everything, leather heated and cooled seats, a voice-activated system, all-weather mats, a large user-friendly navigation screen, ambient and welcome lighting, automatic lift back, and of course, a kick-ass stereo system. Failure to show me a car with my diva list of requirements will result in the salesperson not standing a chance. I'm sure they don't see me coming, but they will catch on quickly, as Alanis Morissette warned in "You Oughta Know." *Hmm.* Maybe I actually am a diva, but only as it relates to my car. Mostly.

I dig a luxury car. I've had Acuras, Infinitis, and Lincolns. I'm in a Lincoln zone right now, and I recently had the good fortune to purchase the 2024 Nautilus. OMG. This car has a huge command center, and the whole dashboard is one giant screen (which I use safely). It's off the chain, and certain details in this car elevate the experience higher than any car I've had. It even has a digital scent, with these tiny little cartridges you put in the center console that diffuse on demand. Yeah, I'm definitely a diva.

To perfect the experience, I set myself up with multiple music options, including a SiriusXM subscription, so I can program channels as diverse as my musical tastes and tailor my ride based upon what I'm feeling in the moment. I also rely heavily upon Apple Music. I'm probably annoying between the variety of choices coupled with my incessant singing. I don't apologize for it; actually, I'm happy as a clam in my little introverted bubble. This is probably why I'm better alone in my vehicle—not sure how many could handle my tendencies. As The Doors sang in "Roadhouse Blues," I'm good as long as I keep my eye on the road and my hands on the wheel.

When I inform people how far I commute, they cringe and say, "how awful." But it's not awful to me at all. Oh sure, I hate traffic jams as much as the next guy, and honestly a lot of people are not deserving to be in a driver's seat. It makes me dream of jumping out of the car and wreaking havoc on the car behaving badly, kind of like Carrie Underwood in "Before He Cheats"—let me take a Louisville Slugger to both headlights. Or perhaps I can subscribe to one of the methods AC/DC identifies in "Dirty Deeds Done Dirt Cheap." Cyanide? Just kidding. Aside from these moments, I've come to appreciate my rides tremendously. On the way to the office, I can mentally prepare myself for the day ahead. On days when I have a complex problem to address or a major presentation, I'll sort through it and brainstorm or practice my verbiage.

For the return home, my ride provides time and space to unwind. I'm so singularly focused on work, not stopping for a minute while operating at top speed. I spend the day wrestling down a million different items from the largest to the most mundane, and though I wouldn't have it any other way, it takes a lot to transition and relax. I'm not sure I ever truly fully get there. Hence, I need every single minute of the car ride home to at least attempt some decompression. Michele usually still has to deal with the aftereffects when I fly through the door. Thankfully she takes most of it in stride, and I appreciate the gentle reminder from her to signal I'm no longer at work.

Over the years, I think I've turned Michele into a car perfectionist, also. Her style is a bit different from mine, and right now she's driving a loaded Ford Bronco, which is a sweet set of wheels. Unlike me, though, Michele actually has some mechanical inclination, and I bet if she set her mind to it, she could do her own maintenance. Due to our location, which gets harsh weather in winter, we both have AWD vehicles, but each of us longs to own a sports car. For me, it would be a brand-new Corvette, and she would opt for a classic Camaro from the '70s. For now it's a dream, but if and when it happens, our diva status may become undisputed.

# Chapter 53 - "Livin' on the Edge"

I don't believe the pandemic was the origination of the crazy, but it certainly blew the cap off. The term "spontaneous combustion" comes to mind. In reality, we've been heading in this direction for years, but it feels as if we've reached the point of no return. Much of what I observe is a non-accepting, intolerant, selfish, and extreme society centered around a lack of understanding and compassion. How the hell did we get here? Aerosmith called it years ago. We weren't listening then, and we certainly ain't listening now—we're "Livin' on the Edge" and something's really wrong.

Probably much like many others, I was in denial about the severity of the pandemic in the beginning. We went about our days leading up to it not listening closely enough to prepare for what was coming, and we failed to consider taking better precautions. In hindsight, I believe I was exposed to it in late January 2020—yes, that early. Michele and I had met up for dinner with a few friends, two of whom were coming off what appeared to be a bad cold or flu. Within a week or so, I began getting the strangest sinus symptoms, bothering me so much I went to urgent care. I probably wouldn't have gone, but Linda was turning 50 and I didn't want to miss her bash. It was mid-February, prior to the real madness, so no COVID test was taken. They provided me some antibiotics and sent me on my way.

The week before the world shut down, rather than paying attention to news reports about the growing certainty of a pandemic, I was more concerned the 2020 NCAA men's basketball tournament had gotten canceled, and my beloved Pirates run was over before it began. We'd had such an amazing year, and our prospects were high. This goes to illustrate my own level of ignorance and imperfection—none of us are immune to being part of the problem, and most of the time we barely realize it. At work, we had a Friday happy hour for one of our associates who was leaving, and the following week, shit got real.

The next few weeks were a flurry of uncertainty as my company was trying to navigate how our staff could effectively work from home. This was new territory, since we worked in the office five days a week, save the occasional workday from home due to a personal emergency or illness. At the time, most didn't have laptops—the majority of the staff used desktops, which led to a lot of time spent ensuring everyone's home laptops had appropriate protections. The one upside was we have always been a Microsoft shop and already had Teams installed. We snapped into action and started creating our communication center around this powerful tool, and so began our evolution into working remotely for the next 18 to 24 months.

I am proud of how proactively we responded to address the multitude of items in the span of a few weeks. Over the next month, we formalized our business continuity plan, created a safety committee, and began a conversion to company-issued laptops. In a lot of ways, we were forced to analyze our use of technology, and it propelled us to evolve faster than we would have otherwise. It led to creation of sophisticated workflows to handle financial reporting and other key processes requiring an audit trail and multiple signoffs. I think we cemented as a senior leadership team in a stronger way during this time, as we were all working in unison, trying to address a whole host of sensitivities. This period led to greater flexibility and redefined how we work, an important aspect for employee health and balance.

Though I was working fully remotely, Michele was going into the office every day, as her job responsibilities were considered essential. Michele took it all in stride, recognizing it was her obligation, but I was nervous for her. At the time we weren't clear if the recommended precautions would be enough, given the magnitude of people dying in hospitals. Michele and I were both healthy, but we are both asthmatic and thus considered higher risk. Despite the uncertainty, I watched in admiration as Michele dutifully performed her job working for the epidemiology division with the Orange County Health Department.

A lot of downsides to the pandemic probably don't need to be mentioned—death, permanent chronic symptoms, fear, isolation, mental health consequences, and a further rift in our society. It was hard losing loved ones, such as John McMurray, who passed away right when the pandemic started. We couldn't properly mourn a person's death, making it harder than it already is.

Still, I took away some positives from this period of time. We were forced to slow down, which enabled a beautiful realization of the simple things in life; the mundane things we often overlook yet are most important. We live most of our lives "Under Pressure," as David Bowie and Queen described, and this period of time asked us to give love one more chance. While Michele and I worked long hours, our spare time was spent enjoying each other's company, spending time with our fur babies, and appreciating the elements of our home life. In the spring and summer months, I paid more attention to the myriad flowers and colorful bushes blooming on our property, walking around every weekend to post pictures on Instagram. As Styx sang to us back in the '80s, it reminded me "The Best of Times" are when I'm alone with her.

In addition to strengthening my bond with Michele and other important relationships, this time gave me the ability to turn the spotlight on myself. I immersed myself in a long period of reflection and was able to critically examine my balance in all the facets of life. That word—balance—is something I'd contemplated for years, and I knew enough to realize when things were off. During the pandemic, I was able to make the necessary adjustments and invest in elements of my physical, mental, and spiritual well-being that I'd never completely succeeded at doing before. I began carving more time into my morning ritual for prayer, reflection, and meditation. I took a pause at lunchtime to walk around the neighborhood, which was good for my physical health and reduced the feeling of isolation. While I don't promote any aspect of the devastation that occurred during this time, I did make the best I could of the circumstances. As Poison sang, I needed "Something to Believe In" and tried to take the high road as much as I could when it seemed very easy to fall apart.

Another unintended result of this reflection was becoming more observant of things going on around me. I've joked multiple times about the singular bubble I often get trapped in (actually, I don't feel trapped at all, which is part of the problem, because it's everyone else around me who's left feeling I'm somewhere else instead of with them). The bubble still exists and always will, but I began questioning more about the world and what was going on around us. I wasn't happy with the findings of my analysis—it was actually petrifying. I guess the trick is to be aware without getting too sucked in, because it would be easy to jump on the "Crazy Train" along with Ozzy Osbourne and everyone else on board. Anyway, back to *what has happened to us as a society?* I certainly don't understand all the root causes or how to go about fixing them. All I know is how certain things make me feel.

Divisiveness and extremes are scary to me, and I think most of us can see them playing out in our politics, religions, and culture. On the political spectrum, extremes on both sides are unhealthy, causing chaos, making the most noise, and overtaking the media. The disruptors create further division, unhinged from reality and somehow causing too many to blindly follow along. The leaders of our country seem to be more focused around being "right" than on how to heal and bring us back together. We need a true leader desperately right now—the person who can see down the middle and get us united. WHERE ARE YOU?

I'm scared for humanity, in addition to myself and my loved ones, and the number of terrorist and violent attacks are unacceptable. The campaign seeking to reverse our basic human rights and equality is dangerous and horrifying, jeopardizing our very democracy. As a gay married woman, I feel our community is under attack, which saddens and angers me. Also a word on immigration: I agree it's a huge mess. I also acknowledge that were it not for immigration, hardly any of us would be living in America.

I know these statements are going to cause a stir, and I've spent most of my life carefully treading away from anything controversial in this regard. In the past, I've discussed hotbed issues with only a small handful of people because I never want things to get argumentative. On social media, I steer away from these topics and instead choose to focus on non-controversial subject matter. I've seen what these conversations can do to relationships and am not sure it's worth it. But I'm exhausted by all of it.

I'm leaning more heavily toward the Democratic party at the moment, but until four years ago, I was unaffiliated and never wanted to declare a party. Why? Because I believe in finding the right person for the job, not blindly following either party into the vast unknown. However, at this moment, the threats to basic humanity and social freedoms are something I cannot and will not ignore. When the Republican party can produce the person who is willing to stand up to right-winged extremists, I will gladly cast my vote if they are the best person for the job. I see no one willing to take a stand. We can't help ourselves from falling.

## TRUE FREEDOM

No creature lives as freely as I do.

Standing fearlessly on this perch of paradise-
  It strikes me as odd so many
  Fail to realize.

I have full reign o'er the water below-

Endless and vast are my sources
Of survival.

Honestly there is nothing finer than this spot.

The rays of the burning sphere shining upon me

The cool breeze caressing my fragile warrior headdress

The shadows of the volcanic monster hovering as protection

Every so often one of those strange creatures
   Who walks on two limbs–
   But can not fly–
   Invades my privacy.

I never fear – they seem to pay me no mind.
   When they do, I can soar away.

There is no end to the beauty surrounding me–

I may go for a short ride over the sea
   But I always return.
   Watch me soar.

# V

# PART FIVE

**AIR GUITAR RULE #5** – *Still hesitating to get started? It's simple. Just play like no one is watching.*

# Chapter 54 - "Piece of My Heart"

March 1, 2021. I entered the month filled with hope and anticipation. The winter slog would soon be behind us, and a buzz filled the air indicating that warmer weather might relax the heaviness of quarantine we'd been trapped in over the past year. I was still holding on to the positives picked up along the way, but for those of us up North, the winter months have a way of emphasizing the feeling of isolation in a good year, so coupled with the pandemic, winter was brutal.

I missed seeing Mom. I missed seeing our family. I missed seeing our friends. I missed my work community. I didn't suffer from Zoom fatigue like many were experiencing, but it was time to return to some normalcy. Michele and I were discussing whether we might finally be able to have a few people over for Easter. The last holiday we'd spent with anyone was in December of 2019. Maybe we'd even be able to head down to Fort Myers in June. A turn for the better was definitely approaching . . .

March 2, 2021. The day started similar to most. I worked through the morning, then prepared to get in my car to head to Basking Ridge for my routine mammogram at Sloan Kettering. I thought about canceling. Routine medical appointments still felt a bit iffy to me since the pandemic. Maybe reschedule when it's warmer weather? A domineering voice took over: *No Cheryll. Absolutely not. You know you cannot cancel. Not this one. You need to keep your peace of mind. You know better.*

I did know better. I'd had a run-in with breast cancer back in 2010. I had Stage 0 DCIS (ductal carcinoma in situ) in my left breast, which basically translates to "it was caught early and was contained within the breast." Despite this treatable diagnosis, it's impossible to underestimate the emotional and mental turmoil. I think nothing is more frightening or mind-fucking than hearing the words "You have cancer." Your knee-jerk reaction is "I'm dying," before you even learn the complete picture. For me, it tugged on my deepest hidden fears after losing loved ones to various forms of cancer. I will never forget the moment I first heard Dr. Kim, my gynecologist, say them to me over the phone.

We were in the middle of a major snowstorm, and I was at Michele's house in Otisville, and she was out shoveling. Dr. Kim didn't mince words; though she is one of the most caring and empathetic doctors I've ever had, it was the hardest thing I ever had to hear. In a few short directives, Dr. Kim (Angel #1) sent me in a direction and it ultimately proved to save my life. In those next moments, she recommended Dr. Capko (Angel #2) from Memorial Sloan Kettering and assured me I would get through this. I was devastated. I hung up the phone, opened the front door, and locked eyes with Michele. She knew by my expression something was very wrong. Cue "Oceano" by Josh Groban—my heart was sinking.

I got through the lumpectomy and recovery followed by five weeks of radiation without fanfare. It was no walk in the park, but my body tolerated everything well. I was tired, though not from the radiation; rather, from having to make daily visits to

Basking Ridge on top of a full workday. I was relieved to have it behind me, and felt incredibly fortunate to have Dr. Capko as my surgical oncologist and the support of the rest of the team in the MSK office.

This explains why I couldn't cancel the appointment on March 2, 2021. A permanent psychological response occurs when you've had cancer, and you are constantly looking over your shoulder. You also never get to the true answer of "why did this happen to me?" which drives you slowly mad. I dreaded every mammogram I had, yet I'd never not prioritized it. Here's why: EARLY DETECTION SAVES LIVES. It is an indisputable fact. Please do not ever delay a routine mammogram (or any other routine critical preventative visit), ever. The slightest delay can be a matter of life and death. If you think I'm being melodramatic, too bad. I have to be bullish on this because my circumstances will not allow anything less. If it helps, I will soften it: Pretty please.

My visit turned into the same drill as always. Waiting. They called me in for the first round of images. Waiting. Dr. Aboody (Angel # 3) looked at them, and they called me back in for more images. Waiting. Dr. Aboody looked at them and they called me back for ultrasound images. Nothing to this point is out of the ordinary, until it is. Dr. Aboody came flying into the ultrasound room looking harried. Something was gnawing at her about the right breast; the slightest nuance or differential she wasn't comfortable about. The challenge with me was always the density of my breasts. It's a common issue for many women, and it complicates things, making it more difficult for the professional team to evaluate and assess what may be lurking underneath. Had it not been for Dr. Aboody's persistence and thoroughness, I'm certain you wouldn't be reading this right now.

Dr. Aboody ordered a needle biopsy, and I knew something was amiss—I had a sudden guttural, intuitive, sensory feeling. The doctors and team at Sloan Kettering know their shit. I knew from Dr. Aboody's reaction she was on to something, because she had been looking at my images for the last 11 years. Problem was, it turned out to be many somethings.

The needle biopsy resulted in a shit ton of bleeding. I drove home, and as I got out of the car, I realized the blood had permeated through my bandages onto my shirt. I called Michele, and she told our friend Heather (Angel #4) who is a nurse. Still panicked, I called Sloan. The nurse practitioner at Sloan instructed me to apply pressure, and asked me if I had fresh gauze to change the bandages on top of the steri-strips. When I removed the top layer, it was like a scene out of the *Texas Chainsaw Massacre.* Blood spraying out everywhere. All over the bed; all over the floor. I'm like, "Oh God, I think I'm going to pass out . . . "

I was convinced I was bleeding to death. I wasn't. Not even close. I was exaggerating. In my fear, I called the ambulance. They found me topless, slumped on the floor in my entry hallway, pressing firmly on my breast for dear life. Heather arrived around the same time. What a crazy scene. The paramedics had to think I was absolutely bonkers. In the moment they were probably right. They asked me to let go, and I realized the bleeding had stopped after my vice grip press. They asked me if I wanted to put a shirt on. *Oh yeah, okay.* I never realized I was an exhibitionist!

After the bloodbath, I painstakingly waited for the results. I got the call from Dr. Aboody, and for the second time in my life, I heard the words that make you feel like someone is jabbing your soul and trying to suck out your essence. This time it was a whopper. I had three different locations in my right breast; one of them an aggressive form referred to as triple negative. Dr. Aboody was leaning toward multiple lumpectomy and radiation as treatment with a possibility of chemotherapy; however, as a precaution she wanted to have an MRI biopsy performed on both sides. Thank God for Dr. Aboody; her instincts are beyond measure. The additional biopsy revealed I had cancer on the left side as well. *Shit.*

The challenge with the left side was I had already had radiation, and they can't re-radiate. The treatment course went from clear to muddled in a heartbeat as the cards were stacking up against me. The best course of action, it was determined, was to remove the left breast, and coupled with the totality of issues on the right, my decision became clear. I talked it through with Michele and Mom, as well as the Sloan team. It was resolved—I'd be getting a double mastectomy. As Kenny Loggins crooned, "This Is It"—make no mistake where you are.

May 5, 2021. Cinco de Mayo and Dr. Capko's birthday. The day I lost both of my breasts. Janis Joplin the legend sang "Piece of My Heart"—just take it. I remember telling Dr. Capko to have a margarita; she had certainly earned it. This particular surgery was hard, as more so than the obvious, because I was alone since no visitors were allowed in the hospital. It turned out fine and the surgery was a total success.

Thank God for Heather; she helped Michele and me with the drains, which was in my view the worst part of the experience. You already know my reaction to blood, so yeah, anything coming out of body orifices freaks me the fuck out. The first couple of weeks was no fun, but I got stronger every day. I was also incredibly thankful the cancer was not in my lymph nodes—we had caught it before the point of no return. Everyone was so incredibly supportive—the medical team, Michele, Mom, family, friends, and my work family—all made the journey feel like a community experience. Echoing Bette Midler, they were the "Wind Beneath My Wings."

Once I had fully recovered from surgery, the seemingly endless process of chemotherapy commenced, followed by the more seemingly endless process of herceptin treatments. I met Dr. Gorsky, my fifth angel and oncologist, a no-nonsense woman who is kind and caring with her patients. But damn, it's a long haul, and you begin to feel as if the hell you are in will never end. You can only deal with it one day at a time. If you ever find yourself in this predicament, which I would never wish on anyone, here are my words. First, put on your fucking armor—you are going to need it. You need every single ounce of resolve and courage, and trust me, it is all there inside you. Having loving people around you to help support you is amazing and affirming. More than anything, it comes down to you and your attitude. Are you going to crumble up like a ball or fight this motherfucker? Because that's all it is—an EVIL, SOULLESS, MOTHERFUCKER. *You*, however, have the heart and soul and the will to live, and it is just trying to trick you into thinking it has the final say—it does not. You do. Listen to everything your doctors tell you to do. Ask tons of questions, because knowledge is power. Talk to people you love about what you're going through and try never to bottle it up. If you feel more comfortable talking to people outside your circle, all cancer centers have support groups and therapists to help. Get ready for the fight of your life—you got this. Take it one day at a time, and you will make it out the other side.

I got through by doubling-down on certain practices to keep me sane—prayer, meditation, reflection. I kept working to keep my mind occupied, and fortunately I have an amazingly understanding team at Hampshire. I'm not one to easily ask for help, but I leaned on Michele and loved ones for support when I needed it. I was able to continue my full remote work situation until my chemo was over. I could have kept working remote through the rest of the herceptin treatment, but I decided it was time to try to create some normal in my life.

My treatments started in early June 2021 and went on for a year, with chemo and herceptin treatments every three weeks. It's hard to explain how many different nuances are involved, and truthfully, it seems you block out most things once they're behind you. In my case I got a surgical port, because it was advised that after a while, sticking needles in your arms becomes a challenge, and also, removing lymph nodes leads to a greater chance of infection or lymphedema. I hated that port; the annoying protrusion above where my left breast used to be was a daily reminder of my illness, but it was a necessary evil.

The herceptin treatment has the potential to impact your heart, so I had to go to a cardiologist every three months for echocardiograms. Additionally, my white blood count was low during most of my chemo, so I had a neulasta shot, which would automatically inject itself into my arm 24 hours after treatment. I had a total of eight chemo treatments and 17 herceptin treatments. Overall, my body handled everything well. I never lost my hair and never vomited. I felt like shit on certain days after my treatment, but in comparison to others, I was darn lucky. Many people have a much harder road in life than I know I ever will.

Still, it's hard when you start losing body parts. I remember feeling a certain depression after my partial hysterectomy in 2007; a part of me was gone, and though I never had children, I still felt a sense of loss. After I lost my breasts, mostly I was thankful my life was spared. It took a lot of time and healing to feel confident about my image and myself in some respects. My boobs had been a part of me for my whole life, and they were no longer. I made the decision to stay flat. Dr. Capko worked with the cosmetic surgeon, Dr. Allen, to keep things looking "neat," with no other enhancement surgery to recreate new breasts.

This is a personal choice and one only the patient can make. In my case, after listening carefully to all the options, I felt like my body had endured enough, and I didn't think further complications and surgery was in my best interest. I was done with surgery relating to my breasts. When I was done, I wanted to move on and leave it in the rear view. I'm certain I made the best choice for me. I'm not going to sugarcoat—it takes a lot of getting used to. The constant numbness and physical aspect of what you're used to takes a lot of courage to squash. My body will never be the same. I remind myself daily that what's inside hasn't changed, which is what matters.

June 1, 2022. Port removal day. Holy mother of God, what a relief. I was pushing to make sure it got done, so I could get the darn bleeping thing out of my body, and we could go enjoy Fort Myers in peace. It was our first trip post-COVID and would be the first time seeing our sisters since November 2019. Too long. It was truly a celebration. Time to rebuild.

The rebuilding is easier said than done. The physical aspects of going through a double mastectomy and treatment are grueling. You physically don't feel like yourself throughout, and at times you wonder if you'll ever feel the same. Once treatment is over, achingly slowly, over time, you do begin to feel better. You start to believe you can move on. You begin to block out the physical elements—as I was writing, I had to ask Michele how many chemo treatments I had, and actually had to look it up.

But. This is so much more than a physical thing. I spent the next seven months, throughout the rest of 2022, trying to crawl my way back into life. I felt an overwhelming sense of loss, roaming around this earth like a nomad with no home. It felt ridiculous. I have a loving wife, family, and friends. It's not something I can explain. I literally had just climbed a mountain, and I was so grateful to be alive, and yet I wasn't myself anymore.

The pre-mastectomy me was gone, and in a lot of respects, I think I had to recreate who I was. The mental and emotional baggage of this thing lingered like an albatross around my neck. I couldn't shake it or figure out what to do about it. As a strongly wired thinking introvert, I can reason my way through anything and talk myself back into good form without any trouble. For this, I had no answers; just a blank page in my brain. Michele knew something was wrong, but I couldn't confide in her, because I didn't even understand it myself. She kept asking me, "Are we okay?" to which I'd reply "Yes, it's just me—I'm trying to figure it out." Later on in reflection, I'd say to myself "Figure out what, you asshole?" Brandi Carlile reminds me in "Right on Time"—I almost lost her in those silent days. Thank God Michele is the amazing woman she is; she was so patient with me.

## WAITING FOR THE STRONGER ME

Somewhere exists
   the stronger version
   of the person I am today

I've witnessed her
   in fleeting moments
   as remnants drifted away

We prayed together
   awaiting test results

We listened together
   grasping comprehension

We talked together
   sharing what became our truth

She was there when I lay
   in the hallway carelessly bleeding

She was there when I lay
   in the scan room shallowly breathing

She was there when I lay
   in the operating room parts forever leaving

We healed together
   watching the hours days months stall

We struggled together
  seeing a new reflection stare back

We persevered together
  recognizing the worst was behind

She was there from day one
  She was there through it all
  She was there . . . but where is she now?

# Chapter 55 - "Live Like We're Dying"

The fog lifted on its own, and by the beginning of 2023, I realized the "Dog Days Are Over" while Florence & The Machine echoed in the background—here come the horses! While I couldn't explain the blur of the last seven months, I was just happy it was gone, and I suddenly had a renewed sense of inspiration. A lot of this probably had to do with my year-end ritual of goal-setting. I've been doing it for years and consider it an opportunity to wipe the slate clean and begin anew. I realize the whole concept of setting New Year's resolutions may be overplayed, but for me it's not about one thing; it's about all the things. It comes back to the one word I am always seeking to master: BALANCE.

I do this planning the last week of the year, before the ball drops. I'm thankful Hampshire closes the office between Christmas and New Year, which allows me to clear my head and prepare my plan. I give appropriate due to celebrate the big accomplishments from the prior year, along with a valuation of the learned lessons—as opposed to failure, I focus on opportunities. I boil down my year into three main themes based on words that resonate with me from the previous year (last year's were health, balance, and relationships), and this is my pool to draw from to set my stage for the coming year based on what is working well and can be built upon, and what needs to be different.

The next part of the process is detailed. I have a journal where I keep my goals, and they cover six facets: health and fitness, spiritual and self, career, home, relationships, and finances. For the first three, Michele and I journal our individual goals; the latter three we prepare together. This allows us to share our personal goals and co-create our combined priorities. I think it's one of the things that keeps our relationship so strong—we respect each other's individuality and recognize the importance of self, but equally respect our joint life needing to be planned and compromised.

This whole goal-setting ritual comes down to being able to analyze what's important, your priorities, and how to best achieve happiness and fulfillment. No one can sell you a magic pill, and what would be the point if you don't earn it? Once the goals are set, I put the highlights in my notes on my phone, so I can reference them often throughout the year. Adjustments get made from time to time based on changing priorities. The plan is a living, breathing entity needing to be flexible around life's curve balls.

The plan serves to form the basis of my daily routines, since I cannot live my life in chaos. I have a certain level of admiration for those who can continually fly by the seat of their pants through life, but it's not for me. The vision and plan is important at a macro level, but to execute it requires discipline and focus, and the routines cement those in place. For me, success and fulfillment is the output. When you can break things down into bite-sized doses and take one step at a time, day by day, week by week, I believe you can accomplish anything. As Boston shared with us in the '70s, "Peace of

Mind" is a beautiful thing—and this is how I get mine.

In 2023, something started to cosmically shift. It was as if Madonna's "Ray of Light" was shining down, like I just got home. Not sure if it was the deeper reflection from the pandemic, my illness, or a combination. For years, I knew my focus of self-exploration was lacking. I had aspirations, but was afraid to prioritize them, feeling that other basics needed to be resolved first. I suddenly realized my routines were firmly in place and wouldn't crack under pressure. Oh sure, I struggle with certain areas similar to the rest of the population—the stubborn 15 pounds refusing to leave, or the 15-minute tape delay I always find myself in, building unnecessary stress and pressure into my day. At some juncture, you have to recognize you're good enough exactly as you are (this concept is hard for me but I'm working on it). Something snapped inside, and I finally started to ask myself, *What are you waiting for, exactly?* After everything I'd been through, the excuses had run out, and it was time to fill the rest of the gaps. As Kris Allen said, time to "Live Like We're Dying." Because we're all staring down the barrel of a gun.

This wasn't an overnight reaction. In the beginning of 2023, I was still focused on doing things to stay relaxed and calm; a routine I had picked up during the pandemic. I continued to cultivate my appreciation for nature, and I didn't need to look farther than our backyard. The four seasons are miracles, and I marvel at how all living things adapt, evolve, and survive. In the winter we feed the birds, providing entertainment for both us and the cats, and we have a large variety of woodpeckers. Have you ever heard the sound of a pileated woodpecker reverberating through the forest in the still of the early morning light?

The spring brings a returning fox family, and the mama delivers babies under our shed. It's amazing to witness; these little puppy-like fur balls romping around in our yard, and watching them grow until they are ready to roam free. Over the summer months, the hummingbirds feed on the rainbow of flowers my wife labors over. This summer we had a particularly friendly chipmunk we named Chip, who has enjoyed feeding on Randy's (our bird's) leftover peanuts. The fall season graces us with the vibrant turn of leaves in the Hudson Valley, and we have several weeks to marvel over the colors Crayola wouldn't be able to replicate. U2 said it—every day is a "Beautiful Day." We shouldn't let it get away.

Other calming techniques established during the pandemic included putting together jigsaw puzzles, which I always loved as a child. Mom and I did them frequently, and I guess it reminds me of those moments together. As an only child, I favored introverted things I could do by myself, since I didn't always have someone immediately available to play with. I think these habits drive Michele crazy at times, but I'm not trying to ignore her. I just need to help my mind calm and make my inner child feel safe. The mind can be a scary place at times, and these tactics help me to not spiral into obsessing about something I can't control. I also got caught up in the Wordle craze, which led to a daily routine of multiple online puzzles through *The New York Times*. We have a little family group text sharing our daily Wordle scores, and keeping each other posted on life—we even got 93-year-old Aunt Lois to join us! In addition to relaxing me, the games help keep my mind sharp. Since it is the best thing I have going for me, I'm determined to keep it that way. The multiple concussions I've had over the years scare me a bit, and I'm afraid one day they will come hunting down their payback.

Great as these items all are, none of them were moving the needle to further grow my exploration of self. There was one tiny victory. I finally had the courage to write something down under my "self" bucket: Writing—how to get started?

## THERE IS A ROAD

There is a road leading to the place where time stands still.

You don't need to excavate for a secret map buried deep
in the ground of an ancient tomb.
You don't need to search for a sacred key floating above
the holy sanctuary in an abandoned church.
You don't need to concoct a mysterious potion that was
bequeathed by a wise old mystic.

There is a road with one requirement to lead you to
a place where time stands still – a deliberate turn
off the three lane highway that is your life.

Away from speeding demons attempting to beat
themselves to their destination
Away from the poison suffocating the air you can
slice through with a dagger.
Away from the state altering pressure you
alone have created.

There is a road, and once you make the choice it
will take you to a place where time stands still.

Drive down the pathway motivated by winding turns
   and sudden twists.
   Drive down the pathway plowing through precious rock
   and tranquil streams.
   Drive down the pathway anchored by God's green
   towers standing strong and tall.

This is the road taking you to a place where
   time stands till, and when you get there, you will know.

Time to hear deer scampering through the woods and
   birds singing on the branches.
   Time to see endless acres of earthly landscape and
   clouds rolling gently by.
   Time to smell perennials blooming and a crisp
   breeze creeping into your nose.

There is a road leading to a place where time stands still–

But it's not the only one.

# Chapter 56 - "Umbrella"

In February 2023, Michele was worried about a pain near her left ovary as well as some random spotting. I chalked it up to residual menopause, as I'd heard it could take years, and she'd had similar pains in the past. Michele and I believe in preventative care and are in tune with our bodies, knowing when something is amiss. There's a difference between us, though—I tend to give more time for things to play out. Michele's hardwired to jump to conclusions, thereby putting her two steps ahead of everyone else. I've seen her do this as it relates to the care of our cats, and it's extraordinary. The average person would never pick up on the signs she does—it's acute.

This pain and spotting prompted Michele to go see Dr. Kim as a precaution. In my ignorance, I thought it was overboard. I'll fully admit when I'm wrong, but in this case I wanted to believe I was right. After a biopsy, followed by a D&C, Dr. Kim found a small sampling right before the procedure was over. The lab results revealed Michele had stage 1B, grade 2 endometrial cancer, and it had made its way halfway through the uterine wall. I was shocked and unprepared. I had been so confident it was nothing. Certain signs are blessings we need to be grateful for. Were it not for Michele listening to her body, the result could have been devastating. As Jefferson Starship advised, if only you believe in "Miracles," so would I.

Dr. Kim sprang into action with another terrific recommendation, sending Michele to a gynecological cancer expert affiliated with Valley Hospital, Dr. Vilardo. She was kind, caring, and empathetic and spent a lot of time explaining everything. The team acted quickly and Michele underwent a full hysterectomy, followed by radiation through Dr. Wesson. She received excellent care. I played the role of note-taker, asking all the necessary questions to ensure we had full knowledge. Knowledge is power—if you become educated, you can advocate for yourself.

Having gone through a traumatic event myself not so long before, I was able to provide some advice, which I'm hoping was helpful. Most of all, I wanted Michele to realize she could stand under my "Umbrella," as Rihanna featuring Jay-Z mixed. I wanted to be present in whatever way she needed me, because it seemed to be raining more than ever. I put up a strong front, but deep down, I was petrified.

Emotionally, watching Michele go through this was infinitely harder than going through my own journey. When it's your own issue, you can compartmentalize how you feel and address the matter at hand, ignoring your own feelings about it. In a sense, you master your own form of control, tricking yourself into believing you hold all the cards. In this situation, I felt utterly helpless, on the defensive side of the ball. As Kris Allen sang on *American Idol*, I was "Falling Slowly," just trying to point the sinking boat home. Like I said earlier, I can't live without her. No joke.

She was so strong throughout her battle, she handled everything like a champ. Everything was successful and caught timely and nothing had spread. Like Ben E. King sang back in the '60s in "Stand By Me," we won't be afraid as long as we stand by each other. I also witnessed something sweet during Michele's treatment. My Mom met Michele at Valley for all her treatments, bringing along ginger ale, cookies, and sandwiches and keeping her company. It meant so much, and I was happy Mom could fulfill a maternal role for Michele during this time.

Michele finalized her treatments by mid-July, and we celebrated by going on vacation with Melissa, Lewis, and Ava. They came to our house, and we traveled first to Boston, followed by a few days in NYC. We had a great trip, but I was concerned it was a lot for Michele. It all worked out okay, though, and she took it in stride. The resilience she displayed was incredible. Still, throughout the rest of 2023, I observed Michele going through the after-stages of cancer recovery.

It's subtle, but having gone through it myself, it was easy for me to pinpoint. When Michele would tell me she was feeling a certain way and didn't understand it, I could remind her. Once you recover physically, the emotional and mental hangover sticks around like barnacles on the hull of an old ship. I watched, knew, and understood. When she was cranky, or just not herself, I could associate without judging. I'm sure I didn't feel good about it at the time, yet I could swallow it down without being critical. As Avril Lavigne bellowed out powerfully, "I'm With You," girl—take me by the hand.

# Chapter 57 - "Enter Sandman"

"Blah, blah, blah, the Jell-O is white" was one of many nonsensical statements I made when Mom would catch me talking in my sleep. I'm sure it was all very cute in the beginning, when the "Dream Police" Cheap Trick warned about originally took residence inside my head. But those crazy buggers decided I should take up sleepwalking as well, making things more complicated. Most of the episodes were innocent enough, and for the most part I'd walk around the apartment until Mom gently told my alter-persona to go back to sleep. One thing about sleepwalkers—most of us are rather compliant. Just don't ever try to wake or startle us—it's best to reassure us all is okay and steer us back to bed.

A few standout nocturnal events gave rise to more of a stir, as Billy Squier navigated with me "In the Dark." I once woke up and found myself standing, wedged between the bed and wall. On another occasion, I woke up on Sunday morning in my church clothes, ready to go pray! On a Girl Scout camping trip, I awoke lying on the bare cabin floor next to all the girls warmly nestled in their sleeping bags—it was a bit premature for hot flashes, so what the hell did I do that for? All I know is I was freezing cold, and I quickly popped back into my bag to get my body temperature up before anyone could discover me. The topper was the time Mom caught me unlocking the door to our apartment. Thank God she sleeps lightly, or who knows where I would have wound up—someone might have found me strolling aimlessly down the shoulder of the Garden State Parkway.

I generally didn't mind hearing about the crazy antics I'd pulled the night before. Back then, I was nonplussed, having remembered absolutely none of it. I relied on the other people in the household to share the encounter. Most led to a ton of laughs, along with some gentle ribbing. All good. I've researched childhood sleepwalking, and a few stats compliments of Google AI are that half of all children talk in their sleep, and about one in five sleepwalk at least once. Given this, nothing about what I was doing would appear to be abnormal. Along with me, many other children encountered the effects from Metallica's character in "Enter Sandman." Hush little baby. A further statistic is the majority of childhood sleepwalking and talking ends by the time the child is a teenager. Good news is, I did eventually stop sleepwalking and talking in my sleep. Hence, I was like every other kid fumbling my way into my teens, right? Wrong.

The sleepwalking was replaced by night terrors in adulthood. Another statistic from Google AI is that only 1 to 3 percent of adults suffer from night terrors, making me a rare bird. I keep hoping for it to disappear, but at 54 I'm guessing it's highly unlikely. You may be wondering what it's like to live with me. Well . . .

When I was married to Seamus, he suffered a punch in the eye at least once (sorry, Shuggy). The best story is when I got him actively involved in my night terror one evening. We had both fallen asleep on the couch, and I awoke him in a frenzy, screaming that Smokey had gotten stuck behind the couch. He proceeded to tear apart our living room, pulling our sectional away from the wall piece by piece. No Smokey . . . *what?* We turned around to find him walking nonchalantly into the living room, looking at us as if to say, "Whatcha guys doin'?"

Michele has had to deal with a different level of crazy. We've graduated from cats on fans to something a bit more disturbing. The nonsensical innocent and funny antics have been replaced with some mind-trippy shit. As Chicago sang in "25 or 6 to 4," at times I wonder how much I can take. Actually, it's probably how much Michele can take, since she suffers the brunt of my condition.

Most times, the night terror causes me to suddenly jolt upright in bed, startling everyone around me. Something utterly terrifying has happened, more terrifying than a worst nightmare, and I'm trying to escape. Just don't ask me what it is. In the beginning, Michele wasn't sure what to do, but over time she learned to deal with it the way my mom did, guiding me back to sleep. The cats don't seem to flinch anymore, knowing it's just their crazy Mom-Dad up to her typical nighttime tricks. At times, Jake will come lay on my chest to comfort me back to sleep. From my vantage point, the aftereffects of these are downright freaky. I often wake up after the night terror filled with an overwhelming sense of dread, believing something bad is happening. It's getting harder to convince myself nothing is wrong, though the song "Silent Lucidity" by Queensryche serves to try and remind me I'm lying safe in bed. I've thought about investing in a sleep study, but for what? For them to confirm the obvious? Just maybe, this is the one time I don't want to understand the why. I just hope and pray I can keep convincing myself, night after night, the Dream Police aren't real and I can survive the night.

# Chapter 58 - "Dancing With Myself"

My ongoing reflection about who I am as a person has led to a growing fascination in understanding why I am the way I am. I think about this often, not being content to simply prescribe to "I am what I am." Certainly this statement is true, and I'm accepting of myself, but I'm also seeking to establish the deeper realm of where behaviors come from. The classic tune by The Who speaks to me—I'm looking for a definition to answer the question "Who Are You." While I didn't formally study psychology or physics, I've always been intrigued, and enjoyed philosophy and ethics classes in college. It's never been enough for me to understand something on the surface level—I will dive down as deeply as my brain will allow me to travel. A great song by Counting Crows is called "Colorblind"—to understand me you'll need to pull me out from inside.

Most of my contemplation has led me to tying my own core personality traits to either my mom or my dad, and in some cases, back to my grandparents. While I consider myself unique—aren't we all?—and certain aspects correlate to environment as opposed to DNA, an overpowering connection of genes explain most behaviors in my opinion. When I look at each of my parents as a person, I know precisely how I'm like them or not like them at all.

This grounding exercise is important to me, because I've traveled through most of my life feeling different from people around me. This isn't an egotistical, narcissistic trip, nor is it an admission of pity for myself. I accept it, but I still seek to understand why. Why do I feel so different? I've already explained a lot of it, including the realization I am gay. This took care of a lot of it, but it doesn't answer it all. I know this because in moments, when I look around among the people I'm with, I feel like I'm on the outside looking in. As Billy Idol sang, in these moments, I believe I'm "Dancing With Myself," and all the empty eyes seem to pass me by. Once in a while, it can feel frustrating, and in those moments I want to ask them to let me into their club. But I'm not meant to be part of their club. I'm meant to be exactly the person I am. This requires accepting myself from top to bottom, backward and forward, inside and outside. It also means trying to understand everyone around me. On the journey of life, I continue to pick up morsels along the way; the arsenal in my tool belt, to help me.

Over the last 15 years, I've gotten a better understanding through Erica, a friend and our leadership coach at Hampshire. As part of our leadership culture, we take Myers-Briggs Indicator Tool tests, designed to increase self-awareness and understand hard-wiring. According to the MBTI, I'm an I=Introverted, N=Intuitive, T=Thinking, J=Judging. While I won't dive deeply into describing all of these, one statistic helps explain a lot—only 2 to 4 percent of the population has this personality type. *Hmm.* Eerily close to the 1 to 3 percent night terror stat. Is there some deeper meaning surrounding this? Okay, I promise not to go down a rabbit hole. But it does help answer why I feel so differently the majority of the time. I'm generally living in a largely empty box!

Over the years, I've attempted to embrace my uniqueness and take advantage of all I have to offer. As a child, I'd try to blend in with the pack at times, but I no longer feel the need to do this. After I revealed the biggest part of who I was hiding away all those years, the baggage along with it also left. Through this discovery and coming out, I could finally start to answer who am I, as Chicago explored in "(I've Been) Searchin' So Long," and I know my life has meaning.

The full acceptance is a relief, but it still raises challenges. I've learned I connect with individuals more strongly in a one-on-one interaction, as opposed to in a large crowd. This makes me steer toward those types of interactions, but I have to be able to communicate in broader settings as well. I've had to learn how to navigate the bigger settings, and it's not as natural to me. The more comfortable I am with the crowd, the easier it is, but if I walk into a room of strangers, it's more challenging. I'm not a fan of small talk, but I've tried to figure out how to get by as a matter of lessening the social awkwardness. If I feel or get uncomfortable, I clam up. All I want to do is get out of the situation as quickly as possible.

The bigger challenge comes in the form of my pensive nature. As an introvert, I draw my energy from within. I've said I'm continually rooting around in there for buried treasure. It's great for me, but not for others around me. When I'm at work or in a social setting I can temper myself, but I spend a lot of time outside of these instances contemplating. I'll admit if it was me on the receiving end, I'd drive me crazy. Michele will exhaustively ask, "Where are you?" and I'll start out being defensive, then recognize exactly where I am and chuckle to myself. I'm just lost in another "Time Passages" loop, as Al Stewart requested—buy me a ticket on the last train home tonight.


## UNSPOKEN

They flow so perfectly when they are all in my head,
    Forming an award winning love story when I'm dreaming in bed.
    They spew out as sarcasm, perhaps a joke,
    Masking the true words that never get spoke.

They crystallize into a diamond on an early morning walk,
    Waiting in pure artistic form for the groundbreaking talk.
    They attack my throat until it begins to swell,
    Subsiding the moment I search for the words I never tell.

They pour out like a fountain as I drive in my car,
    Anticipating that one romantic moment underneath the evening star.
    They pierce at my tongue for endless a day,
    Bleeding in the silence of the words I never say.

They convince me it's as simple as mere child's play
    Believing-
    Until my eyes meet yours-
    They are the words I can say.

# Chapter 59 - "Seasons of Love"

Have you ever heard the expression "fake it until you make it?" I've seen it used most frequently in the business world, and have uttered it myself over the years, equating it in my head as "I'm going to behave into the space I most wish to create for myself." I had never thought about it in a broader context, but upon further reflection, I believe it goes higher and deeper. According to Google AI, the expression has roots in Aristotle's virtue ethics, Alfred Adler's therapeutic technique, and a 1968 Simon & Garfunkel song (interesting combo). It implies by imitating confidence, competence, and an optimistic mindset, a person can achieve the results they seek.

Can't we apply this idiom to anything in our lives? It resonates strongly with me, since I have always lived by Seton Hall's motto, the one I had tattooed across my lower back. "Hazard Zet Forward" is the Latin expression translated to "At whatever risk, yet go forward." Some readers may think, "Easier said than done," to which I would respectfully reply, "What you choose to do with this information is entirely up to you." All I can do is share my experience and give encouragement to others who may be seeking it.

One of the key elements of my success in the level of optimism I hold? How I choose to start my day getting grounded. I get up at 5 a.m.; yes, I'm part of that club. I never read the book; it's just something I've come to on my own accord. I've discovered I can accomplish a great deal in the first two hours of my day, and doing so instills a sense of accomplishment that I carry throughout the rest of my day. After feeding my feline tribe, I pour my first cup of coffee and sit in my favorite chair in my favorite room of my house. As Mötley Crüe lodged into me years ago, there's nothing like "Home Sweet Home" (note: I want this song played in the background at my funeral). I can't underestimate the importance of feeling comfortable, safe, and inspired. Find your space.

My next priority of the day is to enter a period of prayer, reflection, and meditation. I begin with a reflection video offered daily by the United States Conference of Catholic Bishops, and proceed into my own thing, which is focused around what I am grateful for, what I am praying for, and what I am sorry for. Gratitude is an important part of happiness, and I never want to forget how lucky I am in this life. I've made it a point to support charitable causes as a way to return my good fortune. I believe a great song by Mick Jagger, "God Gave Me Everything," to be true, and I also believe God listens when we talk to Him. It doesn't mean we can have everything we ask for. I pray for people who are dealing with difficult circumstances and those I love most in my life, and I realize beyond that, it's all out of my hands. We can't stop pain, illness, or death, but we can pray for someone to reside peacefully in His care and for God to watch over them. We recently lost Charlie, and it was hard to go through for Mom and me, too—it was difficult to reconcile the man we knew in the past with who he was in our present—another family unit disintegrated. I believe our faith got us through it.

I added the "what I'm sorry for" part more recently, as it dawned on me I haven't practiced the sacrament of reconciliation for a long time. My relationship with the Catholic church today is a bit confusing. I have a strong belief in God which will never be altered, and the foundation my family instilled in me is something I'll never take for granted. When I go to Mass, I feel as strongly about the rituals as I always did, and I miss practicing them. The challenge is, the Catholic church gives mixed messages, so I am a bit unclear where I stand and if I'm accepted without condition. Personally, I believe God's primary message is to love one another as you love yourself. As a result, I'm not sure how certain things such as being gay, or divorced, or any other lifestyles can be admonished as they sometimes are. The words in the Bible get twisted into the outcome people want, leading to alienation and discrimination.

I also realize that being religious doesn't equate to being good. Michele didn't have the formalized religious upbringing I had, yet she is one of the best good people I know. In contrast, I've come across so-called "religious" people who are miserable, mean-spirited humans who constantly judge everyone. I'm exhausted by the lack of acceptance, and truthfully, it's getting stale. I'm not asking anyone to understand it or live in my shoes, but rather just to let me live mine without their judgment. Nobody actually gets to judge us—only God can. Also, I think those who judge are off base, and in my case, those folks may be dealing with me and my gay friends upstairs, so they may want to consider resolving this within themselves now. I'm reminded of the song "What the World Needs Now" by Jackie DeShannon—love, sweet love.

After prayer, I go into my Headspace meditation. I've found this app to be great for keeping a meditation practice daily, and it lets you do a meditation session for as short or long a period as you have time for. Audio and video sessions can be used throughout the day, as well as sleep meditation techniques.

Next, I accomplish my writing goals for the day; the length of which varies based on whether it's the weekend or a weekday. Many other writers I've talked to struggle to find time. I get it; it took a lot for me to establish my own discipline. For me, it's about staying on a routine, which builds muscle memory. With no excuses. It's about asking, *how badly do you want it?* If you do, you'll figure out a way. Maybe you have more energy at night than in the morning—perfect. Set your routine around what is most energizing to you.

Here are a couple other mantras I choose to live by. As a rule, I can be strong-willed, and clearly I have a lot of opinions. This is a positive thing in my view, but I've realized it's important not to get so stuck on them you can't see past yourself. We need to listen and understand before being understood. As a society, we don't listen often enough, nor do we always put ourselves in someone else's shoes. I'm far from perfect at this, but as a result of my illness, my perspective has shifted toward it. We never know what someone is going through, so it's important to lead with empathy. I've gotten feedback that I've changed for the better, so hopefully it means I'm doing something right.

I have a strong drive in life, with the basic premise that we should always seek to evolve. We're put on this planet for a purpose, so let's live into it. I don't believe we are meant to figure out everything all at once, but we can keep trying and searching and growing in our discovery. We need to be open, and sometimes it requires shifting energy to accomplish. In the beautiful song from *Rent*, "Seasons of Love" it asks us to answer the question, how do you measure a year? A year in the life? A life?

One last perspective that's helped me with my level of optimism: In any given scenario there are one of two ways a person can go. The choice is ours to look at something negatively and ruminate, or take the positives from a situation and move forward. I will always choose the latter—it's how I survive. It's not to say I'm never negative or don't have bad days. Life is hard sometimes, and we can be kind to ourselves when we're going through a down spell. It's equally important not to stay in a bad place for too long, or risk becoming soured and bitter. It's about trying not to live with regrets, and remembering that all the bad things have made you into the resilient, strong person you are today. Are you ready to drink the Kool-Aid? If so, as inspired by Pink, "Raise Your Glass"—it's 5 a.m. Turn the radio up!

## THIS JOURNEY

This journey of life is a mystery that unfolds,
    Many let it remain one and simply get old;
    Some who ache with a desire to understand,
    Attempt to make most plentiful their God given hand.

It is in this awakening we can truly see the light,
    In this revelation we gain inner strength to fight;
    Pure self-discovery becomes paramount in unleashing the fears,
    We've buried and silenced behind heartache and tears.

Still the greatest blessing in all we learn,
   While it may appear self-empowerment is what we most
yearn;
   We're walking this path intertwined by divine measure,
   Our souls united as one is the gift to most treasure.

# Chapter 60 - "Geronimo"

You'd think I'd be more excited at the last chapter of my book. I've actually been dreading writing this final chapter for some time. As a lifelong avid reader, I've always felt sad when I've invested precious time in a book, reading page by page with building anticipation, and then it's over. Done. Finished, and not the way you expected. No closure; no feeling you've taken a lesson away, absolutely nothing. Hence, it would pain me greatly for anyone reading this to walk away having gained nothing in the process.

The other thing in the back of my mind is feeling the sense of loss and sadness many writers have described upon completing a book. I probably have some PTSD about the feeling I had after my surgery, and God knows I don't want to revert into another solitary nomadic state of being for the next six months of my life. What to do? I'm still not sure how to end this, so I'm going to keep writing, and wait for it to come. In the meantime, let me share what led me to write this book.

I've mentioned I love reading, and it's been a constant in my life. From the earliest of my favorite books as a child, *Pickle, Pickle, Pickle Juice* by Patty Wolcott and *Where the Wild Things Are* by Maurice Sendak, to the present, as I recently finished *Holly* by Stephen King and *House of Hidden Meanings* by RuPaul, I always have a book on my side night table. I consider reading knowledge, power, and enlightenment. Our brains are one of our most powerful instruments, and they need to be fed. As k.d. lang wrote, "Constant Craving" has always been. Naturally, many people love reading as deeply as I do, and a reader doesn't a writer make, do they?

I started writing poetry in high school and have never stopped. I've amassed enough to publish a poetry book, and I've sprinkled some throughout these pages. In high school, I wrote other creative pieces and enjoyed the process immensely. For years, I had the desire to write professionally, but then life happened, and I've spent the last 32 years uber focused on my career. All good, thankfully; the strategy paid off.

Several years ago, I started forming the idea to write a memoir. I have read many, and feel people's stories are inspiring and helpful. Some may ask why a non-famous person has any business writing a memoir. I believe everyone has a unique story to tell, and their story can be equally compelling to the most famous person. We are here on this earth to help one another, offer relatable advice, and share our gifts. This is my way of connecting with you. I decided that sharing some of the things I've been through could help someone else, whether it's a person in the LGBTQIA+ community struggling, a recently diagnosed breast cancer patient, someone searching for hope and inspiration, or anyone looking to escape their own reality. If I can help or inspire one person, my mission has been accomplished. The inspiring song by Stevie Nicks, "Has Anyone Ever Written Anything for You" reminds me that I am doing it for the world, and maybe a little bit for myself.

As the idea was forming in my head, music was the automatic backdrop. When I'm listening to music, I always equate it to something, whether it be past, present, or future. The idea became so strong in my gut I knew it had to be, and I wouldn't exit this earth without telling this story. It became a question of time, which I continued to use the lack of as my excuse. It kept coming at me like an oncoming freight train, but I stood on the tracks, waiting. Playing chicken.

Remember, I wrote the writing commitment down in my goals to start off 2023. Life happened again, and I put it out of my mind for the next six months, rolling around without anything to adhere to. In the second half of 2023, I found out someone I went to high school with had died. Her name was Wendy, and though I knew she had MS, I didn't know she had breast cancer, which had metastasized. Linda and I attended her service, and I came home feeling incredibly unsettled. I consider myself to have an accepting outlook on death, but I feel sometimes people die out of place, against the natural order of things. It happened to me again as I was writing this book, when my friend Robyn passed away unexpectedly, just as I was writing about the great younger years we'd been through together. It's a real mind fuck. Michele said perhaps I struggle with survivor's guilt, and that may play a part.

I was in a dark place for about a week after Wendy's service, then something snapped open within me. I was getting a call I could no longer ignore. I plan on being around for as long as God intends, but no other excuses could be made, and I can't predict what will happen tomorrow. There is only today. Like the band Sheppard, I chose to say, "Geronimo!"

I started to figure out how I could make writing a book possible. In August 2023, I entered a period of conditioning, which included firming up my existing routines and disciplines and getting up at 5 a.m. on weekends as well as weekdays. I began my research; I knew I could write, but knew nothing about the publishing industry. I learned about the pros and cons of self- vs. traditional publishing, editing considerations, and marketing tactics. I spent a lot of time determining how I should go about these things, and what would work best for me. I put my organizational skills to work and created a project plan timeline.

In October 2023, I started crafting my outlines, and my writing formally began in January 2024. It took me eight and a half months to get a final draft to my editor. After this, I'll be focused primarily around marketing and promotion. I started my campaign two months ago on Instagram and Facebook and will be creating my website, launching a newsletter and reader list. If you are planning to write professionally but don't know where to start, you're living in an age when plenty of online tools can help you. Go check out Reedsy.com and consider joining an association like the Author's Guild. If you can hook up with a writer's critique group somewhere, do so. I've found it incredibly valuable.

Okay, okay. Time to get back to reality. I've used enough stalling tactics. As Earth, Wind and Fire sang, the "Fantasy" is over. Still, I promised you I wouldn't end on an uneventful note. *Umm, what should I say next?* I hope you have enjoyed my story as much as I have enjoyed sharing it with you. *Yawn.* Happy trails to you until we meet again. *How utterly archaic.* May all your dreams be fulfilled and realized. *Boring.* Oh hell, I can't do this. I can't it end this way—I need one more song to bail me out. I'll use my friends from Styx and ask you to

"Come Sail Away." We'll live happily forever, so the story goes. Who said it has to end, anyway? Turn the page.

# A teaser from C.L. McMurray's first novel, "The Heartbreaker"

"Miss Hart, we need you to review the photos."

Casey Hart knew someone else had entered the room even though her eyes remained decidedly shut, and her guess was the voice belonged to that dickhead Sergeant Dan Riley. She worried once she opened her eyes, the room would start spinning again. She'd lost count of the Cuervo shots by the time the second set was over last night, and the rest of the evening faded into a messy blur. She'd been brought in for questioning after only three hours of sleep, forced to throw on her rank, sweat-stained clothes from last night. Eww. All she wanted was to go back to bed and tuck this problem out of her mind forever.

"Help us out here, Casey." In comes the voice of Detective Toni Raimondo, who at least is easier on the eyes than that jerk-off Riley. Bracing herself, Casey slowly flutters her exhausted blue eyes back into focus. She knew she'd never be prepared enough for these disturbing images, and along with the last batch she reviewed a few weeks ago, it's a foregone conclusion they will be etched permanently in her worst nightmares.

She unwillingly fumbles through the photos, proceeding

from horrifying to unfathomable. The victim, a beautiful young woman close to Casey's age—late twenties—has a face that appears immersed in a peaceful dream. The rest of her body, arranged like a stake-shielding vampire with arms crossed over her chest, doesn't reveal the butcher job performed underneath. Were it not for the victim's heart, placed like a freshly sliced slab of butcher meat at the center of her two crossed arms, no one would know anything was amiss. Until the eyes travel farther down to the girl's stomach. Written with a thoughtful precision a penmanship schoolteacher could appreciate, the words "The Heartbreaker," using the victim's crimson-hued blood splayed expertly across her soft skin, boasted the maniac's handiwork. The killer finished off each grotesque act by playing Casey's song on repeat in the room of doom, so that when the victim was found it would still be playing. By the fifth picture in, Casey realizes she needs a bucket, but it's too late. She projectile vomits all over the examination floor; the detectives seem nonplussed—this happens in homicide.

Raimondo asks her, "Do you know the victim?" Casey gurgles she does not.

The detective presses her again, "Have you ever seen this woman before?" Choking back bile, Casey shakes her head no.

Dickhead Riley chimes in, sneering. "Why do you think someone would want to use *your* recording to put an exclamation point on their murders?"

Exasperated, Casey replies tersely, "I've already told you, I. DON'T. KNOW."

Raimondo proceeds softly. "It's just that there must be some connection the killer has to you." *Ugh. Clearly,* Casey considers.

357

The last five weeks have seemed to land right out of a Stephen King novel. After the first killing, Casey was nearly arrested, but thankfully she produced an alibi, so they let her go. Since then, she's been called to the police station multiple times. Worse, they keep showing up at the various bars she plays at, which is fucking up her mojo when she's trying to perform.

There aren't enough Cuervo shots in the world to help her forget this horror show. You know, it really figures this would happen to her now. After spending the last decade performing in dive bars all over Northern New Jersey as the lead singer and guitarist for an '80s cover band, Casey was finally getting her break. Someone in the biz had come in to the Hilltop Tavern four months ago and gave them a shot to record after seeing them perform. Dead End released their first single just two months ago; a remake of her hero Pat Benatar's "Heartbreaker."

It's been a whirlwind ever since. Thanks to some social media publicity, the band's exposure was snowballing, resulting in sold-out performances and even recognition by a few fans out in public. But now, this. The old expression "be careful what you wish for" rang in her head.

"Let's go through the sequencing again," Riley barks, shaking Casey back into reality. She nods in agreement. "You recorded twelve weeks ago, is that correct?" Another nod.

"And up to that point, only the band, your agent, and the recording team were aware of this album?" After receiving a third weary nod, Riley continues. "And you said the first single got released on social media outlets eight weeks ago, and it wasn't until then you began performing it as part of your set, correct?" Casey replies with an affirmative and a heavy sigh. She doesn't see how any of this is going to help them figure out anything.

Observing Casey's angst, Raimondo chimes in. "Let's switch gears. Walk us through your relationship history. Do you have anyone in your life who may have it out for you; a jealous ex, anyone like that?"

*Shit.* Here's where things become muddled, and Casey hates this line of questioning the most. She begins hesitantly.

"As I've previously attempted to explain to you, I'm fully entrenched in the music world, and that's been my only focus since I graduated high school. I haven't had any long-term re-lationships, they've been more, uh, temporary arrangements. I don't have time for serious commitments, and no one I've dated thus far is down with living this rockstar lifestyle."

Riley butts in. "But you acknowledge you've had a lot of partners?"

Casey cringes ruefully. "Yeah."

Gruffly, Riley pats the wooden table between them. "We need the names and descriptions of every one of these women; these 'partners,' or whatever you want to call them."

Casey's voice raises several octaves. "But that's impossi-ble!" She struggles to calm herself. "Look, I can maybe give you some first names; some general descriptions but . . . but . . . " Her voice trails off.

Impatient, Riley hits the table with his palm. "Miss Hart, you're not leaving this station until we go through the whole list in painstaking detail. You better call your band friends and your witless groupies and inform them you won't be able to perform tonight."

Fucking asshole. *What a disaster*, Casey thinks to herself. *This is going from bad to worse.* At this rate, she realizes, she'll never get out of this hellhole.

With a deep breath inward, she looks over at Raimondo, tips her head, and inquires, "Can I at least get another cup of your shitty ass coffee?"

# About the Author

After achieving a successful career as a C-Suite executive in the commercial real estate industry, C.L. McMurray is making her professional author debut with the nostalgic memoir, *Air Guitar Rules - Chords of Life.* The writing bug grabbed hold of C.L. in high school when she started writing poetry. Life got in the way, but she's excited to finally pursue the passion that's been burning deep down inside for many years. Raised in Bergen County, New Jersey, C.L. lives with her spouse Michele in the scenic Hudson Valley in New York State with their five cats.

**You can connect with me on:**
- 🌐 https://www.clmcmurray.com
- f https://www.facebook.com/profile.php?id=61562251975249
- 🔗 https://www.instagram.com/clmcmurray
- 🔗 https://www.linkedin.com/in/cheryll-mcmurray-8b31b3154

www.ingramcontent.com/pod-product-compliance
Lightning Source LLC
Chambersburg PA
CBHW020431130626
46549CB00001B/85